To John V. Dorr

with appreciation and esteem

Alan Kennedy

17 May 1946.

D0003116

WITHDRAWN
UTSA LIBRARIES

RHEES OF ROCHESTER

with the good wishes of
John Rothwell Slater

RUSH RHEES

RHEES
of
ROCHESTER

by

JOHN ROTHWELL SLATER

Professor Emeritus of English
The University of Rochester

HARPER & BROTHERS PUBLISHERS

NEW YORK AND LONDON

RHEES OF ROCHESTER

CONTENTS

〰〰〰〰〰

RHEES OF ROCHESTER

I

ALPHA

I am Alpha and Omega, the beginning
and the end, the first and the last.

Our God, our help in ages past,
Our hope for years to come.

∾∾∾∾∾∾∾∾∾∾∾∾∾∾∾∾∾∾∾∾∾∾∾∾∾∾∾∾∾∾∾∾

RUSH RHEES of Rochester was one of the last ministerial
college presidents. He was not a relic but a force—the
force of religion in higher education. If that is a losing cause,
he did what he could to save it.

As an ordained clergyman he not only in later life preached
sermons, taught the Bible, and sometimes conducted weddings
and funerals, as he had when a young pastor at Portsmouth.
He also consoled the sick, helped the poor, kept the secrets of
the distressed, and encouraged the timid and forlorn. Few knew
that, for he was most reticent when most generous. He was not
ashamed to be a Christian, and never apologized for faith, hope,
or charity.

His invariable calmness, which sometimes meant deep feeling
under complete control, restricted surface geniality. He was
kinder than he seemed, practiced more than he preached,
thought more than he talked, and helped many to find themselves who never knew it. Affable to strangers, shy among
friends; fluent in speech, silent under strain; sensitive but
strong; firm but merciful; eyes that saw through you, smile that
reassured—that was Rush Rhees; more than a president, less
than a saint, just about equal to his big job.

This book is neither a success story nor a history of the University of Rochester. It is a study of a rather baffling personality.

1

Where was his secret strength? What did he have that many better known leaders have lacked? Why did he sometimes seem remote even to those who saw him often? To what Puritan principle without Puritan bigotry, what sentiment without sentimentality, can we trace his inner light? Can we trace it at all? He was a man of large reserves; there were barriers beyond which trespassing was not encouraged. Part of him he carried away; it cannot be recovered.

To portray such a man as friends knew him, for the benefit of thousands who saw only protective coloration, is perhaps a task beyond veracious biography. In these days a biography without speculation and invention may be out of fashion. The maxim of pseudo biography seems to be that ironical sentence in Ecclesiasticus, "As well as thou canst, guess at thy neighbors." Such guesswork is trivial and impertinent rather than misleading, for nobody but a fool believes it. Psychoanalytic gossip and invented conversations, however clever or amusing, have been overdone. They catch the superficial, mislead the credulous, and traduce the dead. What a man thought is unknown unless he chose to say. What he did remains.

Overstatement is equally unfair. Rush Rhees avoided superlatives and disliked exaggeration. He did not care for eulogy of himself. Modesty is a kind of disdain. It shrinks even from deserved and sincere praise because conscious of greater things undone and ideals beyond reach. The President of Rochester pushed his college, never himself. Self-advertisers amused him; they were so transparent. To accept or acquiesce in flattery would be almost to join them.

Rush Rhees was partly Welsh. His great-grandfather, Morgan John Rhys, or Rhees (1760-1804), was a radical preacher and agitator of southern Wales. True child of the Revolution, lover of excitement, friend of Jefferson and Priestley, Pennsylvania pioneer, associate of Benjamin Rush, he shared during the last decade of the eighteenth century its devotion, its defiance, and its romantic illusions.

The surname Rhys, Rhees, or Rees (rhyming with "cease," not with "seize"), is common in Wales, and also appears in the forms Rice and Price. It means "ardor," from *rhysu*, to hurry, to rush. The change in spelling from Rhys to Rhees took place after emigration to America. Morgan John Rhys was born December 8, 1760, in the parish of Llanfabon, Glamorganshire, south Wales, near the Bristol Channel. After study at Bristol College he began preaching at Pontypool in 1787. Being a liberal, he published Welsh tracts on abolition of Negro slavery, disestablishment of the church, and other reforms, and traveled through southern Wales on speaking tours rousing public sentiment against political abuses. In the summer of 1791 he was in London, where he met an American officer, Major Benjamin Loxley of Philadelphia. From London he went with his friend Job David to Paris to witness the Revolution at first hand. Though he had to leave the French capital as suddenly as Wordsworth, like him he may have felt

> Bliss was it in that dawn to be alive,
> But to be young was very heaven.

Back in Carmarthen by the fall of 1792, he began publication of a quarterly magazine in the Welsh language. Only five issues appeared in 1793-1794, the enterprise being abandoned for lack of funds. Along with religious articles the periodical contained much radical propaganda. Free circulation of the Bible in Welsh was another of his interests. Since there was much illiteracy among the poor, he was a leader in promoting in Wales a new type of free elementary schools meeting on Sundays to teach children to read and write. These so-called "Sunday schools" had been introduced in Gloucester about 1780 by Robert Raikes. Rhys brought them to Wales.

His strong opposition to church establishment is shown in a tract entitled "The Method of Supporting Religion in the United States of America, and sufficient reasons to justify those who go

from this country to America, and an Advice to the Welsh."
Taxation of Dissenters for support of the Church was to him
intolerable. "If Christianity cannot be promulgated by voluntary supplies, it should not be supported at all." He quoted at
length from the Virginia Act of 1786 providing that "no man be
compelled to support any religious worship, place, or minister
whatever." Reformers were unpopular in British government
circles during the public unrest caused by the French Revolution. Rhys's sudden departure from Carmarthen in midsummer
was probably due to fear of arrest. He sailed from Liverpool
on August 1, 1794, and after seventy-three days of calms and
storms landed in New York on October 12.

From that moment he became in heart and soul an American.
He had but ten years more to live, but filled them with bold enterprise; began much, finished nothing, saw the future before
he left the world behind. At Philadelphia with the aid of Major
Loxley he made acquaintances among the friends of liberty. In
the course of a long preaching tour on horseback through the
southern states he seems to have become as popular as White-
field had been long before. It was on this journey, on July 4,
1795, that he addressed to a military audience and a deputation
of Indian chiefs "An Oration Delivered at Greenville, Head-
quarters of the Western Army, Northwest of the Ohio." This
flamboyant defiance of tyranny throughout the world is still
extant. Its elevated rhetoric is in striking contrast with the plain
and often humorous style of his travel diaries. Not unworthy of
comparison with the Journal of John Woolman, they deal with
the same subjects—hardships of travel, evils of slavery and in-
temperance, prevalence of malaria, dysentery, and yellow fever,
courage and good humor of frontiersmen, patience of their
women, hopes of a great future.

Returning to Philadelphia after a year of travel, he wasted no
time in courting Ann Loxley, a daughter of Major Loxley. He
married her on February 22, 1796. Ann was twenty, Morgan
thirty-five, George Washington sixty-four, American independ-

ence twenty, and the United States only seven years old. Rush
Rhees of Rochester was minus sixty-four.

Ann Loxley was quite a person. In genetics grandmothers
are as important as grandfathers. Ann spent her early life in the
old Loxley house in Second Street near Spruce, down by the
Delaware River, where she had been born June 18, 1775, the
day after the battle of Bunker Hill. Her father, an officer in the
militia, member of the Committee of Public Safety, friend of
Franklin, and leader in local affairs, had seen much of the
beginnings of American liberty. Ann, tenth of twelve children,
grew up a spirited gentlewoman, an active church worker, fit
mate for a pioneer.

Early in 1796 Morgan John Rhees with others organized the
Philadelphia Society for the Information and Assistance of Persons Emigrating from Foreign Countries. In this and other
philanthropic enterprises he became acquainted with eminent
Philadelphians, among them Dr. Benjamin Rush. Since this was
the man from whom all the Rush Rheeses got their name, it is
important to know why Morgan John Rhees named his second
son after him. Benjamin Rush (1745-1813) was a signer of the
Declaration of Independence, and a professor in the medical
school of the University of Pennsylvania. He had been an army
surgeon, wrote many medical books, and nothwithstanding
rather extreme views in favor of bloodletting did much to advance the practice of medicine. He was also a philanthropist
and reformer, established the first American free dispensary,
advocated abolition of slavery, enlightened treatment of mental
diseases, prison reform, better education for women, and other
progressive causes. Being a humanitarian, it is easy to see why
he helped a young Welsh preacher to found a colony in the
Alleghenies, and why the founder named a son for him. Though
the name descended through five generations, all the Benjamin
Rush Rheeses abbreviated Benjamin to B., and were called
Rush. Rush Rhees of Rochester dropped even the initial B. soon
after leaving college, and never used it in later years.

On the western slope of the central Alleghenies, in what is

now Cambria County, Morgan John Rhees with the help of Benjamin Rush bought a tract of 17,400 acres in 1796 for the new colony. At the center of the land, three miles west of Ebensburg, north of Johnstown, a site was chosen for a new town to be called Beulah. Thither Rhees and his young wife removed in 1798. The abandoned site of Beulah is now an isolated spot with few traces of the village that flourished there early in the last century. Though located on what was then a through highway, later and better roads passed it by. It prospered only while Welsh immigrants kept on coming to their hoped-for Utopia.

Beulah is said to be a Welsh word meaning "Land of Freedom," but the Hebrew word Beulah means "married" (Isaiah 62:4). Freedom and marriage are not the same thing, as Ann Loxley soon discovered, for she bore five children in eight years. The family moved in 1799 from Beulah to Somerset, county seat of Somerset County, where her husband became clerk of the court and recorder of deeds. There he died suddenly of pleurisy on December 7, 1804, the day before his forty-fourth birthday. He thought he heard angels singing. Afterward Ann wrote a poem about it; not a good poem, but a good woman; that often happens.

This was the end of the beginning—death and desolation. Beulah was soon as forsaken as it had been before. The only difference was a dream that haunted the ruin, like the tune of an old revival hymn, with a refrain that begins

> O Beulah land, sweet Beulah land,
> As on thy highest mount I stand,
> I look away across the sea,
> Where mansions are prepared for me.

How many hopes men attach to the earth that belong to the sky. How much they expect from life that comes only after death—and not to them. Through his descendants that adventurous Welshman accomplished what no colony, no sermons, could ever have brought about. He and Ann made men and women. If Morgan John Rhees's ship had foundered at sea, or if his mare had stumbled in the Kentucky mountains, Rush Rhees would never have been. The university would have been different. Its library would have borne another name. Eastman's fortune would have gone elsewhere. Music and medicine would never have made Rochester illustrious. Much came from Beulah—which never was, and never will be.

> We are such stuff
> As dreams are made on, and our little life
> Is rounded with a sleep.

Ann Loxley Rhees went back to Philadelphia. Benjamin Rush wrote her a letter of condolence. On limited means the widow brought up her five children, lived to see twenty grandchildren, and died April 11, 1849. She and her husband rest in the Loxley lot in Mount Moriah Cemetery. Their children were:

II. 1 John Loxley Rhees
    2 Benjamin Rush Rhees
    3 Mary Rhees
    4 Morgan John Rhees, Jr.
    5 Eliza Rhees

The fourth of these was Rush Rhees's grandfather. The youngest, who married the Rev. Nicholas Murray, a Presbyterian clergyman, was the grandmother of Nicholas Murray Butler. Besides President Butler there have been several other distinguished members of the family. The second son, Benjamin Rush Rhees the first (1798-1831), from whom the name descended to one boy in each generation, was an eminent Philadelphia physician. He studied medicine with Dr. James Rush, son of Benjamin Rush, and was one of the founders of Jefferson Medical College. In the Rush Rhees Library of the University of Rochester there is a pamphlet written by him, entitled:

An Address Delivered March 6, 1825, in the hall of the Medical Faculty of Jefferson College, located in Philadelphia. By B. Rush Rhees, M.D., Professor of Materia Medica of Jefferson College, Philadelphia: Printed by Stavely & Bringhurst. 1825.

The address defended the somewhat criticized step of founding a second medical school in the same city with the University of Pennsylvania, but was chiefly an exposition of medical ethics. Doctors, of all people, he maintained, should avoid petty professional jealousy of rival practitioners and institutions. There was room for all. Dr. Benjamin Rush Rhees, like his namesake, was a philanthropic leader. He was vice-president of the Pennsylvania Peace Society, formed in 1825, of which his brother John Loxley Rhees was recording secretary. Among the honorary members was Thomas Jefferson, for whom all the Rheeses had high respect.

It was not only Jefferson's strong stand on separation of church and state which they admired, but his liberal and democratic opinions in general, though not his deistic tendencies. To those who think of Jefferson as lacking sympathy with the orthodox of any sect this may seem surprising. But Morgan John Rhees was not too orthodox himself, nor were any of his family. In youth they all declared independence in one way or another, but by the age of thirty most of them had learned, like Jefferson, to work with opposites for the public good. Individualism can condemn a wrong; only co-operation can right it.

Rush Rhees's grandfather, Morgan John Rhees, Jr., was a Baptist minister, who held pastorates in Bordentown, Trenton, and Wilmington, and held secretarial positions in denominational societies. His last pastorate (1850-1853) was in Williamsburgh, New York, then distinct from Brooklyn, where he died January 15, 1853. He had received in 1852 one of the earliest honorary degrees of the new University of Rochester, eight years before Rush Rhees was born. His four surviving children, besides a daughter who died in infancy, were:

> III. 1 Benjamin Rush Rhees
> 2 John Evans Rhees
> 3 Mary E. Rhees
> 4 Annie E. Rhees

John Evans Rhees, Rush Rhees's father, born March 19, 1833, married Annie Houghton McCutchen, of Williamsburgh, and

AN

ADDRESS

DELIVERED MARCH 8, 1825,

IN THE

HALL OF THE MEDICAL FACULTY

OF

Jefferson College,

LOCATED IN PHILADELPHIA.

BY B. RUSH RHEES, M. D.

PROFESSOR OF MATERIA MEDICA OF JEFFERSON COLLEGE.

PHILADELPHIA:

PRINTED BY STAVELY & BRINGHURST.

1825

The author of this address
was the second son of the Rev^d
Morgan John Rhees, a Welsh
Baptist minister who emigrated
to America in 1794 and settled
in Philadelphia, where he
married Ann Loxley in 1796.
In Philadelphia Mr Rhees
formed close friendships
with Thomas Jefferson, Joseph
Priestley and Dr. Benjamin
Rush. He named his second
son for that illustrious physician.

Dr. B. Rush Rhees was
my father's uncle, and I
owe my name to that family
connection. He was born
in 1798, and died in 1831.

Rush Rhees

Rochester, N.Y.
May 1938

moved to Chicago, where he engaged in business as a commission merchant. He died at Williamsburgh in 1862 of tuberculosis, and was buried in Greenwood Cemetery, Brooklyn, where his wife, his parents, and other members of the family also rest. He was survived by three of his four children:

IV. 1 Morgan John Rhees III, died in infancy
    2 Eliza Grace Rhees, married Edward St. John
    3 Benjamin Rush Rhees, born in Chicago, February 8, 1860
    4 Caroline Rhees, who died unmarried

His widow, Annie McCutchen Rhees, removed from Chicago to Williamsburgh in 1862, and in 1867 to Plainfield, New Jersey. She was chiefly dependent on her father for support, and her three children's early years were spent under the shelter of his bounty and the shadow of his piety. William Moore McCutchen (1803-1889), Rush Rhees's maternal grandfather, who ruled a submissive household with joyless rectitude, was of Scotch descent. His parents came from Newton Ards, near Belfast, to New York before 1800. William, left fatherless in childhood, was apprenticed to a carpenter, and soon became a master builder. Later in life he was a successful businessman with a New York office and a comfortable income.

Rush Rhees's early familiarity with woodworking tools and building methods, which he owed to his grandfather, served him well all his life. He spent many happy summer days in later years making furniture for his Maine cottage. A grandfather who gives a boy a chest of tools and skill to use them gives a good thing. He makes a maker. Square, rule, and chisel are not a bad beginning for liberal education, that is to say, liberating education. Hands train the head. To measure is to judge. A boy who has mortised his first good joint has begun to grow up. He has become his own critic. He asks nobody "Is it right?" He knows.

Rush Rhees's childhood until he was seven was spent in his grandfather's large colonial house on Grand Street, Williamsburgh, then a fine residential district with gardens and orchards. Grand Street is now a dismal row of shops and tenements, and where the McCutchens lived stands a meat market. In 1867 they removed to Plainfield, New Jersey. Rush's recollections of childhood and youth were somber. He seldom talked about them. Grandfather's stern religion, his determination to do his duty and see that others did theirs did not encourage play or freedom. When he took his grandson out to walk on Sunday afternoons he would sometimes inquire solemnly, "What is the state of your soul, Rushie?" Rush Rhees eventually became a Christian in spite of his bringing up. Perhaps that is why he took his religion so seriously—it was his own.

Fortunately his two young uncles, Charles and Samuel McCutchen, were men of good nature and high spirits, who, having survived the effects of early piety, mitigated the rigors of Centre Street. To their schoolboy nephew they were always helpful. Their love of fun, their fondness for baseball and other sports, their acquaintance with business, won his admiration and loyalty. Charles McCutchen was one of the strongest influences in the life of Rush Rhees, financed his college education, encouraged all his ambitions, and helped him in many ways in later life. He was a trustee of the University of Rochester from 1903 to 1923, and when he died in 1930 Rush Rhees mourned him as his best friend.

Though his father, uncle, sister, and other relatives died of tuberculosis, Rush escaped that menace. Yet he was never robust. Respiratory infections, recurring almost annually in later life, caused him to lose much time which he could ill spare. Even as a youth he had to take good care of his health, but was able to continue his education without interruption. Graduating from Plainfield High School in 1877, he spent the better part of two years in private study to meet college entrance requirements. Whether he also worked for wages during part of this time is not known. We may be certain he was not idling, for that he never knew how to do. Whatever gaps Plainfield left in his training, he filled them. How much Greek and mathematics he knew when he entered Amherst we cannot discover, but he learned enough of both to teach them with marked success. Foundations must have been well laid, for a teacher weak in rudiments never amounts to anything.

At nineteen he was already a man, a self-made man; older than his years, taller than his height, ready to tackle real learning. His mother and uncles knew he would make good. Others found that out before long. Yet there was quite a gap between Plainfield and Amherst. The top boy from a small school meets equals and superiors in a good college; a shock to pride, but a stimulus to ambition. Youth needs both.

II

AMHERST

The greatest advance in college education during
the last fifty years is found in the emphasis which
is now being placed on self-education as the only
real education.—Rush Rhees

◇◇

AMHERST COLLEGE was more than Alma Mater to Rush
Rhees. He not only studied there from 1879 to 1883 and
taught there two years more, but was throughout his life an
Amherst man. This loyalty was not sentimental attachment to
a place or time, but a strong belief in the kind of liberal education that Amherst men received in his day. At Rochester in later
years he tried, not always with success, to carry over to different conditions ideals and methods derived from his undergraduate experience. Amherst reunions in New York, Buffalo,
and Rochester he often attended, to class anniversaries at the
college he returned when he could, and the varying fortunes of
successive Amherst administrations he followed with critical
but sympathetic attention.

Entering college at nineteen years and seven months, he was
determined to make up for lost time. Unknown, unsophisticated,
unsponsored except by Uncle Charley, he had to make a place
for himself, and did. It was not a first place, but honorable. He
found himself, and little by little his classmates found him out.
They discovered sterling qualities beneath a quiet exterior, and
before graduation friendships were formed that lasted for life.

What Amherst was like in 1879 we can picture to ourselves
with considerable vividness by means of Claude Moore Fuess's
history (*Amherst: The Story of a New England College*. Little,

Brown and Company, 1935). While this lively and diverting volume covers the whole history of the college down to 1935, the chapters dealing with President Julius H. Seelye's administration (1877-1890) are of particular importance for the period when Rush Rhees studied and taught there. *Eight O'Clock Chapel*, by Cornelius H. Patton (Amherst '83) and Walter T. Field, of Yale, contains much Amherst material.

President Julius H. Seelye (1824-1895) was an older brother of Laurenus Clark Seelye (1837-1924), who after a professorship of eight years at Amherst became president of Smith College. Both had been educated as ministers, both were conservative in theology and progressive in education, both were tall, bearded men of commanding stature, and both had great influence on students by reason of sterling character and personal charm beneath stately manners. When Rush Rhees entered college in 1879, President Julius H. Seelye was still in his prime. He had been teaching at Amherst since 1858. In 1874 he had been elected to Congress on an independent ticket, and served out his term in Washington during the exciting years of the Hayes-Tilden campaign and contested election. In 1876, after the death of President William A. Stearns of Amherst, he was elected to succeed him, and in 1877 returned to the college as its head. Political experience had given him wider contacts than his earlier life as pastor and teacher. During the fourteen years of his presidency the college, though still retaining much of the evangelical and pietistic atmosphere of earlier times, was adding to its faculty vigorous teachers of intellectual independence and notable powers of leadership. It was to them that Rush Rhees owed his zeal for scholarship, his belief in the importance of character in higher education, and his concern for closer contacts between professors and students.

The strongest of these teachers seems to have been Professor Charles Edward Garman, who beginning in 1880 as instructor in mathematics, was in the following year made instructor in philosophy, and in 1882 associate professor of moral philosophy and metaphysics. Although his method of teaching differed fundamentally from the President's, Professor Garman was given full rein, and soon became one of the keenest intellectual influences on the campus. The discipline and inspiration of his courses must have been comparable to those of Royce, James, and Palmer at Harvard. Though much less known than they, because he had not time or strength to do much writing, he appears to have made a strong impression on such Amherst men as Dwight Morrow, Harlan F. Stone, and Calvin Coolidge. Many tributes to him appear in *Eight O'Clock Chapel*. Rush Rhees's intellectual habits of independent analysis, discrimination, comparison of not two but three or more sides of every question he may have derived in part from this remarkable teacher. Garman died in 1907, leaving among his disciples some of the ablest Amherst alumni in the teaching profession. Such men, if not immortal, at least live more than two generations, for their survivors shape the future.

In Greek, which became Rush Rhees's special field, one of his teachers was the elderly William S. Tyler, whose connection with the college covered half a century, and whose history of Amherst was the standard reference work until Dr. Fuess's appeared. Latin he had with Edward P. Crowell, a lover of the classics, whose later years were clouded by blindness, and the younger William L. Cowles. In mathematics he must have made a marked impression upon Professor William C. Esty, for upon graduation he was selected as instructor in that subject. Other Amherst figures of the early eighties were Professor Heman Humphrey Neill, head of the English department, to whom Rhees owed some of his appreciation of the poets, and John F. Genung, who began his long career as professor of rhetoric in Rhees's senior year. The required physical training was in charge of Dr. Edward Hitchcock, who was a "character," amusing for his peculiarities but a pioneer in developing a system of physical measurements and remedial calisthenics.

With a combination of elderly, conservative teachers, who doubtless demanded thoroughness rather than originality, and a few younger and more progressive leaders encouraging initia-

RUSH RHEES'S FATHER,
JOHN EVANS RHEES

RUSH RHEES'S UNCLE,
CHARLES W. McCUTCHEN

RUSH RHEES AT AMHERST

RUSH RHEES AT NEWTON

tive, the young man from Plainfield went quietly ahead. He was
elected to Alpha Delta Phi, the oldest Greek letter fraternity at
Amherst, and found its fellowship stimulating and broadening.
In later years at Rochester he never joined in that wholesale
condemnation of fraternities which sometimes arises in a college faculty. The lasting importance which he attributed to
fraternity life is shown by his election in later years as national
president of Alpha Delta Phi.

Few of his classmates now survive, but these all remember
him pleasantly. Mr. Joseph R. Kingman of Minneapolis writes:

He was a quiet, studious man whose record of scholastic attainment is
indicated by the fact that he was a class monitor, which meant that he
was one of the four highest ranking students of the class, his duties as
such being to keep the record of attendance at morning chapel. Since he
was an Alpha Delta Phi and I was a Chi Phi, I did not see him very
frequently outside of the classroom. In senior year we both belonged to a
small group of eight calling themselves a senior society, the name of which
I think was Beta Pi. I came to know Rhees more intimately in later
years from the fact that he was a pretty regular attendant at class
reunions. During later years I became very fond of Rhees as I met him
over the five-year reunion period, and came to regard him as one of my
most intimate friends.

Mr. Everett A. Aborn, of Waukesha, Wisconsin, writes briefly
that "he was genial, studious, and immaculate in attire, a clean-
cut gentleman." Mr. Frank Y. Hopkins regarded him as "one
of the outstanding members of our class. He was much liked
by everybody. Short, and not handsome, but with an impressive
countenance that attracted notice when he had something to
say." The Rev. Jonathan Greenleaf, of Windham, New York,
writes more at length:

Ours was a large class for Amherst in that day, 111 men on the roll at
entrance, and a total membership of 129 during the course. He was a
good student, and took high rank, making Phi Beta Kappa, and winning
the Porter Natural Philosophy Prize and the Hardy Prize for debate in
senior year. Rhees was a quiet, dignified fellow, not given to the frivolities which took up much of the attention of less steady fellows, and as
such he held the respect of his classmates.

At the end of our senior year the class put on a masquerade gymnasium exhibition at which Rhees appeared acting as nurse-girl for a robust

and obstreperous infant, whom he wheeled about in a baby carriage. I have forgotten who the "infant" was.

It was not till later years that I really came to know Rush Rhees, his friendly spirit, his brilliant mind, his broad outlook. At the Fifty-fifth Reunion of our class in June, 1938, as Class President he presided, and his genial influence helped to make it the best of all our reunions. He was greatly loved and admired by his classmates.

Others who have written in answer to inquiries agree as to a quiet, studious personality, friendly but not effusive in manner, better liked when better known. Mr. John H. Manning, of Andover, Massachusetts, adds:

Rush was a high-grade scholar, not an athlete; I was a baseball player, not a high-grade scholar. We were therefore placed according to circumstances. In the classroom, in the gymnasium, on the campus, on the athletic field, Rush Rhees was always a well-meaning, broad-minded, upright boy and scholar.

One of his closest friends in the class, Dr. Edward S. Parsons, formerly president of Colorado College and Marietta College, who died in 1943, wrote in 1939 a tribute for the *Amherst Graduates' Quarterly* entitled "The Fairy Story of Rush Rhees." Others of his intimate '83 friends have passed away, especially Williston Walker, Yale historian, and Howard A. Bridgman, editor of the *Congregationalist*. There are few associates of his earliest years left to speak for him, but in their recollections there is nothing but good.

An innovation in student government which President Seelye introduced in 1880, called elsewhere the Amherst System, so interested Rush Rhees, then a sophomore, that long afterward at Rochester he advocated certain features of it for adoption there. The Amherst System, as explained by Dr. Fuess (pp. 220-222, 252-256, 267), placed responsibility for student discipline largely in the hands of a so-called Senate. This consisted of four seniors, three juniors, two sophomores, and one freshman, elected by their classes, and met once a month. The "catch" in this apparently progressive policy was that the President presided at Senate meetings and had veto power over its decisions. Nevertheless, for a time it improved college morale and class attendance. Instead of constant faculty discipline for absences, students were allowed ten per cent "cuts" from classes to cover unavoidable absences, and were not called to account for their use of this allowance. The system depended for its efficiency upon the quality of the undergraduates elected to office. It fell into disuse, and broke down completely under President Gates in the nineties. Certain features of it, adopted at Rochester, still remain.

At graduation Rush Rhees stood fifth in a class of ninety-three. His Commencement part, an oration on William of Orange, was well received. His mother, Uncle Charles, and Aunt Mary Belle came to Amherst for the occasion. More gratifying to them than even his Commencement honors and prizes was his appointment as Walker instructor in mathematics for the next two years. From 1883 to 1885 at a salary of $700 a year he was assistant to Professor William C. Esty, whose son and successor, Professor Thomas C. Esty, now retired, writes as follows:

He was even in those days a man of reserve and dignity. Small talk was not his long hand; on the contrary, when he talked one always had the feeling that he was giving expression to matured ideas. I do not believe that any one could doubt his capacity for warm friendship, once an adequate acquaintance were established. England and Wales are alike in that they produce men and women who at first give to a stranger an impression of almost complete indifference, but when the ice is once broken, it is hard to match them for friendliness and humor. In his quiet way Dr. Rhees betrayed a keen sense of humor; in fact, it was one of the qualities which made companionship with him a genuine delight.

Those last two years at Amherst were not without compensations. There was the intellectual stimulus of teaching an exact science while preparing for a learned profession which is neither exact nor scientific. A minister cannot use mathematics in preparing sermons, but he can use logic, which is a kind of mathematics, and learn to avoid vagueness and prolixity. Problems in calculus may not help much in meeting the human problems of parish or professorship, but they keep a man from feeling that he could not have succeeded in anything else. Also, the discipline of dealing patiently with second-rate minds is useful in any calling. The pleasure of discovering first-rate minds is rarer but richer. Rhees had both. He learned to go slowly with the dull, not to alarm them with too much truth all at once; and to go fast with the alert, not to bore them with advice or spoil them with praise.

Amherst social life for a young teacher was by no means lacking in the early eighties. It was a small town, but there were old families with traditions of culture, comfort, and travel, in whose homes an eligible young man was welcome. Several elderly professors had clever wives and charming daughters. Certain feminine rivalries for social supremacy may have added both to the whirl of entertainment and to the spice of gossip, but would not have lessened the pleasure of the immediate beneficiaries.

Amherst was a quiet place, but it had atmosphere. Books about Emily Dickinson describe the social life of the village as it was when she was young, a generation before. When Rush Rhees came in 1879 she had already retired into complete seclusion and had become almost a legend, the lady in white who lived upstairs. The public knew little or nothing about her poems until after her death. That strange, elusive figure in the upper room lived and died above gossip, of which there has always been too much. Most of the books about her have little to do with literature, and can be ignored except by the morbidly curious. All that one needs to know about her is her poems, including those recently published, and Professor George F. Whicher's admirable study of her style, *This Was a Poet*. Her unique human quality must have been subtly latent in the spiritual atmosphere of Amherst while she lived, but few were sensitive enough then to have perceived it. Rush Rhees was not among them. Of course he met some of the Dickinsons, as anyone living six years in the college circle often met them, but never Emily. It is possible to live longer than that in a town without knowing its most interesting person.

MINISTER

He preaches well that lives well, quoth Sancho.
That's all the divinity I understand.—Cervantes,
Don Quixote.

〰〰〰〰〰〰〰〰〰〰〰〰〰〰〰〰〰〰〰〰〰〰〰〰〰〰〰〰〰

BETWEEN Amherst and Rochester, Rush Rhees spent fifteen years in three religious vocations. From 1885 to 1888 he was a student at Hartford Theological Seminary. After several months of further study in Berlin, he became in 1889 pastor of a church in Portsmouth, New Hampshire, where he stayed three years. Accepting in 1892 a chair of New Testament interpretation at the Newton Theological Institution, he remained there until the end of the academic year 1899-1900. Since in most professional careers these fifteen years from twenty-five to forty are the most decisive and often the most fruitful, though not the most rewarding, we cannot pass too rapidly over this theological period. It had more to do with his presidency than might seem to those who never met him before 1900. A college president should be a scholar; he was a scholar. Religion was his field of scholarship. His Biblical teaching at Newton was more significant than the two years of mathematical instruction at Amherst, for it was advanced vocational training for college graduates.

His teaching of the New Testament he continued for some years in a single college class at Rochester, which pressure of executive duties eventually forced him to relinquish. Since he was a born teacher, especially of superior students, this complete abandonment of instruction was one of the major disappointments of his later career. The gradual reduction of his scholarly research and writing in the Biblical field was another deprivation. It was only part of the price he paid for undertaking in middle life a large task totally different from what he had expected.

Yet nothing was wasted. His Rochester classes in the life of Jesus and the life of Paul, and the chapel addresses and baccalaureate sermons which he continued for thirty-five years until his retirement, formed an important link between the ministerial and university periods. He was still, and always, a preacher. He was in much demand as a speaker in other university chapels and in churches of several denominations. In no sense did he abandon one profession for another, but added a new one to the old.

At Amherst in his time, as in other small colleges of religious origins, many of the older professors and all of the presidents down to the end of the century were former clergymen. Many of them continued to preach, and all were expected to make chapel addresses when their turns came. It was therefore natural that Rush Rhees, turning from the pastorate first to teaching and then to a college presidency, should carry on so far as time permitted his ministry to the religious as well as the intellectual life of young people. He was equally interested in both. The spirit in which he chose the ministry as his profession and the equipment which he brought to it will be the subject of this chapter and of the following one on the Newton Centre period. These pages can be skipped by those interested only in secular education, but without some knowledge of those fifteen years one cannot rightly estimate his achievement in beginning a new career at Rochester in middle life. That he was then already a mature productive scholar and a successful teacher, though without executive experience, will become evident as we examine the record.

The Hartford Theological Seminary, where he studied from 1885 to 1888, was a scholarly Congregational institution, since then greatly expanded into a group of affiliated schools. Emphasis was laid on mastery of the Biblical languages, on

Biblical theology historically studied, and on systematic theology correlated with the philosophical background already acquired in college. There were learned and well-known scholars on the faculty. From one of Rush Rhees's classmates at Hartford, the Rev. Thomas M. Hodgdon, the following reminiscences add something to what little we know of those seminary years:

The class of 1888 at Hartford Seminary was small in numbers. I knew Rush Rhees as intimately as any man in our class. His was a great soul, a rare man in every respect. I considered him the ablest man in our class, one of the ablest in the Seminary. He was so regarded by the faculty, especially by President Hartranft. Rhees had carefully considered what the theological schools had to offer and decided on Hartford. Doubtless he was influenced in this decision by some of the Amherst men then students at Hartford.

I knew him both at play and at work. I often played tennis with him and Henry Kingman, his dear friend, and Weedon, an Amherst man. Rhees was a steady and dependable player, never brilliant, but always companionable and stimulating.

He was a friend of Professor Ernest Cushing Richardson, the librarian, an Amherst man, and through him he had access socially to some of the first families of Hartford.

In the classroom he was at his best in systematic theology and kindred subjects in Dr. Karr's classes. They had many friendly tilts on mooted questions, much to the enjoyment of the boys and Dr. Karr, who appreciated a brilliant and worthy antagonist. In Dr. Hartranft's classes in church history and ethics Rhees was an outstanding student. We were proud of him as the best man in our class, strong in mind, radiant in spirit, sweet and friendly in heart.

His first sermon in a church was preached during his senior year at the Asylum Avenue Baptist Church, Hartford. His text was: "Blessed are the pure in heart, for they shall see God."

When he returned from his study abroad he did not contact a church at once. As I had lived in Portsmouth, New Hampshire, and had relatives and friends in the Baptist church there, and as the church was then looking for a minister, I called the attention of some of the people to Rhees, saying that he would be an ideal minister for them if he could be secured. He was soon called by the church and had a very fruitful and happy ministry there. He was greatly beloved both by his own people and by the church people of the city. Dr. Lucius Thayer, an Amherst graduate, then minister of the North Church, Congregational, was his most intimate friend. While in Portsmouth I have reason to believe he made a thorough study of the New Testament, using the Greek language. Some of the results of this study appeared later in his *Life of Jesus of Nazareth.*

He became deeply interested in the study of the New Testament in his work under Dr. Riddle, a great teacher and a dynamic personality.

Seminary life was not solely an intellectual discipline, but an opportunity for enlarging his knowledge of men and of social problems both in Hartford and elsewhere. During summer vacations, like most theological students, he preached in country churches, mostly in Vermont and New Hampshire, and saw something of rural life. He had also brief summer vacations with the McCutchens in the Adirondacks.

With financial aid from his uncle he rounded out his theological course by a sojourn at the University of Berlin in the summer of 1888. Little is known of this, his first trip to Europe, except that he enlarged his knowledge of German by intensive tutoring from an expert teacher of foreign students, and that he valued most his lecture courses with the famous church historian Dr. Adolf von Harnack. In his chosen field of New Testament criticism and Biblical theology he made rapid progress during these few months in Germany, and was familiar with the best recent German treatises, then still untranslated, which he used freely in later teaching at Newton.

He may have begun in Berlin his special interest in certain late Jewish books of the period between the Apocrypha and the New Testament, such as the so-called Psalms of Solomon. These and other books written in Greek not long before the time of Christ throw much light on the later Messianic concepts of the Son of Man and the Kingdom of God, to which Jesus gave new significance. Without some knowledge of these late extra-Biblical books no adequate interpretation of the Gospels is possible. Between the Maccabean period and the writing of the Gospels there were more than two centuries which can be filled only by research.

Acquaintance with Harnack, then a leading figure in the theological world, was in itself worth a trip to Germany. Some other leading Biblical scholars then at Berlin, whom Rush Rhees cites freely in his books and articles, he probably saw and heard in this summer quarter. Though it was a brief sojourn, it gave him standards of exact scholarship and knowledge of opposing schools of thought which kept him always from becoming provincial.

He could state clearly and fairly the opinions of men with whom he totally disagreed, without feeling always obliged to attempt a refutation. This ability is not common among theologians—nor among scientists, critics, or politicians—most of whom become partisans for what they believe to be the only tenable position on some controversial question. He did not get this power from Germany; it is neither German nor American, but exceptional everywhere. It endeared him to his best students and puzzled the rest. Untrained minds do not wish to hear more than one side—their own.

Returning from Berlin to Plainfield in the autumn of 1888, he resolved to undertake, at least for a time, the work of a regular pastorate. He supplied various pulpits, but for several anxious months received no call, and devoted his enforced leisure to study. He was never idle while waiting; a delay was an opportunity. Whether he then looked forward to the ministry as a lifework, or rather as an apprenticeship for theological teaching toward which his later studies had been tending, is unknown. In either case, he was probably relieved when in December, through a classmate's friendly offices as above mentioned, he received an invitation to preach as a candidate at the Middle Street Baptist Church, Portsmouth, New Hampshire. He seems to have pleased the congregation, for on January 28, 1889, there came a formal call to the pastorate. The salary offered was $1,500, payable quarterly, with a month's vacation. From Plainfield on February 13 he sent his acceptance. He was never in a hurry when he had an important decision to make. He was deliberate but not dilatory. If other people often kept him waiting for their convenience, he sometimes kept them waiting for time to think; for when he had once made a promise he kept it.

For his ordination to the ministry on March 14, 1889, according to the custom of the denomination, a council was called consisting of pastors and laymen of other Baptist churches in Portsmouth and vicinity. The candidate's mother and his favorite uncle and aunt came to Portsmouth for the occasion, as they had for his Amherst Commencement. It was a notable day for them all, the beginning at twenty-nine of a career for which he had been long preparing, and which might be his for life. With faith and hope those four faced the unknown. If they had known then where he would be in twenty years—or in fifty— would they have been happier or wiser?

The hymns chosen for young Mr. Rhees's ordination, when he became the Reverend, included according to the printed program Tate's metrical version of the Te Deum, sung to the tune St. Anne. He might have preferred for old St. Anne that other metrical version by Isaac Watts of the Ninetieth Psalm, "Our God, our help in ages past." That was one of his favorite hymns, which he always gave out at the first college chapel of every year. "Sing all the stanzas," he used to say. Once when for variety the pianist began to play an alternative tune of the same meter on the same page, the President stopped him with a wave of the hand. "The right tune is St. Anne," he said, in an eighteenth century voice. (Wales and Scotland speaking; grandfathers all there.) St. Anne is the right tune for his biography.

The Ninetieth Psalm seemed to mean for him the beginning and end of all great things. Its words were what one day says to another when they meet. It was a mountain song for hazards and crises, for war and the end of war, for life and the end of life, for the certainty of trouble and of its final passing. A hymn for high places, fit to look out over the grand canyon of the world. A glimpse of the vanishing present, joining an irrevocable past to an unknown future; time under the aspect of eternity. Few ever heard Rush Rhees read that psalm at a funeral or give it out as a hymn to be sung when change was coming who did not feel that here was a quiet man who lived with the changeless and was never appalled.

Portsmouth was an old town, older than Boston, almost as old as Plymouth. There were traditions of early seafaring days among the old families, and there was the navy yard group, and a new industrial element coming in. The church was conservative, with that linkage of money and orthodoxy not unknown to young pastors. Rush Rhees was accustomed to delicate situations, and this additional experience did not come amiss in later years. Finesse without evasion, good manners without surrender, were among his social assets.

He was popular in Portsmouth. People could not easily forget his pleasant, slightly quizzical smile, or his interest in young people and their ambitions, even in old people and their complaints. They recalled, too, that his long complex sentences always came out triumphantly to a grammatical conclusion. His predicates never forgot his subjects. No relative clause got lost. He could catch a runaway verb by the tail and tie it. Schoolteachers admired his syntax; schoolboys wondered, "Will he make it?" He met his people more than halfway. Where he saw good will he gave back more than he received. Rush Rhees could talk fifteen minutes to a country boy and make a lifelong admirer. Yet in later years some thought him distant. Why? Was it not their own self-distrust?

Life in Portsmouth was not monotonous or lonely. One summer the McCutchens spent there in order to be near him. One winter his mother was there. At the boardinghouse of the three Misses Pillow, maiden ladies of culinary distinction and complete propriety, lived two young bachelors, the Rev. Rush Rhees, Baptist, and the Rev. Lucius H. Thayer, Congregationalist (Amherst '82). Both were temporarily immune to the shafts of Eros. The two parsons got along splendidly. In later years it was not always "pie like mother used to make" but "piecrust like Miss Pillow's." Long afterward Rhees used to speak with laughing affection of those three comfortable sisters, now gone where all good cooks go. Some of their recipes survived in the Rochester kitchen.

The young minister was always a worker. He not only prepared his sermons as carefully as if for a large city congregation, but kept up Biblical studies beyond the demands of the pulpit. His daily work on the Greek Testament was not a mere search for texts. Like a teacher, a preacher must know much that he never directly uses in discourse. A speaker who ventures too close to the edge of his knowledge is in danger of guessing beyond it. There are many sermons based on misinterpretation of motto texts, in which sound exposition is abandoned for fanciful playing with words. The Bible is made a point of departure for speculation. Rush Rhees always wanted people to know first what the Scripture really meant when it was written. Then, if he chose to talk about something else, after fair notice he could.

Except for formal occasions he did not write sermons in full or read from manuscript. He spoke from rather full notes, written in expanded outline form on small slips of paper convenient to hold in the hand. These sermon notes were later filed in envelopes, on the outside of which he wrote the title, the text, and the date and place of delivery. Many are still preserved. In addition to the main divisions of the discourse the notes contained all the subdivisions, hints of illustrations to be used, the first sentence of every paragraph, and the complete words of the conclusion. He knew what he was going to say but not in detail just how he would say it. The advantage of such a method over reading from a complete script was that he could keep his eyes on the audience, and also that he could easily omit or interpolate as occasion required.

To illustrate his method of preaching as well as its prevailing substance, we may choose from his pulpit notes a sermon on the text, "The things which are seen are temporal; but the things which are not seen are eternal" (II Cor. 4:18). He began by explaining that "eternal" does not mean endless. The reference of the Greek word so translated is to a conception inherited from older Hebrew thought, distinguishing the existing world order from the coming age, or "aeon." "Things which are not seen" belong to a kind of life not yet fully realized, life better than we know. The point in the phrase "aeonian life" or "eternal life" is not duration but quality. Not how long but how fine is the life of the soul?

After this exposition of the text, he next made the point that, although such contrasts between the two ages were originally meant to console an oppressed and despondent people, they were equally applicable to times of prosperity. "Things which are seen" are not unimportant, not to be despised, for they furnish motive power for most of the ordinary concerns of daily life. They include good health, successful work, comfort, possession of power. These are visible goods, but not the highest goods. The history of human progress shows "the ascendancy of the new and higher influence over the strong and obvious." Among the higher goods in the realm of the unseen, or kingdom of God, he enumerated the ultimate triumph of righteousness over evil, the realization of human brotherhood, and fellowship with the divine.

Social and ethical progress, he held, comes only by individual effort based on ideals. This was the burden of all his preaching—the long pursuit of the difficult and beautiful. Nothing good is easy. Choice between lesser immediate goods and greater distant goods cannot be based merely on reason, for reason lacks impetus. It comes, if at all, by a vision of some higher perfection than any but the saints have reached—by attempting the impossible.

This was his message to the young. He did not preach much about sin and personal salvation, vicarious atonement and satisfaction of divine justice, not because he did not find these doctrines in St. Paul, but because he did not find them central in the serious thinking of a new generation. This generation at its best is more concerned than the old with social justice, less with safety first. He preached for the present, not the past; for conduct, not for speculation. He confronted young men not with abstraction but with action.

Religion in his view was not a set of opinions but a way of life. It comes partly from beyond us. The Supreme Reality is also the Highest Good. God, who is both in one, must be concerned not only with cosmic energies and designs but also with the moral life of men and nations. The Great Spirit must be better as well as wiser than the best of men. Why? Because otherwise the Creator would be lower than the creature, the cause less than the effect.

These metaphysical axioms or postulates, based not on "wishful thinking" but on the pagan logic of Aristotle and the Christian logic of St. Thomas Aquinas, as well as on the Scriptures, Rush Rhees rephrased many times. They do not supplant revelation but confirm it, and support a faith possible even for an agnostic age.

If there is no higher sanction for good life than social science, expediency, and self-respect, if reverent religious feeling and devout observance are to be eliminated from higher education, replaced solely by lectures on comparative religion, then Rush Rhees was behind the times. If what he stood for was a broad idea of religion on which good men of all faiths could agree, preserving in addition their separate creeds, then he was ahead of his own times and farther ahead of ours.

The Portsmouth pastorate, so promisingly begun and happily continued, was not long. Within two years he was first approached by the Newton Theological Institution as to a teaching appointment. He declined the first overtures because he felt that it was not fair to a church to leave it so soon, even for a wider opportunity. He owed it to his people and to himself to prove that he could be a good minister. More than once in later life he expressed doubts about men who shifted their positions every year or so to better themselves. It seemed to indicate lack of stability and fidelity to a self-imposed task. But after a third year, and renewed urging from his friends that he should not, at the age of thirty-two, longer delay beginning a new professional career toward which he was strongly inclined, he resigned his office. The church on May

18, 1892, accepted his resignation with great regret. In addition to the conventional expressions of appreciation there was a more unusual note that seemed to indicate that the people knew what a prize they were losing.

Apart from weekly preaching and daily pastoral experience at Portsmouth, it is not unlikely that he had a better opportunity there than later in Newton Centre to see at close range something of community problems of poverty, housing, need for playgrounds, treatment of juvenile delinquency, and improvement of public schools, in all of which he was active in Rochester from the beginning. The pastor of a small church in an industrial town, with a sprinkling of poor children in the Sunday school, cannot fail to learn in pastoral visitation something of those social needs. Whether he acquired his social conscience at Portsmouth, or earlier at Hartford, he had it, and it drove him into constantly widening fields of philanthropic interest.

The three years were not wasted. It may be doubted whether a larger city church, with a higher salary and more public notice for his sermons, would have been so good for his development. At Portsmouth his inner life had time and space to widen and deepen. Never again—until retirement—would he have so much spiritual leisure. Years crowded upon him tasks beyond the reach of meditation.

Not only as minister but as man, not for three years but for life, Rush Rhees's religion was himself. In that Supreme Reality of which he was always a part and often aware, he lived and moved and had his being. When he ceased to live and move, it was still his being.

IV

TEACHER

—quando nel mondo ad ora ad ora
m'insegnavate come l'uom s'eterna.—Dante

≈≈≈≈≈≈≈≈≈≈≈≈≈≈≈≈≈≈≈≈≈≈≈≈≈≈≈≈≈≈≈≈≈≈≈≈≈

NEWTON THEOLOGICAL INSTITUTION, where Rush Rhees taught from 1892 to 1900, was not in his time the equal of the best seminaries of other denominations. Founded in 1825, its long history as a school for preachers and missionaries was honorable, but in scholarship it was inferior to Hartford. There were two good scholars on the faculty, and one of them was leaving. The two were Charles R. Brown, Old Testament, and Ernest D. Burton, New Testament. Burton was going to the new Divinity School of the University of Chicago. He was already the author of several scholarly books, and an excellent teacher. It was his place that Rush Rhees was invited to fill, after an older candidate had declined the appointment. The other departments were not strong. Newton was perhaps doubtful about Rhees, but Rhees was certainly doubtful about Newton.

On the other hand, the progressive spirit in the Newton administration was sufficient to ensure a welcome for young scholars of liberal tendencies, a policy that did not prevail in more reactionary schools. The location of the institution, on a hilltop with a magnificent view, in the pleasant suburban village of Newton Centre, with good railroad service to Boston, was superior to that of many more famous seminaries. Since Rush Rhees was already turning toward New Testament scholarship as a career, and since no openings for him were then available elsewhere, he accepted President Hovey's offer of an associate professorship at a salary of $2,000. In his letter of acceptance he wrote: "With the understanding that so far as is practicable the subjects that will ultimately be assigned me for teaching will be those that are associated with the theological phases of New Testament interpretation as distinguished from the philological features of the work." In so carefully delimiting the future field of his professorial labors, Rush Rhees presumably looked forward to a lifetime of teaching theology. Little did he guess what was ahead.

At the beginning he had to face the difficult position of being Burton's successor, and had to overcome in himself a certain tendency toward overfastidious and sarcastic criticism of his students. He was also antagonistic to some well-established policies of the institution. It had not only its regular course for college graduates with Greek, but a special curriculum for so-called English students less thoroughly prepared, and also a small group of French Canadians training for Protestant mission work among their own people. With neither of these latter departments was he in sympathy. The former he regarded as lowering the scholarly standards of the seminary, the latter as an unjustified anti-Catholic enterprise. One who knew him in those first years says of this latter protest:

He said that the Catholic rector must, he thought, be a very fine man. Rhees had frequently wished to call at the rectory and make his acquaintance, "But as long as we are conducting an anti-Catholic propaganda institute on the hill, such a call might be embarrassing on both sides." I dissented, bringing up the familiar trustee argument that the French were not being trained as controversialists but as missionaries, that thousands, of French Catholics had left the Catholic church, were without religion, and Protestants ought to give them the gospel. Rhees answered with unusual heat that if I would examine the instruction I would find that it was largely an attack on another branch of the Christian church, the branch that was associated with the historic church and the transmission of the gospel.

He never changed his opinion on this point, and after going to Rochester had pleasant and friendly relations with some of the Catholic clergy there. His opposition to the nongraduate courses at Newton did not help his standing with members of those courses, though he did his duty by them. The letter continues:

Just how much Rhees himself knew of these undercurrents of opposition I have no means of judging. He never whined or complained. He spoke out against things that he disapproved, but not to air personal grievances. He was, however, too sensitive and alert a spirit to be unaware of some antagonisms. Even among the men who admired his work there was some resentment. His fastidiousness made him very critical of some of the boorishness on the hill. Beyond question he was a bit officious in corrections, especially as the youngest professor. The adjective "fussy" was applied to him very generally.

During the years 1894-96 a great change came to Rhees. The last of the mourners for Burton graduated in 1894. Also the trustees advanced Rhees from an experimental associate professorship to a full professorship. He now had an assured status. His hard work and experience were beginning to flower. It was pleasant to get letters from friends in 1896 and have them say, "One of the most noticeable things this year is the change in Rush. From the most ridiculed man on the faculty he is turning into its most popular member."

The faculty had taken him at his real value from the start. By conscientious straightforward work he had won his way with students, and at least in part with trustees. They gave him full status, but held back full salary until his marriage. He took it laughingly, saying that he quite agreed with them that an unmarried man ought to be able to live on less salary.

The Rhees of the last two years at Newton had mellowed up remarkably. A few of us, fearing that our scanty German was going to waste, asked for the catalogue promise that a professor would read German with students who desired. Rhees proposed that he would take us if it was understood that it would be no class-and-instructor affair, but a group reading some theological work which he wanted to use in his New Testament work. I still smile to think how we climbed to the third floor of the Hartshorne house for those genial, almost jovial sessions. Nearly always there was discussion of what the long sentences meant after they were transferred to English, often of their philosophical bearing. We got all that we applied for, and that Rhees was no sarcastic, snappy pedagogue, but almost one of the boys.

Such testimony shows that he had to get over feeling superior before he could be accepted as equal. Many young teachers have had to learn that. When they have learned it, their real superiority, no longer claimed, is cheerfully conceded.

He began his new career with thoroughness. He placed

knowledge above opinions. As a motto for the first page of his *Life of Jesus of Nazareth* he chose a quotation concerning "the demand for an intelligent faith, which shall transcend but shall not despise knowledge, or neglect to have a knowledge to transcend." His teaching method placed emphasis on facts, on concrete mastery of the body of New Testament literature studied in relation to its background. His classes were provided with syllabi of the lectures, copies of which still survive. These were at first mimeographed, later privately printed, with wide margins for notes. The method would have been liable to abuse if it had merely saved students the labor of taking their own complete notes, but since they were held responsible in examinations not only for the outline but for the much fuller discussion based on it, the saving of time for all concerned was considerable. When teachers dictate an elaborate outline or place it on a blackboard, slow writers with one-track minds pass the hour copying when they should be listening.

These syllabi, revised and reprinted from time to time on the basis of experience, and of new material which had just appeared, had some of the advantages of a loose-leaf index, kept up to date by marginal annotation. Eventually, however, they were intended to be made into books. The lectures on *The Life of Jesus of Nazareth* did so appear in 1900 (Scribner's), the last year of the author's Newton service. The book has since been widely used as a textbook. Even though it contains none of the contributions to New Testament scholarship of the past forty-six years, it is still more readable and useful than many later books, because free from partisanship and prejudice. As is so often the case, having originally represented a rather liberal position, it would now be classified as conservative. Advanced opinions on such questions as the late date and the nonapostolic authorship of the Fourth Gospel were not ignored, but the author did not share them. He felt, however, no doubts as to the scholarship or the Christian character of those who did, nor did he misstate or underestimate their views. There was nothing belligerent about Rush Rhees as a

Biblical scholar. His gospel was peace—even among Christians. Seeing both sides of truth, he claimed no monopoly of either.

The Life of Jesus of Nazareth was chosen by a Japanese scholar, Tatsu Tanaka (Hartford Theological Seminary '05) to be translated into Japanese, and appeared in Japan in 1906. The Rochester author never expected to derive any profit from this foreign edition, but suggested when his permission was first requested that any royalties which might accrue should be paid to the Doshisha University, founded by an Amherst graduate, Joseph Neesima, in 1870. It was explained by Mr. Tanaka, however, that such books are rarely profitable in Japan, being published only as a contribution to learning. After the lapse of a generation, it may be wondered how much or how little influence Rush Rhees's life of an "author of peace and lover of concord" may have had in the history of Japanese Christianity.

Those who desire to get a clear impression of Rush Rhees's intellectual outlook before he became a college president should examine his one full-length book. If already familiar with the general outlines of New Testament criticism, they should turn first to the appendix, in which sources are evaluated and special problems considered. This appendix, not meant for the general reader, represents the technical residue of the original syllabus on which the book was based, and shows how thoroughly the author had studied the critical, chronological, and geographical questions of the Gospels.

In view of his initial request at Newton that his teaching be rather in the field of New Testament theology than of critical or philological investigation, it is surprising that only the last fifty pages deal with the teachings of Jesus. This fact is partly explained by the scope of the series to which the book belonged, and partly by the author's later articles in the *Biblical World* and the *American Journal of Theology* on related subjects, listed in the bibliography at the end of this volume.

A privately printed syllabus for *The Life of Paul: Notes of*

*Lectures to the Junior Class in The Newton Theological Insti-
tution* appeared in 1897, but the corresponding textbook in the
Scribner's series, announced by the publishers as in preparation, was never completed. Studies for it were undertaken
at various times, such as a pamphlet monograph on *Saul's
Experience as a Factor in His Theology* (Chicago, 1896), an
Amherst M.A. thesis on "The Life of Paul" (1897), and an
unpublished paper on "St. Paul as Prophet and Scholastic."
The author expected when he came to Rochester to find time
to finish his second book, but leisure never came. For some
years at Rochester he continued to teach the life of Paul, using
materials collected for the book, but these classes too were
finally abandoned. This inevitable loss to himself and to Biblical scholarship is the more to be regretted in that, judging from
the syllabus and the published magazine articles, his interpretation of Pauline theology would have been somewhat unusual. "He was the apostle of Christianity as a world-religion—
far-sighted, radical, and bold."

In sermons on Pauline texts, such as that referred to in the
preceding chapter, he was able to continue his interpretation
of the apostle. But few who listened to these can have known
that they carried with them the intensity of a renunciation
that had changed his life. In later years he had other hidden
disappointments, all like this beyond his control. One does
not like to be reminded of unavailing regrets. When nothing
can be done nothing should be said.

Returning to his eight years of successful teaching at Newton, we find that his classroom lectures were often followed by
discussion. Questions of conservative students frequently
turned on apparent contradictions in the New Testament narratives. If one account is really at variance with another, what
about divine inspiration? If the author of the Fourth Gospel
or of the Acts expands actual sayings of Jesus or of His apostles
into longer discourses, like the speeches in Greek and Roman
historians, how do we know which part is the original nucleus
and which the author's interpretation? Such questions the

teacher often met by asking questioners first to define their terms and then to offer their own tentative explanation of the difficulty.

On miracles he was cautious, neither denying their possibility nor admitting that they involved suspension of natural law. He did not question Matthew's and Luke's narratives of the miraculous birth of Jesus, but pointed out that neither St. Paul nor the author of the Fourth Gospel based his belief in the divinity of Christ on those narratives. Likewise with regard to the resurrection, he surveyed without prejudice all attempts to explain it on some vision hypothesis, but pointed out the difficulties of accepting any such theory. The supreme miracle that we all accept, as he often used to say, was the moral character of Jesus. He wished to shake no man's faith, to blame no honest doubt. He always lifted such discussions above the level of orthodoxy or heresy into the region of spiritual aspiration and endeavor. Faith is a force for action, and most men believe enough to do something about it.

His relations with students were informal and friendly. As a bachelor living in a boardinghouse he could not entertain them often, but he could walk with them or welcome them to his room. He called on them when they were ill, helped them when in trouble, encouraged them when despondent, and recommended them when they were seeking appointments. He did these things not professionally but humanely, because he liked sincere and unselfish young men, whether brilliant or not. He wished to see them make the most of themselves. The world could use them all.

The difference between a mediocre student working at his top level and a superior intelligence retarded by lazy complacency is not always easy for a teacher to detect at first acquaintance. Once found, it would lead Rush Rhees to praise the plodder, and spur the clever idler to try something beyond his powers. This was what both needed and neither expected. He taught by surprise.

If there were now and then a few students of the other sort, glib, self-important, and superficial, they probably did not like him, because he saw through them and smiled. When he met such ministers in later years, and heard them call him "brother," it must have been a strain. Bores bored him, hypocrites made him tired, but he had a poker face and could hide disgust. This helped later to make him a good president; he never exploded, though sometimes the pressure ran high.

His social life in Newton Centre and Boston was naturally freer than at Portsmouth, because it was in a wider, more cultivated circle, and because he was not quite so restrained by his position. Being now a member but not pastor of a church, and only one among half a dozen reverend professors, he could and did make friends in other neighborhoods and other communions, as well as in his own. Even now, after half a century, he is pleasantly remembered in Newton Centre by people who knew him then as an agreeable and friendly neighbor and companion. Mr. William H. Rice, of Newton Centre, writes:

Professor Rhees was a charter member of The Villagers, a club formed in January, 1894, for "mutual improvement and social culture." At the meetings of this club the members in turn read papers on subjects which might be of interest to the other members. Professor Rhees's first paper was given at the meeting on October 16, 1895, and was entitled "Dr. MacClure and his Patients." It was an instructive analysis of the principal characters in the Reverend John Watson's book *Beside the Bonnie Brier Bush.* Professor Rhees acted as toastmaster at the first Ladies' Night held April 26, 1898 at the University Club. At the meeting on January 17, 1899 Professor Rhees read his second paper, "The Educational Value of Sloyd." At the second Ladies' Night, held at the Hotel Somerset on April 4, 1899, he informed The Villagers of his intention to marry. His resignation was accepted at the meeting of October 16, 1900 and he was elected an honorary member of the Club, and a copy of his inaugural address as President of the University of Rochester was ordered to be placed on file. As I remember Mr. Rhees he was a highly educated young man, full of fun and wit. He was decidedly sociable. The members of The Villagers all spoke of what a great loss it was to the Club when he moved away from here.

Professor W. N. Donovan, of Newton Highlands, who for Rush Rhees's last two years at Newton Centre was a junior colleague, speaks of long tramps which they took together. Rush owned a horse, and rode almost daily. He also belonged to a golf club. Dr. Donovan mentions Rush's membership in the Twentieth Century Club of Boston. He and others refer to his activity in the First Baptist Church of Newton Centre, where he taught a training class for Sunday-school teachers. He also assisted in maintaining a Sunday afternoon Sunday school at a village several miles from Newton Centre, supported by visitors for the benefit of children who would otherwise have been without religious instruction. In many ways he did more than he had to, and more than he was paid for.

The most vivid pictures of his social life at Newton Centre come from those who met him daily at his boardinghouse. His rooms were at Mrs. J. C. Hartshorne's, but he got his meals at Mrs. C. H. Rowe's, from whose daughter come several glimpses of the lively circle:

Dr. Rhees had two rooms at my aunt's. She and my grandmother with the maid were alone in a large house. They had burglars, and Dr. Rhees was supposed to be a protection. He was always kind and pleasant, thoughtful and friendly to my aunt and to my aged grandmother, who was in her nineties. Dr. Rhees's mother used to come to visit her son, and came to our house for meals with her son. Dr. Rhees was devoted to her, and she was a friendly, gentle woman.

Dr. Rhees was with us only for meals, and seldom lingered afterward. At the table he sat next to Dr. Edward Sullivan, who was rector of Trinity Episcopal Church for over forty years. Dr. Sullivan with his Irish wit and funny stories was much appreciated by Dr. Rhees; the room was often filled with laughter.

When Dr. Rhees took his first trip to Europe we wanted to celebrate, so the men wore dress suits to dinner and the women dinner gowns. Some extra nice food. A Boston University student that mother gave a home to blacked up and waited on table with all the airs of a Negro waiter. There was much joking and fun during the meal, and Dr. Rhees entered into it with enjoyment.

Then when Dr. Rhees was engaged he was still with us for meals. He was radiantly happy and we joked him about it, saying we never thought he would do such a thing, and he said, "I thought you would know by the size of my mouth," for his smile was wider. He had a pleasant smile. People liked him. The students used to say that if one of them was sick he was the first professor to go to see him, and would be thoughtful and kind.

The Boston University student who acted the part of a colored waiter at the going-away party was William F. Rogers, now an associate commissioner of the Metropolitan District Commission of the Commonwealth of Massachusetts. Here is his testimony:

I knew Rush Rhees in the early nineties when I was working my way through Boston University. I got my board for tending the furnace, shoveling snow, etc., at Mrs. Rowe's. Rush Rhees was the star boarder, and the fact that I was the chore boy made no difference in his attitude towards me. He was always kindly and considerate. It was a rare privilege for a boy from the backwoods of Maine to sit at the same table and to be in on the wit and learning.

When he was called to be President of the University of Rochester there was no question in the minds of his table companions of his fitness for that position. Now that I am a Trustee of Boston University, I can better appreciate his qualities for an administrator of a large university.

Fifty years have wiped out memories of revealing incidents, but the impression remains that Rush Rhees was a big, kindly man.

Mr. Harry J. Carlson, of Newton Centre, a leading Boston architect and trustee of the Massachusetts Institute of Technology, was also a member of that cheerful boardinghouse group. In response to a request for recollections, he writes:

I knew him well, for we ate at the same boardinghouse, where the conversation might well have interested the "Autocrat" himself, for Rush Rhees was then at his best, full of fun, keen of wit, and with a lightning retort. There was a Boston Latin School teacher who delighted in starting him off and then prodded him to still greater verbal battle. The rest of us would just sit and grin; the pace was too fast for us. I think people in general were a little afraid of him. He was always a little better dressed than anyone else, he looked always perfectly groomed, and he had an air of aloofness and an incisive manner of speech that rather kept people at a distance, but his boardinghouse manner was so frank, boyish, and full of enthusiasm that we all loved him.

Some of his associates on the faculty of the theological school were old, long-whiskered fossils, full of the stern traditions, while R.R. seemed like an up-to-date version of the *new* testament.

He and I took many long bicycle trips together—Blue Hill, Wayside Inn, Concord, Lexington—but in our many rests we never discussed theology but enjoyed the trees, the hills, and the joys of the country road.

Wife and I came out of the Metropolitan Opera in New York one night and saw him coming out immaculate in evening dress; said he often came over to New York just to enjoy the music of the opera.

I remember in Rome, Italy, meeting two New Zealand young ladies, and they asked where I was from. I answered, "From a little town near Boston that you have never heard about, Newton Centre." One of them smiled and said, "Do you know Rush Rhees?" Their picture of him was the friendly, companionable man that I knew so well.

I treasure his wedding present, a beautifully bound set of Lowell's poetical works. He too soon married, and we saw less and less of one another, except at church and occasionally at prayer-meeting, where his simple statement of faith was in contrast with the heated, dogmatic, positive utterances of the old die-hards.

I wish I could have seen R.R. and George Eastman, whom I also knew as a member of the Corporation of the Massachusetts Institute of Technology. He (G.E.) was so quiet that I wonder if R.R. could stir him up. At least he appreciated him.

Mr. Carlson's reference to Rush Rhees's going to New York just to hear opera is characteristic. He always had a season ticket to the Boston Symphony concerts, and was a true music lover, though neither a performer nor a critic.

Summers during the Newton Centre period were not spent wholly in recreation at the McCutchens' Adirondack home. In 1893 he taught at the University of Chicago, visiting the Columbian Exposition then in progress. He spent one summer in Germany to study again in Berlin. Another summer he went to Denver, where his mother was staying. In several later summers he spent some weeks at the Chautauqua Summer Assembly on Chautauqua Lake, lecturing on the New Testament, conducting classes in the Institute of Sacred Literature, and giving devotional addresses. His friend George Vincent, son of Bishop John H. Vincent, was then prominent at Chautauqua, as were Ernest D. Burton, Shailer Mathews, and William R. Harper.

At the home of friends in West Newton in 1897 he first met Harriet Chapin Seelye, of Northampton, daughter of President L. Clark Seelye of Smith College. She was a member of a distinguished New England family, descended from Robert Seely, who came from England in 1630 and was one of the founders of Watertown. Her mother, Henrietta Chapin, daughter of

Lyman Chapin of Albany, was descended from Samuel Chapin,
one of the founders of Springfield. He was the original of
Saint-Gaudens's ideal statue of "The Puritan" in Springfield,
that bronze figure with a broad hat, a long stride, and a big
Bible. Clark and Henrietta Seelye, being thus wholly of seventeenth century New England ancestry, brought up their six
children in the fear of the Lord and the love of learning.
Harriet, though she spent her early childhood in Amherst,
where her father was a professor before becoming president of
Smith College, had been brought up in Northampton. Her
biography of her father (*Laurenus Clark Seelye*. Houghton
Mifflin Company, 1929) bears indirectly on this biography of
her husband. Since she was as much a product of New England
higher education as he, and had been longer and more intimately associated with it by reason of her family connections,
the first meeting of these two, so long delayed, was an event
to be remembered. They had much in common: their intellectual interests, their love of music and art, their European
travels, their Puritan inheritance, mellowed by tolerance and
humor. In March, 1899, they were formally engaged.

Soon afterward the first overtures from Rochester were
received. Informal inquiries such as always precede an important appointment were continued at Northampton in June,
when Rush Rhees was visiting at the Seelye home. The chairman of the Rochester Board of Trustees, Mr. Rufus A. Sibley,
interviewed him and, satisfied with the candidate who was
warmly recommended by his prospective father-in-law, Mr.
Sibley sent to Rochester a favorable report.

The detailed history of these negotiations, which led to Rush
Rhees's election as president on his wedding day, July 6, 1899,
belongs to the next chapter. But since he decided to postpone
for a year the assumption of his new duties, in order to complete his book, and to give the Newton trustees the usual
year's notice before leaving, the wedding was celebrated at
Northampton without further delay.

During the honeymoon the two discussed the Rochester offer carefully, in view of all the factors involved, the complete change of work with accompanying responsibility and uncertainty, and on the other hand, the great opportunity for a career of broader possibilities than a theological professorship. Mrs. Rhees says of this decision:

It was characteristic of him not to make decisions off-hand. He always balanced the pros and cons with scrupulous conscientiousness. In general he disliked having to make a decision, but, once made, he no longer worried over it. So, once he had made up his mind that the Rochester offer was the thing for him, he cheerfully sent his acceptance, and we adjusted our minds to the prospect of life in Rochester. . . . He agreed, therefore, to begin his duties in the University on July 1, 1900, and the first year of our married life was spent in Newton Centre, where he kept on with his work at the Seminary, and worked hard on the book, which was published in the spring.

The Rochester appointment was accepted by letter dated July 24, 1899. At the age of thirty-nine years, five and one-half months, exactly one-half of his entire life, Rush Rhees began life all over again.

It was a risk. Most of the reputation he had begun to build up for himself in theological scholarship would count for little in his new career. Only his methods of study and teaching, his interest in young men, his slight but increasing acquaintance— through the McCutchens—with men of affairs and business practice, his capacity for long-range planning and execution, then latent but not unnoticed by his friends, would be available. Idealism was not what was wanted. Religion was not what was most wanted. The University of Rochester needed most of all a strong and tactful leader to restore somewhat impaired public confidence in its future. It was a going concern, but it was not going far—unless new resources could be found. The trustees thought Rhees was the man to find them. They were right, but they took a long chance, and so did he. Life gives to many a man a second beginning, but to few a third. He had made good elsewhere, but he must make better here. *Meliora* was the college motto. He took it for his own.

V

ROCHESTER

Difficulties are things that show what men are.—Epictetus

Nel mezzo del cammin di nostra vita mi ritrovai—Dante

〜〜〜〜〜〜〜〜〜〜〜〜〜〜〜〜〜〜〜〜〜〜〜〜〜〜〜〜〜〜〜〜〜〜〜

IN THE middle of the road of his life Rush Rhees found himself; not, like Dante, in a dark wood, but in a riverside city
where light was growing. He found himself not by groping or
random experiment, but by using his head. From others' mistakes he learned what to avoid; from their timidity, where to
be bold. The first ten years were the worst; the next ten mildly
encouraging. Only in his third decade did things happen in a
big way. Culmination came in the last five years. Not many
things in America were culminating after 1929 except calamity,
but Rochester's harvest had been sown long before. He was
the sower; others will reap.

It must be remembered that the history of the University
of Rochester is not the subject of this book. That is larger than
the life of any one man, or any ten. It has already been partly
covered in Jesse Leonard Rosenberger's two historical studies,
*Rochester and Colgate: Historical Backgrounds of the Two
Universities* (University of Chicago Press, 1925) and *Rochester: The Making of a University* (published by The University
of Rochester, 1927). Mr. Rosenberger studied the origins,
material progress, and personnel of three-quarters of a century.

Not the college but the man is what we are after. How did
the new president meet the situation that he discovered when
he arrived? How far had he been prepared for it? How did he
face the inevitable disillusionment of early years, financial

43

stringency, and relative public indifference—in some quarters
—to the university? What chief objectives did he set before
himself, first, for making a good small college into a better
small college; second, for meeting demands and opportunities
for expanding this college into a university and so earning a
new right to an old name; and third, for keeping the university,
when at last amply endowed, from becoming one-sided?

Rush Rhees as an educator, rather than as a financial wizard,
is the figure we are to consider. If money and buildings had
been chiefly what he stood for, the first ten or fifteen years
would be merely background for the more spectacular growth
that followed. But knowing what we do of the first forty years
of his life, and the lofty spirit in which he approached the
tasks of higher education, we may perhaps find that he did
some of his best work before rather than after the money
began rolling in. After that, he was a cautious spender of trust
funds; before that, he was a prodigal giver of time and thought
for goods that money cannot buy.

Money would never have come if he had not already shown
that he could use it well. Trustees of great fortunes and men
of great wealth avoid academic beggars. When they are ready,
and not before, they seek out the wise man who goes about his
business and lets them alone. He has been watched. What he
could do so well with little money he can do better with more;
so they reason. But of course the wise man must have a few
friends who know a few confidants of rich men, or they might
never hear of his existence. To interest them without scaring
them off is where tact comes in.

When Rush Rhees began, he did not think in millions. A few
thousands for annual deficits, a few tens of thousands for endowment, a giver for a building—these were his concern. He
had to pass the hat. He had to scrimp in order to stop passing
the hat. Those were days of small things and large hopes.
They were days when a smaller man would have regretted his
choice, a prouder man would have rebelled, and a weaker
man would have retreated. But they were also days when

determination was strong, when older helpers bore even more than their share of the burden, when unexpected encouragement, small gifts and quiet words, kept up good spirits and lighted the way. He brought cheer with him and kept it. When he began giving it away he had more. Men began to look to him for evidences of things not seen, not because he was an optimist or a prophet but because he believed in the future of Rochester. *Felix qui prospicit.*

How did he get that call in the first place? Why did Rochester trustees, some of whom did not want a ministerial president, finally choose one? If they wanted a money raiser, why did they pick a Greek teacher? He must have wondered himself, until he learned the whole story, and had to revise any notions he may have had of Divine Providence determining the call. As it now looks, at least to the ungodly, it was anything but that. To put it bluntly, Rush Rhees, who had been second choice at Newton, was fourth choice at Rochester. Many good men who were last choices have come out first in the end. Let us review one curious aspect of the preceding decade in order to understand why he was called.

After fifty years of struggling along on inadequate resources, the college was still holding its own, because it had strong teachers and a good reputation. But it was not growing. Its out-of-town ratio was dwindling. It was becoming chiefly a local college for boys who could not go elsewhere. Years before, it had been more than that. The shadow of a great name still lingered, that of Martin Brewer Anderson, who retired in 1888 and died in 1890. President David Jayne Hill (1889-1896) had bravely tried to begin a new era. He had attempted to convince the Rochester public that the university belonged to them and should be loyally supported regardless of denominational affiliation. But this made some conservative Baptists of the state suspicious that the traditional status of the institution, dating back to its foundation in 1850, was about to be weakened or abolished. Custom, not charter requirement, still kept a preponderance of Baptists on the Board of Trustees.

There had always been some trustees from other churches, sometimes the most active and generous, but they had been in a minority. The university was not strictly speaking a denominational institution, and the only aid received from the Baptist organizations of the state was in the form of scholarship grants to give free tuition to ministerial students during their college course. In 1892 a member of the Board of Trustees, the Rev. R. S. MacArthur, of New York, introduced a resolution which he apparently thought would clear up the denominational situation, as follows:

> That it is the sense of this board, alike in harmony with the spirit of its founders and the character of its history, that two-thirds of its members shall be members of regular Baptist churches, and that the remaining one-third be composed of persons irrespective of their religious associations or beliefs.

Mr. Rosenberger, historian of the university, says that "after a motion that the resolution lie on the table was lost by a vote of six ayes to seven nays, the resolution was unanimously adopted. . . . Some of the speakers doubted the propriety of the formal resolution." It was certainly an unlucky thirteen, that "unanimous" vote which was not really unanimous, and caused trouble for president and trustees in later years. It did not really represent the spirit of the institution, which under President Anderson had never been narrowly sectarian. There were members of all churches in its student body and of several in its faculty.

President Hill naturally did not like the MacArthur resolution, which failed to stop criticism of the university in reactionary quarters. He resented "ecclesiastical interference" and felt that his honest efforts to raise the standards and improve the educational methods of the college had not been appreciated. Since he had already become interested in international law and diplomacy, he resigned in 1896 to go into the Department of State as assistant secretary. His later distinguished career as ambassador and author showed that the university

had lost an able administrator because of lack of timely
support. The mistake was not repeated.

This forgotten denominational controversy, though it long
ago ceased to have any importance, had an indirect bearing on
the election of a new president. There was no legal requirement that he should be a Baptist, but there was a restricted
fund of $20,000 dating from early days known as the Burbank
Foundation, the income from which helped to pay part of the
president's salary, so long as the office should be held by a
Baptist. In case a member of any other denomination should
be elected, the $20,000 would revert to the Burbank heirs.
Finances being what they were in the nineties, when annual
deficits averaged several thousands, it was unlikely that $20,000
would be paid out of permanent funds in order to get a non-
Baptist president. For practical reasons, therefore, centering in
the treasurer's books, President Hill's successor had to be a
Baptist.

During the period from 1896 until 1899 the acting presidents,
Professor Samuel A. Lattimore and Professor Henry F. Burton,
kept the college running smoothly. The trustees considered
three eminent candidates for the presidency, all of whom in
turn declined. The nominating committee had an instinct for
discovering potential presidents but could not get them. In
1898 it had reported to the board:

> We were severely handicapped by the unwritten but imperative law
> demanding the appointment of a member of the Baptist communion. We
> desired an experienced educator, and highly accomplished. But we also
> wished the rare combination of the man of learning and the man of
> affairs in the same person. These requirements we find in but few persons.

What led them in 1899 to suppose that the New Testament
professor at Newton was a man of affairs, we do not know. He
was not, though later he became one under the stress of necessity. How they happened to think of him at all is an interesting
story. Women started it. In 1898 the late Mrs. Joseph T. Alling,
wife of one of the Rochester trustees, while visiting Mrs. Lucy
Waterbury (later Mrs. Henry W. Peabody) in Newton Centre,

was invited to a Ladies' Night meeting of the Villagers. There she was introduced by her hostess to Professor Rhees and had some conversation with him. The next year, when Mrs. Waterbury learned that Rochester was looking for a president, she wrote Mrs. Alling that the young New Testament teacher was too good a man for his job and might be interested. Mrs. Alling told her husband, he told the committee, and so it all began. If the Villagers had not invited the ladies that night or if Mrs. Alling had not been there, the whole story might have been different. This is one more link in the chain of chance.

The Rochester committee sent Mr. Rufus A. Sibley to Northampton in June, 1899, to interview the candidate at the Seelye home, as stated in the previous chapter. After this conference with the chairman of the committee and a visit to Rochester, Rush Rhees wrote as follows:

My dear Mr. Sibley:

Since leaving you I have been considering seriously the proposition made to me by your committee. I will say frankly that it has impressed me more favorably than I had any idea would be the case. In many ways I am drawn to Rochester. Yet I am unable at present to give you a definite answer, since the problem has for me so many phases. Some things seem increasingly clear, however, and I will report them.

1. As I intimated in my conference with your committee, it seems clear to me that I cannot discharge obligations already contracted in time to enable me to enter your service in the near future. It is most probable that the delay of a year—as suggested in our conference—would be necessary. I can easily appreciate that this may seem to your trustees too long a time to wait.

2. I should not feel that the Rochester call is imperative unless it can be extended with virtual unanimity. The move would be a serious one for me, and I should not dare to make it unless I were confident that your Board is very cordial and earnest in asking me to make a change in my work. I am in no doubt about your committee. But if you should make any informal canvass of your Board with reference to my nomination I should be glad to know its result. I hope I need not assure you that I appreciate the importance for you of keeping this matter out of the papers. I shall be scrupulously careful.

3. I am sorry to be still undecided, but it is not easy for me to see duty in so radical a change of work. So I have to ask further time for consideration. As for the incidental details of house, work in classroom, etc., your attitude while I was in Rochester has shown me that consideration of

them may be postponed until the main question is settled. I think I will be able to give you a definite answer within a week or ten days at most.

Thanking you and your associates for all the courtesy shown me, and with cordial regards for yourself and Mrs. Sibley, I am

Sincerely yours,

RUSH RHEES

After further correspondence he wrote on July 4, 1899:

1. Would your Board be ready, as a body and as individuals, to push energetically a movement for increase in the endowment funds? You have told me that the funds of the University are sufficient for present expenses. Of course I assume that by "present expenses" you mean the present scale of appropriations including the $4,000 a year that you offer to your president. But it is evident that some advance must be made in the near future. The report of the Acting President indicates some present needs. I myself saw some others, and my mind readily finds directions where expansion is needed if the institution is to do the work that it must do to attract me to the administration of it. If I accept the presidency of Rochester, I shall not try to shirk any duty belonging to that office. But I shall be unwilling to accept it unless I can see that those already interested and responsible are ready to move energetically for the increase of the resources of the University. Kindly tell me what I might expect in this direction.

2. As you know, I am not accustomed to the arrangement by which your President has no vote in the Board of Trustees. So far as I am aware it is customary in our eastern colleges for a president not only to be a member but the presiding officer of the Board. I can see some possible advantages in having another for presiding officer, but it seems to me important that the President of the University should have an actual vote with the Board of Trustees. I understand from you that he does serve as adviser of the Board, and that may signify virtually the same thing. But it does not seem to me the desirable relation. Now I do not know what conditions your charter may contain to interfere with my desire, should I become your President, to be a member of the Board. Kindly tell me, and also tell me whether, if it is possible, I might look for an election to the Board when the next vacancy occurs.

There follows a passage concerning the house and grounds provided as a residence for the President, which with free rental, heat, and necessary repairs were a part of the compensation offered. The letter concludes:

I see I have omitted to mention that I should want to be relieved from all responsibility for the teaching of "intellectual and moral philosophy," and to be allowed to do what teaching I undertake in the department of biblical literature. This I understand you think will be possible. Please investigate and reply definitely.

Here was a man who knew what he wanted, and why. They liked his frankness, and his terms were promptly accepted. The Board of Trustees met on July 6, 1899, and unanimously elected him to the presidency and to their membership. In accordance with his desire to have one more year at Newton in order to finish his book, as previously explained, his term of office was to begin on July 1, 1900. The Board of Trustees, knowing that July 6 was his wedding day, telegraphed the news with its congratulations. It was no surprise, but it was a triumph; one more vindication for Rhees tradition, for his long letter of inquiry and requests had been written on July 4. Various other Rhees family events in earlier and later years, whether by choice or by coincidence, fell on Independence Day.

On July 24 he wrote to Rochester accepting the presidency, and to Newton resigning his professorship, both to take effect on the following July 1. The die was cast, the man was married, the new life was begun. It was just one hundred years since Morgan John Rhees had left Beulah for Somerset in 1799. Morgan had five years more. Rush had forty. Both filled them full.

During the remaining year in Newton Centre the Rheeses lived quietly in their own rented house, some distance from the Theological Institution. He worked on his book, and taught his courses for the last time. He was in Rochester for a brief visit in the autumn of 1899. He missed being present at the semicentennial Commencement of the university on June 15, 1900, because that was the day his son Morgan John Rhees was born in Newton Centre. It was announced at the Commencement dinner in Rochester that Amherst had made Rush Rhees an LL.D. and Mrs. Rhees had made him a DaD. He had sent in advance the following letter, which was read to the alumni by Professor George M. Forbes:

It is difficult for me to express the regret with which I find that illness in my home makes it impossible for me to be in Rochester at this time of jubilee. . . . As I study the task which I am soon to undertake at your call, every new insight I obtain into the elements of that task deepens my sense of the priceless heritage Rochester possesses from the long and noble services of Dr. Anderson. He belonged to the old type of great teachers, men who were supremely great in their personal influence over those whom they taught. If I mistake not, Rochester can never become a rendezvous for pedants so long as that practical, lofty soul holds any place in our memory and affection. There are other good inheritances from the more recent past. I can never be unmindful of the strong constructive work that was undertaken for the institution during the service of President Hill, nor can I deny myself the satisfaction of speaking of what is to me the remarkable work of Professor Lattimore and Professor Burton and their allies in the faculty during the years when the administration of the affairs of the University has been added to their ordinary academic duties. I am glad that we remember today the devotion and foresight of the godly men who were instrumental in planning our college in Rochester. I am equally glad to remember today the other men of catholic spirit and like earnestness who for the sake of their city and the youth of their neighborhood devoted themselves and their wealth to the interests of the University. We shall not build well if we do not meet them with like catholicity and generous encouragement to expect great things of us. Let me reiterate that I count it most auspicious that I am to enter on my work with the memory of this worthy past fresh in all our minds, and to acknowledge that I have it as my firm purpose to build on the foundations already laid a structure worthy in some measure of the wisdom and the courage of the men who before me have put their lives and their wealth into this godly and exalted enterprise.

Among the semicentennial addresses, which the President-elect did not hear but read afterward, was one by Governor Theodore Roosevelt on "Promise and Performance." It had to do with the duty of college men in public life. Its first sentence was characteristic: "Before making a promise think of what you are doing, of what you say you will do; and in the next place, do it." The "next place" for Rush Rhees was twenty-five years off, but when it came he did what he said he would do. He built on the foundations.

When the Rheeses arrived in Rochester on a morning early in September, the first to welcome them at the Powers Hotel, where they went from the train for breakfast, was Mayor George A. Carnahan. The new Mayor, recently elected on a reform ticket, who happened to be there that morning, greeted the new President, similarly chosen. The Mayor, having at the semicentennial in June spoken on the relations between the college and the city, which he said should be cordial, immediately began to make them so.

Ever since that day, and indeed before it, city officials have often shown their helpfulness to the university. This happy relation, though occasionally imperiled by such issues as assessment of university property, has generally prevailed. The new President soon found that neither the municipality nor the press would present such problems of indifference or antagonism as have sometimes arisen in other university centers. This was partly because Rush Rhees was as good a citizen as he was a scholar. Rochesterians know that a university is the best friend a city can have.

The President's house at 440 University Avenue, at the corner of Prince Street, opposite the campus, had been put into thorough repair during the summer. It was originally the Van Zandt homestead, erected in 1857, purchased by the university and enlarged for President Anderson in 1867. An old-fashioned but commodious house, with large rooms suitable for social purposes and several acres of land, it was the Rheeses' home for thirty-two years. There they brought up their children, entertained their friends, welcomed students and faculty at college receptions, hospitably received visiting lecturers and distinguished travelers, and often had the pleasure of family visits from the President's mother and Mrs. Rhees's father and mother.

There were guest rooms, but not always enough for special occasions. When numerous guests had to be accommodated, there could be complications. President Seth Low, of Columbia University, one of the out-of-town speakers at the formal inauguration on October 11, 1900, was installed in Mother Rhees's room, she being shifted to the sewing room. At the last minute before starting for the ceremonies, Grandmother discovered that in moving her possessions she had left behind an organdy bow belonging to the widow's bonnet which she

ANDERSON HALL, 1861. AS IT WAS IN 1900

THE PRESIDENT'S HOUSE, 440 UNIVERSITY AVENUE,
NOW A WOMEN'S CO-OPERATIVE DORMITORY

always wore in public. Without that bow, no inauguration for Grandma. So with much embarrassment she had to knock at Seth Low's door and rescue the sacred ribbon from the Holy Bible, where it was always kept neatly pressed.

The inauguration was an impressive occasion, with a long list of distinguished guests. There were at least ten presidents on the platform, Low of Columbia, Harper of Chicago, Seelye of Smith, Merrill of Colgate, Taylor of Vassar, Jones of Hobart, Gunnison of St. Lawrence, Davis of Alfred, Stewart of Auburn Theological Seminary, and Strong of Rochester Theological Seminary. Of course the McCutchens were there from Plainfield. Alumni attended in large numbers. The exercises were held in the afternoon at the Alumni Gymnasium, erected the year before at the southeast corner of the campus, now no longer standing.

All three addresses now read almost like warnings against temerity, but President Rhees did not need them. His inaugural address on "The Modernizing of Liberal Culture" showed no rash intentions of premature expansion, innovation, or autocracy. Surveying the changes in college education during the preceding generation, he found them mostly good, but requiring higher standards and better equipment than the old. Recognizing that decline in classical studies might be irresistible, he inquired whether equivalent values may be looked for in other fields. The teaching of history should be so broadened as to take in the whole development of human culture. There should be courses in aesthetics and in religion as branches of that culture. Economy of time is as important as economy of money. Students looking forward to professional training should in some cases be allowed to count part of their graduate studies toward the college degree. The degree in science should mean positive emphasis on science, not merely —as it then did—absence of ancient languages. Such were some of his concrete suggestions. At the close he made this promise, which for thirty-five years he gradually fulfilled: "As new demands arise and new resources are found, we pledge

to you that we will meet the demands most eagerly, and use
the resources with the broadest wisdom we can attain."

A pioneer starts something that he can never finish, because
it is too big and life is too short. An incompetent, by haste,
waste, or vacillation, can soon finish what he could never have
begun—finish it by ruin. This is true of a business, an
organization, a college. There is a risk for any man taking over
a small college which has had a long, slow growth and trying
to make it over quickly on some new and unwelcome pattern.
Many colleges and some universities have had that misfortune.
Rush Rhees knew better. He felt his way. His first duty was
to meet immediate problems, his next to get acquainted with
the constituency and the community. Only when these were
accomplished did he begin to move for important academic
changes. He had come to a small college fifty years old, with
two hundred students, seventeen teachers, four buildings,
twenty-five acres, a tall iron fence, and a small endowment.
There was much to be done, but he took his time. A current
student pun was, "You can't rush Rhees."

Instead of being precipitate, he was a deliberate man in
every way. Dr. W. N. Donovan, who knew him at Newton
Centre, said:

I used to admire his lack of any appearance of haste. He seemed to me
like a well-adjusted, well-oiled machine, working to the exact second
without hurry or fuss. I was puffing up the hill one day. Rhees said,
"Plenty of time." He then told me that after much experience he had
calculated that if he was at the tree at the corner of Chase Street by
the time the bell rang in Colby Hall tower, his usual pace would land
him at his classroom desk in ample time to be composed when the buzzer
rang. If the bell rang before he reached the tree, he must put on steam,
and that he disliked to do. I took it that this was an application of his
mathematical training to affairs of daily life. He was quick in thought,
speech, and action, but I have no recollection of any sign of nervous
haste or "rush" in my five years' association with him.

Three problems at once confronted him. They were not
surprises, but they could not have been adjusted or even prepared for until he reached Rochester. He had to be on the

ground, see the people, talk with the leaders, learn the previous history of each problem before attempting to solve it. These three immediate problems were deficits, women students, and faculty appointments.

He had been informed that the annual net income was slightly below the necessary annual budget, but that the accumulated operating deficits were being carried along without difficulty pending further efforts to secure increased endowment. This did not satisfy him.

He had also been informed that as the result of negotiations extending over nearly ten years the trustees had finally voted to admit women students as soon as $50,000 could be subscribed. But since pledges were still far short of that amount, it was hardly expected that the guarantee could be completed in time for the opening of college. Barely a week before that date subscriptions for the balance were hurriedly obtained, forcing immediate admission of thirty-three women. The whole subject, which for the first few years caused many complications and some friction, is dealt with in a later chapter.

The third problem, faculty appointments, arose from the increase in the number of students by admission of women and from the approaching retirement of several senior professors. All three problems were interrelated. Annual deficits would be larger because of admitting women, since tuition covered less than half the cost of a student's education. Faculty appointments would be more difficult because adequate salaries could not yet be offered. Neither was there at that time any sufficient fund for pensioning aged professors.

The pump was nearly dry. The alumni and the Rochester public had for years been solicited for college subscriptions for this, that, and the other, and were in no mood for further demands. The alumni with great efforts had raised money for a gymnasium, just finished and not entirely paid for. Repeated unsuccessful attempts to raise a quarter of a million for endowment had drawn in many conditional subscriptions and further limited the field for a fresh campaign. Rochester women and their friends had made themselves responsible for the $50,000 fund, subscriptions to which would run for years. Moreover, it was already evident that a new laboratory building for physics and biology was an urgent need. Where the money for that was coming from, unless from still another subscription by many small givers, nobody knew.

It was as hard then to raise $100,000 as it was to get $1,000,-000 twenty years later. In considering the early financial struggles which Rush Rhees and his trustees had to face, one must remember the scale on which they had to work. Poverty is a relative thing. Universities always feel poor; but after all, when a president must think long and hard before he can consent to increase the deficit by adding a cheap instructor to an overworked department, when coal bills are a burden and a new boiler a luxury, that is something which the University of Rochester of today knows little about.

The President himself was not rolling in luxury on his modest salary. Two more children were born, Henrietta Seelye Rhees and Rush Rhees, Jr., and as the household increased, and necessary entertaining required more domestic help, the family budget needed close scrutiny. Clothes and luxuries had to be considered carefully. They had no automobile until 1921, and went to formal dinner parties in the trolley cars in evening clothes in all kinds of weather. Like everybody else, in addition to household bills they had to subscribe to local charities and church funds, but unlike faculty members, who could afford not only to be poor but to seem poor, they had a position to maintain. Those who thought Rush Rhees had an easy time should know that at first he was often just as "hard up" as men with half the income. One would never have guessed it by his immaculate attire and perfect company dinners. In matters of family expense thoroughbreds do not talk about money or lack of it; when they have it they use it; when they don't they worry along. In later years, as faculty salaries were gradually raised, of course the President's also increased, but his scale of living remained modest while his giving grew.

During the first five years he had to give much of his time to writing letters and interviewing prospective givers for the long-postponed endowment fund. He also initiated inquiries as to the possibility of interesting John D. Rockefeller, Andrew Carnegie, Mrs. Russell Sage, and other rich persons. The story of how he got from George Eastman the first $10,000 for the science laboratory, and how that sum grew without further solicitation to the whole cost of the building, will be found in another context.

In addition to the Eastman Laboratory and a new central heating plant, campus improvements less necessary but desirable were made possible by special gifts. Sibley Hall was renovated at the expense of Mr. Hiram W. Sibley, son of the donor. A bronze statue of President Anderson was erected in front of the hall bearing his name. As early as 1904, President Rhees was writing to Mr. G. L. Heins, of Heins and LaFarge, New York architects, directions for a comprehensive plan for the location of future buildings for the Prince Street campus. At that time, when the mere cost of making such drawings was not a small item, he was dreaming in such terms as these:

> I suggest herewith certain buildings which should be located on our plan for the campus:
> 1. The new science building, southwest from Sibley Hall.
> 2. An engineering building, east of Reynolds Laboratory.
> 3. A chapel and auditorium.
> 4. A museum for art.
> 5. A geological museum, perhaps between Anderson and Sibley.
> 6. A group of dormitories; near the Gymnasium seems a natural place, but may be impracticable.
> 7. At present our telescope is in a small building directly east of Reynolds. It should probably be removed if our engineering building is erected.
> 8. The Rochester Academy of Medicine may put up a building on our campus. We should consider its location. We shall be able to dictate its architecture.
> 9. It might be well to bear in mind a possible building for a music school—though that is in the somewhat distant future.

Such studies were made from time to time, and large ground plans and even conjectural perspective drawings came from

New York to the President's office in Anderson Hall. With no prospect of funds for any of these buildings in sight, except the science laboratory, and with negotiations for Carnegie gifts toward engineering still in an early stage, the location of imaginary halls on the campus was not a pressing problem. But the survey gave pictures to show to people who cannot see with their minds, and diverted the President, who liked to study architects' drawings. At present it is interesting to consider what the Prince Street campus might have become if so developed, and whether it would have been adequate for the future expansion.

The slight but definite financial improvement of the university during those early years would not have been possible without the greatest economy in small expenditures, and personal supervision by the President over petty details of work on the buildings and grounds. As a homely but graphic illustration of this supervision, in contrast with grandiose designs, it may be worth while to give space here to a letter received by President Rhees at his Maine home in the late summer of 1902 from James H. Craigie, an old-time head janitor and Jack-of-all-trades:

Rochester, Aug. 28, 1902

Dear Dr. Rhees:
    I think that everything you mentioned has been attended to. Mr. Ernisse has just finished the floors and I think you will be pleased with the work. The inner doors and mantel also were done. Everything in the large building has been done that you authorized. Professor Burton and Mr. Hoeing each want pieces of blackboard in their rooms. I did not order this done as I wished your sanction before it was undertaken. I had the conductor pipes on your house overhauled and quite a lot of the old pipe was rotten and had to come out. It is in good shape now.
    Ten new benches arrived today. They are darker than the old ones but may look all right when finished. I have cleaned and shellacked all the benches in the chapel and they look very much better. We did the same in every classroom as we cleaned and the improvement is marked. I have run quite a bill for shellac but I feel justified in the result.
    It has been almost impossible to get anything done this summer but cut grass. All through the season we have had to keep at it, and it takes the time of two men almost constantly. We are trying to get our cleaning

done but have to break off and start the lawn mowers before we get very far along with the inside work.

Mr. Ernisse says you did not wish him to start on the Sibley Hall work until you got home, so unless you send word to the contrary he won't start it. Shall I have him do the work in Latin department? Professor Esty wished to have a section of his board lined in squares. This can be done when he gets back, some Saturday or sooner if he wishes.

My man John has been greatly afflicted in the loss of his wife. He is left with seven small children and no one to care for them while he is at work. I don't see how he can manage to care for them all at home. He hopes for the coming of his sister from the old country, as she has been written to asking her to come out and help him.

Our man Herman deserted and hired out to the railway company. He is trying to become a motorman. I have another man who does very well and I am much pleased with him.

I wish we might have the front doors of Anderson Hall coated. Do you think you could authorize the doing of that?

It is going to be a problem what to do with the seats in the Gym. It won't do to put them where they will get dampness. If you could suggest some plan, I will carry it out. Anything you require will receive my prompt attention.

Respectfully yours,
J. H. Craigie

Craigie was a retired sailor. In overalls, with his old pipe in his mouth and his seagoing vocabulary, he could be one kind of man on a Saturday night facing a crowd of students when hell broke loose on the campus, and quite another man next morning when he and his family, all in their best clothes, sat in their pew at the First Baptist Church, not far from President Rhees, who was also a pillar there. Craigie was always sweeping, raking, shoveling coal or snow, mending plumbing, cleaning blackboards, grumbling to himself when things went wrong, but talking politely to those professors who called him "mister" and said "Thank you" for a favor. One October day in 1926 while raking leaves in front of Anderson Hall he fell dead, was carried to his basement room, and the whole college mourned him. Men like that helped Rush Rhees, because they respected him and he them. President and janitor knew good work and did it; so did the rest. Something besides money the old college needed and had—men.

Faculty appointments to fill existing vacancies and to plan for future replacements were perplexing the new president before he had been long in office. Of the older faculty several had already retired; others would reach retiring age within a few years. In selecting younger men to take their places he was determined not only to get good scholars and good teachers, but men who would win the respect of students and maintain the morale of the institution. In this problem, as has already been made evident, he had to face two handicaps: not only that the salaries offered were small, but that future promotion and increased income could not always be promised.

There was one aspect of the faculty problem which must be included in this chapter, because it marked the end of an era. When Andrew Carnegie's representatives, who had already been approached with reference to an Applied Science Building, were asked as to conditions for admission to the pension benefits of the new Carnegie Foundation for the Advancement of Teaching, the denominational issue came to the front again. Carnegie would not give one penny for any sectarian purpose. The trustees of his foundation, after careful investigation of the university's educational and financial status, agreed to admit it to the benefits of their academic pension system if the Rochester trustees would adopt the following resolution:

Resolved, that no denominational test is imposed in the choice of trustees, officers, or teachers by The University of Rochester, or in the admission of students, nor are distinctly denominational tenets or doctrines taught to the students.

By passing this resolution on June 19, 1906, the board obviously reversed its action of 1892; but since Dr. MacArthur himself was the seconder of the motion to adopt the Carnegie formula, no ill feeling or misunderstanding remained. Fourteen years had changed the situation. The university was sacrificing no real obligation and breaking no promise in order to become eligible for faculty pensions. It was merely recording a fact which for some years had been evident to all, that while Bap-

tist in origin it had in fact become undenominational long
before those pensions were announced.

In the winter of 1908, provision for retiring allowances for
retiring professors having been completed, and funds for the
erection and endowment of the building for applied science
being well advanced, Rush Rhees decided to make a thorough
study of European industrial education and technical research.
He had worked hard for eight years, had been successful in
raising considerable funds for general expenses as well as for
buildings, and desired before proceeding further to get a wider
view of the next stage in the development of the university.
Also, he needed and deserved a rest. He therefore requested
and received from the Board of Trustees a year's leave of
absence for the following academic year, 1908-1909. While he
was in Europe, Professor Burton became again an efficient and
acceptable acting president. The results of his European studies
of new methods in applied science, and the use made of them
in later developments at Rochester, will be the subject of the
next chapter.

The eight years had been difficult, more difficult perhaps
than had been expected, but not without reward. If the sums
of money so far raised were not large, possible sources of much
larger gifts had been discovered. The spirit of the faculty was
good, and of the student body as well, with some possible
exception in the matter of coeducation. Many kind words were
doubtless said to the President in private when he seemed in
need of them. From letters found in the files of his correspondence during the first six years the following passages are
chosen to show that he did not lack appreciation. An alumnus
wrote in 1905:

If you could have known as some of us did a few years ago the almost
heartless indifference of many of the older alumni to the college after Dr.
Anderson's death, and under the checkered experiences that followed,
how difficult it was to secure their interest in anything that concerned
it, and then could make the comparison in that one respect which we
can do now, you would feel immensely encouraged at the present outlook.

Dr. Talcott Williams, an eminent Philadelphia editor and friend of the President, to whom the university had given an honorary degree in the previous year, wrote on July 27, 1903:

I have thought much in the quiet of summer of the three days with you; days which were full to me of great encouragement. Your own problem grows upon me. I do not think I had ever realized its difficulties till I was in Rochester, though I knew something of them. It is, I must say, more important work than I feel you can do anywhere else, though there will be hours of depression in the future when you will wish that there were more tangible results in the work of the scholar, fully accomplished and visible on the printed page, instead of the work of the educator, poured into human lives, which pour it out again to others, a perpetual stream.

I hope you have got some rest, for I felt you were much closer to the point of over-strain than you could yourself possibly realize. You are close to the years when almost all Americans push themselves to the point of breaking down, and then learn their limits. It is so much easier, though in these things we never learn from the experience of another, if you will avoid a breakdown and keep the freshness which never returns after one has once parted with it, at the expense of a long illness, or what is sometimes harder to bear, an acute malady, or a long period of malaise out of which one slowly emerges.

From Professor Samuel A. Lattimore, revered head of the Department of Chemistry, who was soon to retire and was on his way to Europe, President Rhees received the following letter. The gracious spirit of the writer, himself an acting president of the college in earlier hard times, is as well revealed as that of the equally reserved executive whom he addressed. One quiet man spoke to another at long distance, which was the only way they could.

June 10, 1906
Nearing Gibraltar

·I was so sorry to leave home without seeing you, as I wished very much to say two things, one of which ought to have been said long ago, but the conventional reticence so curiously characteristic of college life is perhaps in part to blame; but I do wish you to know that, specially during all this last year, I have been most sympathetically aware of the tremendous burden of care and responsibility you were carrying so uncomplainingly and silently. My associates, I am sure, have shared the same feeling, and yet we have seen no way to relieve you except by trying to see that our several departments should add nothing to your own burden. These assurances may have slight value, but it relieves me to express them.

An old man nearly over the sea thought, like many other voyagers far from home, of words that should have been spoken to the silent. Gibraltar was near, the ship's mail would soon be closed; but he still had time for those words before he reached the Strait.

VI

UTILITY

Science is nothing but trained and organized common sense.—Huxley

ROCHESTER, a technical city, needed more technology. This need had become evident long before Rush Rhees arrived in 1900. He found already in existence under efficient private management a nonprofit trade school for industrial education. Then commonly known as Mechanics Institute, it has become since 1944 the Rochester Institute of Technology. Its full name until then was the Rochester Athenaeum and Mechanics Institute; a merger in 1891 of a time-honored association founded in 1829 for library and lecture facilities, the Rochester Athenaeum, and the Mechanics Institute for industrial training established in 1885 by Captain Henry Lomb and his associates. It had no connection with the public school system, being supported by private philanthropy supplemented by modest student fees. Leading manufacturers had encouraged its service in preparing young people for factory and commercial positions.

In early days, because of the sagacity and personal sacrifice of Captain Lomb, there was at Mechanics Institute something of the spirit of Benjamin Franklin. There was frugality and expectation in its humble beginnings. John J. Bausch used to say: "Those who make it easy for a young man make it hard for him." Those pioneer opticians taught young men to see. They roused ambition, self-help, and thrift, which is more than a college can do.

At the beginning of the century a large gift from George Eastman provided additional land and an adequate building

64

for its use. In later years more land, buildings, and increased resources have made possible a mechanical equipment and a technical staff unsurpassed in its noncollegiate field. This field has included almost from the beginning household economics, mechanical and freehand drawing, applied art, and academic subjects, as well as the use of tools and machines. For evening instruction of young men and women employed in factories and stores, as well as for full-time students of high-school age desiring vocational training, it was already at the beginning of the century a remarkable example of co-operative support by businessmen and philanthropists of an educational plant outside the public schools.

But at the college and university level Rochester had no corresponding technical school authorized to confer degrees. A young man desiring to become a mechanical or electrical or hydraulic engineer, an industrial chemist, a machine designer, an expert manager or superintendent in any of the city's great manufacturing plants, had to go to Cornell or Columbia or the Massachusetts Institute of Technology for his advanced work. Moreover, owing to the uneven preparation of its students, Mechanics Institute was not in early years giving enough mathematics or physics or chemistry to enable its graduates to enter with advanced standing a college scientific course. Its mechanical drawing and shopwork were indispensable for pretechnical students in the university, and arrangements were soon made for such instruction by agreement between the two institutions. College women also were able to get domestic science courses at Mechanics, and those with artistic talent could practice drawing, painting, and modeling in its studios long before the university had an art department.

President Rhees was elected to the Board of Directors of Mechanics Institute in 1903. As a lifelong member of its committees he was active in promoting its growth. He regarded it as an important part of the city's educational system, and while for a variety of reasons no actual merger with the university was ever seriously considered, close co-operation was maintained. His fellow members on that board were leading manufacturers and businessmen. From them and from some of the trustees of the university he learned that the local demand for more advanced collegiate work in applied science was well founded. These men did not view the question from theoretical educational premises but as a practical community problem. Engineering, machine design, and testing of materials might or might not be classified as legitimate parts of a liberal college course; but both defenders and opponents of such an addition to the curriculum agreed that technical students should have basic training in language, literature, history, and economics. That they should if possible have some free time for further elective work in cultural subjects was held to be desirable though difficult.

Rush Rhees had many friends and acquaintances in Boston, New York, and elsewhere who were engineers, architects, and successful industrialists. Some were self-made men without much general culture, though expert in their fields. Others were well read, cultivated, versatile, good writers and fluent speakers, able in any company to explain a plan, defend a project, or convince a doubter. It was his firm conviction that the latter group, mostly graduates of liberal colleges with postgraduate technical study, had a great advantage, well worth the extra four years which their education had cost them. But he was also aware that self-supporting students or those dependent upon hard-working parents of small income could not afford four years of undergraduate study wholly without vocational value. They could manage perhaps five years of higher education after high school, but not seven or eight. Moreover, he firmly believed that the arbitrary line sometimes drawn between pure and applied science to the disparagement of the latter was spurious, snobbish, and contrary to the public good.

That the addition of applied science to the college curriculum was no contradiction of the aims of liberal education was repeatedly pointed out by the President. He reminded supporters of the university that such instruction was con-

templated by the founders in 1850, though never undertaken
during the first half century. Yet extracurricular contacts of
pure science with its useful applications had already existed for
many years, through the co-operation of Professor Lattimore
in chemistry with the Water Department and with local industries, and of Professor Dodge in biology with the Department
of Health.

The beginning of some prevocational courses dated back to
the earliest years of the new administration. They probably
would not have been tolerated before. There was now a many-
sided man in control, a champion of culture who knew that
culture depends on utility more than utility on culture, and
that they are not opposed but complementary. The angle from
which applied science came to be accepted as a legitimate part
of what was still a college, not actually a university, was this:
It is the duty and privilege of a college in a city to serve the
city in all practicable ways that do not interfere with its major
educational aims. These ways include technical assistance to
local industries when requested and possible. Furthermore,
liberal college education for prospective technical experts
requires addition to the undergraduate curriculum of pretechnical studies necessary to save the student's time in postgraduate
technical schools.

If any of the more conservative alumni or faculty members
felt that engineering and shopwork were an intrusion on the
cultural program of a liberal college, they soon discovered that
the President had no apologies to make for the new departure.
He had not been forced into it, but had become convinced of its
desirability. His only concern was that whatever technical work
was undertaken should be as thorough as that of the best
institutions, and that it should not usurp more than its share of
the time of teachers and students, or of university funds. Himself a product of a different type of education, that of an old-
line literary and classical college in a small New England town,
he had seen enough of Rochester's needs to make him not only
willing but eager to meet a new situation with new methods.

This factor in the evolution of a theological professor into a large-scale executive is important to those who would comprehend the growing versatility of Rush Rhees. What finally made him into a big businessman with the dignity of a scholar was not primarily the constant demand for increasing the university's funds. It was his power of adaptation for any specific service. When he saw that a man with a machine is just as important to American progress as a man with a book, he studied machines, in order to make them serve rather than rule the mind.

An irrational scorn for utility marks some academic circles. Rhees never shared it. He defended no useless knowledge— nor unused knowledge. His most severe indictment of half-educated bachelors of arts was that they did not use what little they knew, or thought they knew. Utility is not the test of truth, but it is the test of achievement, invention, progress, and prosperity. A generation is judged not by its speculations or its opinions but by what it creates for human betterment.

Without utility there could be no learning; without learning, no permanent utility. To call them incompatible is a pedant's folly. Every professor's salary comes from some past invention or business enterprise, or from public taxation of such enterprise. Laboratories for pure science are founded on the profits of applied science. Libraries are not built by scholars, but by the utilitarian rich. One man buys the book, another reads it. Neither thanks the other, or needs to; each to his own job. Some truth pays, some does not, but it is all useful. The best truth is given away free, and few know how to use it.

In keeping with his enlightened views of utility in education, President Rhees in his report for 1902-1903 announced an arrangement for pretechnical studies which would permit students intending to become engineers to enter third-year classes at Cornell, the Massachusetts Institute of Technology, or the School of Applied Science at Columbia. This was made possible by some adjustments in the curriculum and by providing shopwork for such students at Mechanics Institute. His interest in this matter was not merely a desire to save time for such students in their later vocational studies, but a conviction that some substantial part of a liberal education should be included in the training of engineers.

In 1905 the offer of Andrew Carnegie to give $100,000 for an Applied Science Building on condition that the University should raise an equal sum for endowment led to a money-raising campaign extending over three years. In announcing this advance step in the field of technical as distinguished from pretechnical education the President said:

This is a field which it is extremely desirable that we should enter. Students in our territory are increasingly seeking technical courses. Moreover, the city of Rochester is peculiarly well adapted to technical instruction, owing to the fact that the great variety of high-class industries carried on in this city would offer opportunity for most advantageous observation on the part of students of the practical commercial working out of technical conclusions. Moreover, it is universally true that the average standard of work in technical and professional schools is more exacting than in colleges of liberal arts, and the presence on our campus of such a technical department would certainly react with valuable stimulus upon the work of the college.

An early illustration of the President's growing interest in applying science to his own executive duties was the detailed attention which he gave in 1904 to the design and construction of a central heating plant. His correspondence with heating engineers on such matters as automatic stokers, correction of early defects in the insulation of underground conduits for steam pipes, and smokeless combustion of soft coal, shows that he mastered the physical and mechanical principles involved. He was competent to co-operate with contractors in making necessary changes in plans, and to hold them responsible for miscalculations. With habitual foresight, in placing the heating plant due attention was given to its probable future use not only for heat but for power.

Likewise in 1905 the construction of the Eastman Laboratories for physics and biology was closely supervised by President Rhees in co-operation with the architects. Inasmuch as special conditions called for construction of this building by separate contracts let at different times for each of the several trades involved, instead of by a single general contract with subcontractors, the necessity of saving money and time led to constant checking of details by the President. If there was any field of administration in which he was too unwilling to delegate power over details to others, it was building. He knew something about it to begin with, having had a builder for a grandfather, and was constantly learning more. Architects and builders may at times have felt somewhat hampered by his insistence on careful checking of details in plans and construction, but they soon saw that he was no ordinary meddlesome client, but a man who knew what good building is, and how to get it.

As plans for the new Department of Applied Science progressed, it was made clear that the program could not include full preparation for an engineering degree. The curriculum was so arranged that graduates entering Sibley College at Cornell or the Massachusetts Institute of Technology could receive the M.E. degree in five or six years from the time of entering college. The President's report for 1907-1908 contained the following announcement:

The new work, as we hope to develop it, will be genuine college work. The introduction of courses in Applied Science into our curriculum is not regarded by us as a departure from college ideals. These studies are simply further agencies for general culture by means of work which may prove practically useful to the student. It is difficult to estimate justly the possible culture value of the training in accuracy, the demand for efficiency, the checking of theories by practical results, which characterize applied science.

At that time, when the prolonged effort to match Mr. Carnegie's gift for the building with an equal amount for endowment had just been brought to a successful conclusion, and when studies for the building and the new curriculum were well under way, Rush Rhees decided to find out more about both before going ahead. In his report to the trustees for 1907-1908 he thus explained his decision:

From a source highly friendly to the University the suggestion came to me last December that it might be advantageous to the work with which I am charged here if I were to plan to spend the next year in Europe. The fact that we are soon to introduce new work in applied science made the suggestion seem to me to be timely. I believe that in connection with our new project it will be profitable for me to observe the practice and the equipment in technical education in England and on the Continent. I shall also seek to acquaint myself with other aspects of current practice in higher education.

Whenever any important new step was under discussion at the university the established policy was, not to devise some scheme out of one's head, but to find out what other institutions were doing and proposed to do, what their experience had been, what had succeeded, what had failed, and why. This principle was followed at every stage in the expansion of a small college into a university. It was followed later in the matter of the Memorial Art Gallery, the co-ordinate College for Women, the School of Music, the School of Medicine and Dentistry, the gradual evolution of University Extension, the honors system, the comprehensive examination—in short, Rochester never played a lone hand. The President wished to know, and wished his colleagues to know, what those who had already tried experiments understood better than those about to begin them. The European trip of 1908-1909 was therefore not a case of going away from home to study methods arising under different conditions, perhaps not applicable in detail to the local situation. It was rather a characteristic application of the inductive method. Rush Rhees could deduce from sound premises a sound conclusion, but deductive logic has less to do with constructive policies than wide and accurate knowledge of facts. This he needed and this he got. He generally got what he went after.

The Rhees family on this first extended journey together traveled simply and economically, crossing in a slow steamer, staying at pensions or cheap hotels, riding third class, making every dollar go as far as possible. There were six in the party, including the three children and a nurse. They sailed from

Montreal, July 4, 1908. At Liverpool they were met by Mrs. Rhees's father, mother, and sister, who had preceded them, and the entire group, though not traveling together, met several times during the summer. After short stops in Chester, Warwick, Kenilworth, Stratford, and London, the Rheeses settled in lodgings at Dorking in Surrey. The Seelyes also were there for a part of the time. Rush and Harriet visited cathedral towns, explored Devon, and often went up to London. Rush went alone to Oxford, Cambridge, Birmingham, and London to study the universities, more especially the science laboratories and technical institutes.

Wherever he went he knew what to look for, whom to see, what questions to ask. He was never an aimless traveler nor dependent on guidebooks. In all his many journeys he not only enlarged his knowledge of natural scenery and ancient buildings, as all travelers do, but also of the manners and customs of the people, their folk speech and folkways, means of livelihood and diversion, arts and crafts, fairs and festivals, holy days and holidays.

As a frank digression from utility the following account of a week in a Scottish castle shows how science may be applied to holidays. It could be a parable on the relation between money, brains, and happiness. But it is not a parable, it is true; though in 1898 Rush Rhees at Newton and Harriet Seelye at Northampton would hardly have supposed that ten years later they would be following bagpipes to dinner with lords and ladies in the Highlands.

In August an invitation came from Mr. and Mrs. Andrew Carnegie to spend a week at Skibo Castle in early September. This came about because Mrs. Carnegie's brother was architect of the new Applied Science Building at Rochester. The laboratory had not been built, only planned. Mr. Carnegie's $100,000 had not been paid, only promised. It was all in the future. And now it is all in the past. For Carnegie Hall, built for engineering, has been transformed into a women's dormitory, engineering being more commodiously housed at the River Campus.

So the end has been achieved as a new beginning. The giver is gone, the gift remains. The years are gone, a week survives. Shops and engineers are gone; instead of durable machines there are transient girls—more agreeable, though sometimes less useful. Anything can happen in thirty years. But Rush Rhees never feared change; he liked it.

Those who now pass Carnegie Hall may perhaps associate that utilitarian building with the following interlude. It is a long way from College Avenue to the Highlands of Scotland. But the link is the word "Carnegie," which besides a building and a man also stands for steel, engineering, professors' pensions, science, art, libraries, heroes, and international peace. Words are queer things; they take us swiftly from dreams to facts, and back again to dreams.

Leaving their children in good hands at Dorking, the Rheeses said good-bye at York to the Seelyes, who were on their way home. They stopped to see Durham Cathedral on its hill above the river Wear, with memories of Bede and Cuthbert. At Edinburgh they took a night train for the north, and arrived early next morning at Bonar Bridge, in the northern Highlands, the nearest station to Skibo Castle, an hour's drive away.

This was not another castle in the air. It was real, as was proved by the castle motor that met them at the station. As they passed through a village the car was stopped for a stout gentleman in black clerical dress who came running down a path, waving in his hand as a sort of distress signal a round clerical collar. Climbing breathless into the car, he introduced himself as vicar of the village church, put on his collar, and explained that Mrs. Carnegie had invited him to spend the day at the castle.

The Skibo house party was made up partly of the heads of the Scottish universities and their wives. Mr. Carnegie as lord rector, an ornamental appointment of which the duties were mostly social, had invited the principals of Edinburgh, Glasgow, Aberdeen, and St. Andrews, and other notables in the scholarly world. Among them all moved as genial host the short, gray-bearded ironmaster with his Santa Claus smile, democratic as Dunfermline, plain as Pittsburgh, inscrutable as Wall Street on Sunday; yet in hospitality more than a baron to the manner born.

Each morning a Highland piper in kilts and full regalia marched around the outside of the castle, playing his pipes to wake the guests. Each evening he played them to dinner in a column of twos. Skibo had to move briskly with his skirl and drone. There was quieter music too, from the organ in the great hall. Days were spent in walks, drives, and games. One morning all the guests were driven to a mountain stream to watch salmon leaping up the waterfall. One day ladies accompanied Mrs. Carnegie to a distant village where she opened a charity bazaar. Another morning Mrs. Rhees played golf with Mr. Carnegie and Lady Balfour. Those Highland days were few but memorable.

The Rheeses had been ten weeks in Britain when they crossed late in September to Ostend. Their goal was Göttingen, but they stopped a few days to see Bruges, Brussels, and Cologne. At Göttingen they settled down in a pleasant pension, where the children learned German, and Harriet felt at home, having lived in that town years before as a girl. The quiet old streets and ancient churches, delightful villages all about, ruined castles for picnics and forests for rambling, were as restful as Dorking, and as fascinating as Heine's *Harzreise* and his *Buch der Lieder*.

Rush Rhees had selected Göttingen as the center of his travels devoted to the study of technical development not only because of its natural attractions, but because at the Georgia Augusta University and the institutes for applied science which had sprung up in its neighborhood he knew he should find a welcome. Quotations will show how readily his inquiries were answered.

Soon after our settlement in Göttingen I sought an interview with Professor Felix Klein, a world-renowned mathematician, concerning whom I had learned that he could give me more information about the institutions I wished to visit than any other man in Germany. In response to my letter seeking an interview—accompanied of course by my credentials—I received a very cordial reply naming an hour. I found a man of most delightful and friendly bearing, who put himself wholly at my service, and gave me suggestions of the highest value for my work in Germany. Later I met many of his colleagues at their laboratories, and found the same simplicity, cordiality, and readiness to serve me in every possible way. Professor Voigt himself conducted me throughout the new physics laboratory, explaining the whole construction and equipment, although I asked him to designate one of his assistants for the purpose. Professor Prandt at the Institute for Applied Mechanics introduced me to a social custom of his laboratory, inviting me to drink a cup of tea with his assistants there at five o'clock one afternoon, and afterward he also guided me through his rooms and illustrated the use of his equipment.

Like cordial reception was accorded me by Professor Rung at the Institute for Applied Mathematics, by Professor Simon at the Institute for Applied Electricity, by Professor Tamman at the Institute for Physical Chemistry, and by many others. So I found it wherever I went all over Germany. I made the acquaintance of the equipment and some of the leading men at the technical high schools at Aix la Chapelle, Berlin (Charlottenburg), Dresden, Munich, and Vienna. The men have the same characteristic eminence of attainment, devotion to science, and the same patrician simplicity and cordial friendliness and approachability of manner which I found at Göttingen, and which years ago as a student I had found at Berlin.

He described at some length the use in the Institute for Applied Mathematics at Göttingen of various complicated calculating machines and other timesaving devices, the emphasis in all these institutes on problems such as those actually met with in manufacture and invention, in short, the triumph of efficiency over tradition. He also reported his visits to commercial high schools of university grade, manual training secondary schools in various places including Cologne, Elberfeld, Düsseldorf, and Munich, and studied the methods of the well-known German Museum at Munich.

During the two months in Germany he filled his mind with many projects for Rochester, but also with ideas too big for that relatively small enterprise on the campus. Why not learn just enough? Does not too much confuse the observer?

Rush Rhees always knew so much more than he could use

that his mind was clear to the edges. He could see all around his subject. This was just as true of applied science as of Bible teaching, mathematics, civic development, educational reform, business management, art galleries, libraries—anything he had to do with. In later travels, even for health or recreation, he never missed an opportunity to investigate on the spot what could not be so well learned elsewhere. The utility he valued was not merely immediate need but preparation for the unforeseen. Such men are good travelers. They wear out shoe leather, but bring back power. The more they travel the more they are at home.

After studying technological developments in Germany the Rheeses went to Italy for the winter, and spent the spring in the château country of France. There was also some time in Paris and Switzerland. The remainder of Rush Rhees's educational inquiry was a trip which he made alone to England and Scotland, visiting the universities of Glasgow, Edinburgh, Cambridge, and London. He was then concerned not solely with applied science, but with university methods in general. The year abroad had been of the highest value in many ways, and its fruits were large in later years. He was no longer a stranger to science.

Returning to Rochester in September, 1909, the President proceeded with plans for the Carnegie building and with organization of the new department. It was decided not to undertake work in civil engineering but only in the mechanical and chemical branches of the science. With equipment ample for the mechanical engineering first established, and a small group of well-prepared students, the new enterprise was begun in 1911. It remained a college department, not a separate division of the university, until a number of years later, after President Rhees's retirement.

Utility continued to be one of his many interests in the following decade. As a member of the Board of Trustees of Mechanics Institute he had an important share in its reorganization for closer relations of its departments with one another under a single head. In co-operation with its department of domestic science, arrangements were made for carrying out the provisions of a large bequest by Lewis P. Ross which became available in 1917. Mr. Ross was a trustee both of the institute and of the university, who left his residuary estate amounting to over $800,000 for physiological research and popular instruction in the field of nutrition. In his report for 1915-1916 the President said:

It is certain that this gift lays upon us a large task, but it also opens before us a great opportunity to be of service to mankind. Mr. Ross clearly intended that his estate should help people to understand better than most now do how to order their physical lives for their own greater health and happiness.

Mr. Ross chose as the title of the new department the name of "vital economics," which he had taken from lectures and books of Professor Irving Fisher, of Yale. A part of the income from his estate was designated for the food administration work at Mechanics Institute, and the remainder was devoted to research and teaching of physiology in the College of Arts and Science. After the opening of the School of Medicine and Dentistry in 1925 the offices and laboratories of the Ross Foundation were transferred from the Eastman Laboratories on the Prince Street campus to the medical school. Instruction in physiology for college students was still carried on there, as well as physiology of nutrition for medical students. The public dissemination of recent scientific progress in this field for the benefit of the laity, which in earlier years was promoted by popular publications and lectures of the department, has been reduced. Through other agencies, however, including the city Department of Health, the Chamber of Commerce, and some of the large industrial organizations of the city, Mr. Ross's desire "that human life may be prolonged with increased health and happiness" has been partially realized. The university has done its part to see that Rochesterians eat what they ought. When they transgress the principles of hygiene, it is no longer through ignorance. Education does not cure everything.

Another example of community service in applied science has been in optics. Over a long period of years under the encouragement of the university there has been theoretical instruction and practical training for optical technicians, lens designers, photographers, and others in allied fields, maintained chiefly at the expense of the large optical industries of the city. At one time a course in optometry was included in this group in response to what appeared to be a local demand for adequate preparation of persons desiring to meet state requirements for a license to prescribe glasses for defective vision without a full medical training. This was soon withdrawn, however, partly because few applicants could meet the high standards of the course, partly because such work was available elsewhere in the state. An Institute of Optics on a much more advanced basis, affiliated with the Department of Physics and by no means chiefly vocational in aims or methods, has replaced the earlier experiments. Rush Rhees investigated in Germany and elsewhere the best schools of this type, believing that when the time came for a complete Institute of Optics on a graduate basis, with a building and endowment of its own, Rochester would be the best city in the United States for its location.

Shortly after his return from Europe in 1909 Rush Rhees was requested to address the opening session of the Second Annual Convention of the New York State Branch of the National Society for the Promotion of Industrial Education. His subject was "The National Importance of Industrial Education," which he presented in no conventional or commonplace way. The point he made was that, whereas in pioneer times every American brought up on a farm had to turn his hand to almost any trade in order to repair tools, vehicles, and buildings, urban life and mass production have left us without a native class of craftsmen. Since industry and labor unions no longer provide adequate equivalents for the apprentice system we have become dependent on immigration from northern and central Europe for skilled labor.

Whereas a generation ago the men who supplied the needs of the factory came from the farm, today the workmen who come to us have no such training as they did before. The life and training they undergo now is more adapted to producing men skilled in buying and selling than in manufacturing. . . . Industries must rest upon the productive power of the country or they will have nothing to do. If we are expecting to supply the country with a mass of youth who are ready to keep books and sell goods, and are to depend on immigration to supply us with people to manufacture the goods, we certainly are placing a false emphasis in our task of preparing the youth of our country to elevate the country's life and to defend its interests and advance them.

A generation ago, when many Americans were still speaking complacently of the past and optimistically of the future because of native inventive genius, he closed with this warning:

We had immense advantages in the characteristics of the pioneer Yankee. We can no longer congratulate ourselves on these advantages. We must find some equivalent for that former versatility and energy and efficiency in the future plans for the education of tomorrow.

By connecting applied science and industrial training not merely with the prosperity of American industry but with its survival, Rush Rhees showed a broad view of utility in relation to social welfare. He was thinking not only of profits but of human freedom, health, and happiness. A scholar who cannot think clearly on such themes has been ruined by his books. Because Rush Rhees could think without books, he interested industrialists. He commended himself as a potential leader to George Eastman and to the advisers of Andrew Carnegie and John D. Rockefeller. Like those three, he saw the future republic as a nation not of scholars but of skilled, responsible, and independent workers, with freedom to be themselves and ambition to become something more. The big three had more than money; he had more than brains. He had common sense and uncommon sense. They were keen, he was canny. Therefore they trusted him, and things began to happen.

VII

CITIZEN

Let us raise a standard to which the wise
and the honest can repair. The event is in
the hand of God.—George Washington

The danger of democracies is the domination
of demagogues. What is the safeguard? Widespread intelligence reaching beyond the limits
of a particular vocation.—Rush Rhees

※※※※※※※※※※※※※※※※※※※※※※※※※※※※※※※※※※※※※※※

OF POLITICS in the debased American sense, meaning a
tricky game by which a few seek to control the rights of
all, Rush Rhees knew enough to shun it. In politics as the
honorable science and art of good government he was an active
participant. City, state, and republic as they should be are
ideal concepts, which the good citizen works for because they
do not yet exist. He cannot make government perfect, but he
can make it better. If he does nothing, it grows worse. Only
a leader who says what he thinks, does what he says, works
with men of like and of unlike opinions for gradual improvement by reasonable compromise, and believes in the American
idea, can deserve civic approval. Rush Rhees deserved it, had
it, and valued it. In his later years he was Rochester's leading
citizen.

In civic leadership while holding academic office he had
good examples. Martin B. Anderson and David Jayne Hill
were as much concerned with city and state as with church
and school. They used their prominent position as college
presidents to utter wise and sometimes daring words on public
themes. Educators generally avoid partisan political advice

except when moral issues are involved, unless they are prepared to sacrifice for temporary advantage the respect of part of their constituency. But emphasis on reform of evident abuses, on improvement of government machinery, and on honesty and intelligence in legislation should be expected of a college president. For only as government is based on public interest rather than on private prejudice and selfish advantage can education succeed. Schools and colleges alike suffer in a badly governed community, as has been amply demonstrated in many American cities.

Rush Rhees in this respect welcomed the change of residence from Greater Boston to Rochester. He came to a city where population was more compact, the general level of intelligence higher, and racial conflicts less acute than in most parts of Boston proper. He had been a member there of the Twentieth Century Club, where discussion of public questions by progressives was encouraged even by conservatives. In Rochester, though at the beginning there was no such public forum as the City Club, founded in 1908, there was an active Chamber of Commerce, whose committees worked not only for business growth but for civic improvement, public health, and educational progress. As a member of that body he had many opportunities to become well acquainted with businessmen outside the group of university alumni and trustees, and to discover how many of them held public service to be as important as their business. It was the usual thing for merchants, manufacturers, and bankers to be trustees of hospitals and charitable institutions and philanthropic societies. In this Rochester did not differ from other industrial cities, except that since the leading citizens were too few to go around so large a circle, many had to double up. There were times each year when some of them spent so many hours a week working for the public good that they had little time left for their own.

Rush Rhees also found, on the other hand, that the traditionally Republican city had been in some respects under machine control. A reform movement, initiated before his arrival, in which some trustees and friends of the university participated, began with the schools. Against bitter partisan opposition in some quarters a progressive school board of five members gradually transformed the system. In this movement Rush Rhees did not share, but it had his sympathy. When the appointment of teachers and the supervision of studies were freed from partisan control there was rapid improvement.

Machine methods, though they ceased to affect the schools, remained for a time sufficiently powerful to affront good citizens of both parties. The only occasion on which Rush Rhees, so far as is known, varied from party regularity was when he voted for a Democratic congressman in order to defeat the boss. Ordinarily he confined his efforts at political reform to using such influence as he had within his own party. His characteristic independence of thought and action did not lead him to favor third parties, even that of Theodore Roosevelt, whom he had admired. But being a believer in representative government, he took frequent occasion to communicate with those who were supposed to represent; to remind them of causes likely to be neglected, to remonstrate with them when they failed in their duty, and to congratulate them when they served the public interest at personal sacrifice. This last-named duty of constituents is often forgotten. A good congressman has a rather thankless job.

Improvement of city government was one of his chief interests, as it was of George Eastman, Joseph T. Alling, James G. Cutler, and other friends and benefactors of the university. He was always an advocate of local self-government and local responsibility. The Rochester Bureau of Municipal Research, of which he was a director, had been founded by George Eastman and a group of public-spirited citizens for the study of possible economies in city administration. In the movement for a new city charter and for the adoption of the city manager system he was not a leader, but a wise adviser. Studies of municipal finance and methods of taxation, in the improvement of which lay all hope of future civic progress, were of particular interest to him. For this reason, as well as for proper performance of his duties in the administration of trust funds, he found it necessary to go much further into economic theory and practice than his previous experience had led him. Gradually he became a businessman as well as a citizen of foresight and good judgment.

City planning and housing also were prominent in his non-academic interests. There are in general two types of city planning—that of the architect or landscape gardener and that of the traffic engineer, emphasizing respectively beauty and convenience. Rochester had as one of its most honored citizens a nationally known expert in both fields, Charles Mulford Robinson. It had also two of the leading park men of the country, Calvin C. Laney and John Dunbar, who had developed in the outlying districts of the city an unsurpassed group of parks. Rochester, long a horticultural center, was known throughout western New York as the home of lilacs, trees, and roses. Rochesterians were proud of their parks and boulevards, and had a right to be.

But much of the main business street was shabby and discreditable, consisting chiefly of obsolete low buildings with false fronts and gaudy signboards. A few modern banks, stores, and office buildings scattered along the way only emphasized the desolation. The skyline was depressing, except where the river gave vistas; and that river, flowing right through the heart of the city, was totally concealed from the main street by decrepit buildings on the bridge. Side streets were chaotic; every journey was triangular. Long-standing business rivalry between east and west sides, overassessment of shrinking land values, high tax rates, and public apathy retarded the correction of obvious defects. Tax-poor owners would not spend the money, and the city did not have it. Therefore Rochester stood still, while poorer communities surpassed it.

These faults were as evident to Rochesterians in 1900 as they are today, but comparatively little has been done about them. Repeated surveys by experts from other cities, calling for a civic center and parallel streets to relieve congestion, have been received, paid for, and filed. They looked well on paper; but the high cost of condemning land, erecting adequate public structures, and tearing down ugly buildings in the heart of the city has delayed realization. Rush Rhees was a member of various committees which tried to advance these plans. He knew better than most people why so few of them have been carried out. But he never ceased to remind his fellow citizens that the burden of remaking the heart of Rochester cannot be ultimately evaded. In one of his earlier letters on this subject he wrote:

We are the fortunate possessors of one of the most beautiful sites for a city to be found in this or any other country. Our experience during the first hundred years of our community life makes it clear that notwithstanding the fact that individual taste and initiative have given us a unique position as a city of beautiful homes, as a community we have not sufficiently realized the importance of beauty and dignity of setting in our municipal buildings. We are now conscious that we have allowed ourselves to ignore too much the priceless possession which the city has in its river, to mention but one feature of natural beauty. We are all grateful to our city government for the steps that have been taken to transform the lower river from a source of offence to a source of joy and pleasure which its natural beauty destined it to be. I am confident that all our citizens must welcome the fair dream which your committee will set before us of something worthier, lovelier, and more significant which the Rochester of tomorrow may hope to become. Our mistakes in the past have been due to our lack of such an ideal. The fact that the dream cannot be completely realized at once will be no reason why we should not cherish it.

Nearly two decades later in a public address at the Rochester centennial celebration in 1934 he added:

When we consider our shapeless city plan we think with longing and chagrin of the earnest studies which have been made by most eminent experts for correction of some of our haphazard street arrangements, some of our neglected potentialities for civic beauty, some of our narrow preferences for local over general interests in our civic growth. Our city government has paid the lip service of acceptance of some features of the latest studies submitted. But eternal vigilance is requisite at each step of civic development if local clamor is not to deaden our ears to the dictates of larger convenience and beauty. Our hope for the twentieth century's contribution cannot be better phrased than in George Eastman's oft repeated vision—Rochester as the best place in the world in which to live and bring up children. We have a long way still to go. We have a great opportunity given by those who have gone before us.

Even transformation of the central business district, however, if it could have been brought about, would not have satisfied the civic conscience of Rush Rhees. That, after all, was a matter of pride, a saving in embarrassment and apologies when distinguished visitors came to town. Of much more real consequence for social welfare than boulevards and show places was housing of working people and low-income racial groups. For playgrounds near enough to the tenement districts to keep children off the streets he was equally concerned.

Rush Rhees's interest in social welfare, as well as in the physical improvement of the city, led to his share in the movement which came to a head in 1910 for organizing the many charitable enterprises of the city for common advantage. It was no new subject to him; since Newton, even since Hartford, he had been acquainted with the need for improving the business methods of philanthropic bureaus, and with the progress already made in that field in Boston, Buffalo, Cleveland, Chicago, and many other places besides New York. In 1903 he had been one of the delegates appointed by the governor to represent New York State at the National Conference of Charities and Corrections in Buffalo. The supporters of Rochester hospitals, homes for children and for the aged, shelters for the unfortunate, and agencies for relieving distress without the publicity and humiliation of municipal support had long felt the need of getting together. In order to prevent overlapping, duplication, and fraudulent appeals, as well as to ensure careful investigation of family problems underlying poverty, a central bureau for pooling such information was proposed. The university co-operated in bringing to the city an economist and sociologist who took charge of the newly organized central bureau and also taught a course at the college. Some of his successors have maintained a similar connection.

Emphasis on fact-finding surveys in the field of public relief, as well as in municipal finance, was in part due to George Eastman's objective bent of mind, but Rush Rhees also was influential in promoting it. He had no use for unsupported theorizing. To study social phenomena just for the sake of talking about them did not appeal to him. Collection of miscellaneous data, paper work for hired investigators, was in his judgment overdone, as well as passing resolutions and sending petitions to legislative bodies, when regarded as ends in themselves. What can be done about it?

Since bad housing conditions in crowded parts of the city were hardest on families of foreign ancestry, Rochester citizens did what they could to prevent human deterioration. One of the causes in which Rush Rhees was interested was the civic education of immigrants. He was a member of a Chamber of Commerce committee which promoted knowledge of American institutions among the Italians, Russians, and Poles who had thronged to Rochester before immigration was restricted to a quota. To prepare them for naturalization and to welcome them upon admission to citizenship by an annual dinner for new citizens was a Rochester custom as early as 1910. By his public addresses on Washington and Lincoln and patriotic themes the President of the university contributed to this significant cause.

It was also his privilege to know personally some of the more ambitious sons and daughters of the foreign-born in their efforts to win an education. Without much opportunity to study their home conditions, he nevertheless helped the gifted, cheered the disappointed, and congratulated the successful. Nothing pleased him better than to be able to award a prize or a scholarship where it meant changing the whole current of a life.

Adult education in citizenship beyond that provided by the public schools was a favorite cause of two of the more influential trustees of the university: Joseph T. Alling and James G. Cutler. For some years through their efforts and with the approval of the President a course in citizenship was given in the college, combining study of municipal and state government with that of the United States Constitution and its workings. Students visited the courts, the City Council, and city institutions to observe government in actual operation—sometimes different from what appears on paper. In later years this instruction was taken over by the Department of Government in the college, changing its title and to some extent its scope, but remaining always popular and influential among the students.

Rush Rhees was a student of American legislation, whose command of that field was much increased by an interesting experience in 1915. At the state election of November, 1914, he was elected one of three delegates from his senatorial district to the Constitutional Convention which was to meet at Albany in the following April. Since the previous revision in 1894 many sections of the constitution had become obsolete. Many other parts of it were in the nature of statutory legislation on special subjects which had no proper place in the fundamental law. The state government had become unwieldy by multiplication of bureaus, many of them overlapping. The civil service had been impaired by special privilege. Conservation of state lands and natural resources was endangered by business interests seeking the removal of barriers in forests and water-power facilities. What was most needed was a simplification of state government, so that the people could understand it and the politicians could not abuse it.

Rush Rhees's experience as a member of the Constitutional Convention was his most definite and concentrated public service. That it ended in apparent failure because of the defeat of all the proposed amendments at the polls in November was not so disappointing as it seemed at the time; for in later years nearly all of the more important reforms proposed by that convention were finally enacted into law. Of these the short ballot, reorganization of executive departments, reform of the court system, and complete transformation of state finance, with an executive budget and an independent audit, were the most important. Although Rush Rhees's summer was used up in protracted committee meetings and debates at Albany, so that he got little real vacation, he never regretted it. Inside knowledge of practical politics and intimate association with eminent men like Elihu Root, George W. Wickersham, Henry L. Stimson, Seth Low, Jacob Gould Schurman, John Lord O'Brien, and Alfred E. Smith more than compensated for the apparent anticlimax on election day.

Elihu Root, president of the convention, appointed Rush Rhees chairman of the committee on civil service, and a member of two other committees, one on the short ballot, the other on conservation. The heavier part of the work was done in committee meetings during the earlier part of the season. Public hearings were held at which arguments were heard for and against about eight hundred proposed amendments. Every one of the 119 amendments which came before his own committees Rush Rhees had to study carefully, in order to be able to speak on some and vote on all. His many short speeches, printed in full in the official proceedings, afford an interesting contrast of style to that of his educational and religious addresses. All three classes differed in vocabulary and cadence from literary papers written to be read to small groups. He had many styles.

One significant point in the Albany debates was that even there, where sometimes it might have seemed legitimate, he was never sarcastic. Clever sarcasm is a form of egotism that costs more than it is worth. It amuses the speaker, alienates the victim, and convinces nobody.

Progressive in principle, conservative in method, he wanted not more legislation but less. Instead of increasing the complexity of government he would have made it simpler. More attention to fundamentals and less to machinery would in his opinion improve the American system. He once wrote: "The cure of any evils which develop in representative government will be found through an awakening of patriotic interest on the part of the electorate, rather than by means of modifications in the political machinery."

During the two years before the beginning of World War I he did not share the comfortable optimism of those who thought Europe's internal rivalries unlikely to affect us. Preparation for national defense he regarded as indispensable. Early in 1912 he wrote:

Anything which will shake our people into a realization of the fact that raw recruits cannot be immediately transformed to soldiers, and that arms cannot be manufactured over night, will be of great value. The greatest danger from our present complacency arises from the rashness with which our excited people are sometimes inclined to tread on the toes of other nations. This country ought to keep on hand an adequate supply of arms and ammunition to equip a large civilian army if emergency should arise.

Through the efforts of Dr. Benjamin Ide Wheeler and others, he had been invited in 1913 to accept the Roosevelt professorship in Berlin for the academic year 1916-1917 and had agreed to go. When the war broke out he had already spent considerable time in preliminary research for his lectures. The subject was to have been the relations of church and state in America in the seventeenth and eighteenth centuries. The study was abandoned. Those Berlin lectures were among various interesting things in Rush Rhees's possible career that never came to pass.

In the spring of 1914 talk of preparedness was in the air, though without apprehensions of an immediate explosion. Summer military camps for college students were planned by the War Department on a volunteer basis, and several Rochester students were assisted in attending these camps through the generosity of Mr. James G. Cutler. When war came in Europe in midsummer, it became evident that the position of the United States would be increasingly difficult. It was hard for the President of the university to guard against any utterance or act which might violate American neutrality. He himself avoided either attacking or defending the policy of the national administration.

After the American declaration of war on April 6, 1917, many students volunteered for army or navy service. Though the President advised against haste and urged them to finish the term, some left at once for the training camps. Military training on the campus was begun, at first without uniforms or proper equipment. The War Department was slow in providing instructors and facilities for such training. President Rhees, knowing that sometimes silence is the best patriotism, suppressed his opinions of official delays in his effort to co-operate completely with the national government. Throughout the war he showed his power to ignore his own personal judgment as to methods, and to take suggestions or orders from Washington whether he did or did not see any sense in them. Because he could obey, he could command. It was no time for individual dissent. The best men complained least.

By 1918 there was no one left on the campus, man or woman, young or old, who did not do his part in the noncombatant part of the war. Not only the 862 University of Rochester students, alumni, and teachers in the national service, but all the rest who stayed at home, were busier than they had ever been before, doing what they could for victory. To students about to leave for the war the President said: "Your life's next task is the world's most serious crisis. Glory in it, for your lives now will count for all that they are worth."

As chairman of the budget committee of the Community Chest, or Rochester Patriotic and Community Fund as it was then called, he rendered public service of great value. Rochester was not the first city to combine all annual solicitations for community enterprises and national philanthropies in one short campaign, but it was one of the best organized and most efficient. The Community Chest raised immense sums at the height of the war, and spent them freely but fairly for the good of all. Rush Rhees had little to do with raising the money, but a great deal to do with spending it.

Two fundamental principles controlled this important community movement: (1) For all the thirty-six local agencies and the many national and international causes to which contributions were asked, full and accurate statements of income and expenditures were required, as a basis for allotting specific sums in the annual budget. (2) Rochester's quota, the total sum to be raised, of which about one-tenth was for local agencies, was fixed at three-fourths of one per cent of the national budget. This ratio was not a mere guess. Rochester's population was one-fourth of one per cent of the whole country; Rochester's bond subscriptions were about one-half of one per cent; desiring to deal generously with war relief, the committee at George Eastman's suggestion added these two figures for a Community Chest goal.

Distribution of funds raised for agencies outside the city, national and international, was an even more perplexing task. Rush Rhees was a member of the executive committee of the National Investigation Bureau of New York, set up by large givers for checking waste and overlapping in war relief. Not infrequently it was discovered that two societies were soliciting funds for the same purpose, or that commissions were paid to solicitors, or money wasted on expensive offices and staffs. Only such organizations as could pass a searching investigation received money from Rochester. Therefore every Rochester subscriber, whether he gave ten dollars or a million, could feel sure that all his money was going directly to the needy. Overhead cost was met, not out of charitable contributions, but from separate funds subscribed for that purpose by those who could afford it.

Rush Rhees retained his position on the budget committee after the war, but eventually relinquished it as other duties increased. He derived from it a remarkable capacity for spending other people's money. This was not without its compensations; for example, there was a certain satisfaction in being able to vote $50,000 in one year to feed French and Belgian children, with Herbert Hoover to spend it. Decorations and diplomas received years after the war from the Yugoslav and Polish governments for his efforts in behalf of their impov-

erished peoples were not without their pleasant reminiscent
value for Rush Rhees. Most of all, it was the demonstration in
administering those large war budgets of his financial soundness and wise judgment that led George Eastman and the
General Education Board to entrust him and his university
with a fortune. He knew how to save small sums and spend
large sums with equal firmness and foresight. He was penny
wise, pound wiser.

An unpleasant war episode that he had to handle was the
persecution by certain individuals and groups in Rochester of
Ewald Eiserhardt, a professor of German, who happened to
be in Germany when war broke out and was unable to return.
President Rhees had interceded on his behalf with the German
government in the fall of 1914, representing that he could be
more useful in Rochester teaching classic German literature
than as a recruiting officer in the German army. This appeal,
which resulted in his return to teaching at Rochester in 1915,
may have been an error of judgment on the part of the President; for after American entrance into the war in 1917 Professor Eiserhardt was of course an enemy alien. His position
then became anomalous, and he was a target for unjust suspicion among the suspicious. Nevertheless, those who knew his
sterling character, his antimilitarist principles, his unsurpassed
power of winning the loyalty and affection of students and
colleagues, hoped that the President would stand firmly behind
him. President Lowell at Harvard had done that for a less
admirable and more aggressive German scholar. It took a good
deal of courage for Rush Rhees to write on April 9, 1918, an
open letter to the press, in which he said:

We have found no reason to believe that Professor Eiserhardt's influence is in any way subversive of most positive Americanism in his
students. His colleagues in the faculty are a unit in confidence in his
integrity. Should the Trustees of the University act on suspicion unsupported by discoverable evidence and ask Professor Eiserhardt to withdraw, what would be gained for the public good, in the absence of a
government provision for the internment of all Germans? What would be
gained in America's war for ideals of honor and justice and good will,

if in the absence of evidence to justify such action we should yield to
mere suspicion and discharge a man of whose honorable integrity of
character we have every reason to be confident? We are convinced that
justice and the larger patriotism which shuns injustice as a most subtle
undermining of patriotism dictate the course the University has followed
of retaining Professor Eiserhardt upon our faculty, as long as constantly
watchful observation leaves us still convinced, as we now are, of his
integrity, honor, and readiness to observe strictly the regulations which
must order his life and speech in our land, which is at war with Germany.

Notwithstanding this spirited defense, Rush Rhees could
not stand the pressure. He had the backbone, but he could not
endanger the university's position in the community in order to
satisfy his own convictions. Some of the trustees would not
support him. Public feeling ran high. Eiserhardt offered his
resignation, and it was accepted. Apparently Rush Rhees was
defeated in a clear contest of reason against prejudice.

But he was a hard man to beat. When the war was over,
doubtless not without some opposition, he got Eiserhardt back
on the faculty. Because the war had greatly decreased the
study of German, and there was no real need for his full time
in that department, the President made a place for him in the
history of art, for which also he was well fitted. The President
encouraged his advanced studies, and helped him to carry out
a long cherished design for a seminar in the orientation of art
with philosophy and religion. He gave Ewald Eiserhardt a new
career. He made possible travel in the Far East for further study
of early Asiatic sculpture and architecture. For his few remaining years Eiserhardt taught great things to small groups, which
will never forget him. Then on his way back to Asia for one
more look at the temples of the oldest gods, he contracted a
fatal disease, and died in Germany with a dream still un-
realized. But his students and friends have made his dream
their own, gazing in silence at the subtle smile of an ancient
stone sculptured head of a Boddhisatva in the Memorial Art
Gallery, given in memory of him. A Boddhisatva is an adept
who has attained, but lingers among men; wisdom amidst confusion; in the world, not of it. Thus Ewald lingered, thus he

departed, yet his essence remains. His was a beautiful and tragic life. Rush Rhees knew that, showed in the long run justice and mercy, and never talked about it.

Intolerance in all its forms he opposed. Among the many irrational consequences of both our wars with Germany has been a decrease in the study of the German language. No clearer illustration of unreason in the name of Americanism can be found. It is not merely a folly of the young; they could hardly be expected to know better when their elders write to a college president, as one did to President Rhees in June, 1918, demanding "that all teaching of German in the University as well as the high schools should be discontinued for the period of the war." He replied:

I cannot agree with you with reference to the propriety of discontinuing the teaching of German in the universities during the period of the war, any more than I can believe that it would be wise for chemists and physicists and biologists to discontinue the use of German periodicals devoted to their special sciences. The colleges exist to train men and women who may become competent to assume positions of importance and leadership in later life. After the close of this terrible war it will be of the utmost importance that such persons be able far more perfectly than before the war to know what Germany is thinking, so far as that can be disclosed by what she is publishing. A refusal to give the young people who are preparing for possible service in this time the opportunity to qualify for the acquiring of such knowledge of Germany's thoughts and purposes seems to me most unwise and unnecessary.

Reason was always his solution. He was aware that many people think they are thinking when they are merely feeling resentment or fear, but he would not encourage this delusion. A friendly opponent once wrote to him: "You are a very hard man to convince. You are always asking, Why?" It was true; and few could answer when they suddenly saw they were wrong. The Socratic method can sometimes be crushing; it crushes self-deception as well as sophistry.

Reason rather than emotion was likewise his approach to other forms of intolerance. A man can be judged by finding out not merely what he thinks about race relations but on what grounds. Rush Rhees believed in equal rights and opportunities for Negroes, Jews, and other classes of Americans still subject to discrimination; but this was not because he had worked himself up into an excited feeling that they needed some sort of holy crusade to help them out. They were citizens and human beings, capable of contributing their full share to the common good. To deny them that opportunity did not make sense. Furthermore, it would merely give them a grievance, and lead them, like their oppressors, to act on prejudice rather than reason. Victims of intolerance become themselves intolerant. The enlightened have always known that, but some of the so-called elite do not know it yet.

As a friend of the Negro he supported the work of the southern Commission on Inter-racial Co-operation, and various educational institutions for colored people in the southern states. In the kind of industrial education given to Negroes at Tuskegee Institute he had strong interest, visited that school on several occasions with its chief benefactor, Julius Rosenwald of Chicago, and contributed regularly to its support. But reason showed him that Negroes also need higher education for their professional leaders, especially for teachers and physicians, and he was well acquainted with Negro colleges and medical schools at Atlanta, Nashville, and elsewhere. He could not see why friends of the Negro need take sides, as champions either of Booker T. Washington or of William E. B. DuBois. Both were good men, both were needed. There was no true opposition between intellect and handicraft; George Washington Carver had both; the race could not have too much of either. It was because, in the judgment of Julius Rosenwald, George Eastman, and many other benefactors of the Negroes, they needed more artisans than artists, more potatoes than poetry, that a mistaken cleavage of opinion has arisen in some quarters. When the problem of Negro education became a matter of feeling rather than of judgment, Rush Rhees deplored this aberration. To the president of a Negro university he wrote:

Be assured of my great interest in the work you are carrying on, which interest is coupled also with the profound conviction that the indispensable basis for strong higher institutions for colored people is the multiplication of such facilities for elementary education as will serve to raise the level of the mass of the colored people. It has always seemed to me unfortunate and a mistake that so many educated Negroes have failed to recognize the significance and importance of the work of such institutions as Hampton and Tuskegee. On the other hand, the development of such institutions calls with increasing clearness for the maintenance and improvement of the opportunities for more advanced education for colored people.

In 1931 he was invited to deliver an address at the fiftieth anniversary of Tuskegee Institute. The following passage shows further his position on Negro education:

Booker Washington was great in the contribution which he made to the solution of the perplexed problem of race relations. At the expense of being misunderstood by many of his own race, he had the insight and the courage to take the long view and to dedicate himself and his school to the task of compelling respect for Negro work and Negro character—respect based on recognized service and worth. He was not blind to evils nor deaf to the cry of the oppressed, but he sought to lay a foundation on which mutual good will and respect of whites and Negroes might be built up.

Reason rather than emotion likewise governed his attitude toward Jews. If they were sometimes too aggressive, this might be a compensation for centuries of persecution. If they were too suspicious of discrimination, he would give them no ground for it. When Jewish students at Rochester formed a fraternity and asked for recognition, meaning a share in student elections and social events, he pointed out that no other society based solely on either race or religion had claimed similar privileges. The college has always had Jewish students and they have not been denied their rights. As a citizen Rush Rhees believed in complete civil equality. As a Christian he maintained cordial relations with Jewish rabbis, scholars, businessmen, lawyers, journalists, scientists, and philanthropists, and counted some of them among his best friends. On anti-Semitism and the cure for it he wrote to a Jewish friend in 1929:

The effort to secure and to make more widespread an attitude of mutual respect based on increasing accurate knowledge between Jews and Christians is one which merits continued interest and support. Such an effort seems to me to be more likely to be successful if not identified with official committees representative of either Jews or Christians. The intense and bitter controversies which exist between liberals and reactionaries in the Christian churches suggest the almost insuperable difficulties in the way of any official cultivation of the mutual understanding and good will which we believe to be as essential as it is desirable to the advancement of pure and undefiled religion. It is for this reason that I look with more hope upon the quiet cultivation of acquaintance and respect between Jews and Christians than I do upon any official activities seeking to accomplish the same result.

He distrusted attempts to change the world by legislation. He disliked "pressure groups" of reformers almost as much as other lobbies. On national prohibition his views would have been misunderstood at the time by his fellow churchmen, for it was generally supposed in orthodox circles that temperance was synonymous with the Anti-Saloon League. He did not like saloons, liquor advertising by brewers and distillers to increase sales, or their underground political power. Neither did he like some of the methods of the opposition at Albany and Washington. Two quotations from his letters will sufficiently indicate where he stood:

For over fifty years I have been convinced that the legalistic effort to control the habits of people in the matter of alcoholic beverages was destined to precisely the failure which the prohibition experiment has met. I am very heartily in sympathy with all efforts to cure the drink evil by persuasion and the control of the sale of alcoholic beverages.

I am profoundly interested in and concerned for anything which will advance the cause of temperance. I am also equally interested in the advancement of respect for law in our country, which respect is put in jeopardy by disregard of the prohibition law. I never have believed and do not now believe in prohibition by constitutional amendment. The experience in this country with the Fourteenth and Fifteenth Amendments is rather ominous. As a consequence it would seem to be rather inconsistent with my convictions to become a member of your board.

Reason rather than emotion also controlled his attitude toward the question of the postwar settlement. He had long been a member of the League to Enforce Peace, an advocate of the Permanent Court of International Justice, or World

Court, a believer in partial disarmament, and in international co-operation. He was anything but an isolationist, yet he could not approve President Wilson's obstinate insistence on the adoption of the Treaty of Versailles and the Covenant of the League of Nations without amendment or reservation. Reason told him that it could not be adopted at all without some concessions to the Senate.

President Rhees was one of the signers of a declaration published just before the election of 1920 calling for the defeat of Wilson on the ground that Harding was the more likely of the two to bring about American adherence to an international peace organization. They actually thought Harding meant what he said. In this bad guess he had good companions, who have been silent ever since about that prophecy. He never gave up hope that at least our adherence to the World Court, endorsed by every president for a generation, would finally be approved by the Senate, but in this hope he was disappointed.

On Armistice Day, 1930, by request of a local newspaper, he contributed the following statement on international peace:

The peace which the world needs is not a passive quietism. It is rather the abolition of the appeal to physical force and the preparation for such appeal to physical force to safeguard national life, so that the safeguarding of that life may be seen clearly in its rational and moral aspects, and may be striven for with all the moral and intellectual force which a nation possesses.

In the second place, the peace which the world needs is not a surrender of rights by the peoples of the world to the groups or individuals who may make a guerrilla warfare on social order and equity. It does not imply the abolition of police power. It seeks rather a substitution of police power acting under recognized laws for all forms of sabre-rattling which threaten and often result in the surrender of considerations of justice to the bold demands of national self-interest.

In the third place, the peace which is sought for the world is not an abolition of the "struggle for existence"; it is rather a recognition of the truth that the issue of the struggle for existence must be a fitness to survive; and an insistent and confident affirmation that such fitness is and must be measured by moral rather than physical standards, if indeed mankind is to justify the claim to be higher than the beasts. Such a continuous struggle for a triumph of truly human life over brute force will so engage all the intellectual and moral powers of man that there will be no chance of that softening of manhood which the foes of disarmament so eloquently fear.

In that same month of November, 1930, still believing in disarmament as a means of maintaining peace, he received the following letter from the president of the University of Louvain, to which the University of Rochester had contributed £100 for rebuilding its library, and a silk Rochester flag to be hung with many others in its great hall. This letter, which reads like a too literal translation from the French, has now a melancholy interest for those who then thought that war was over:

My dear President:

It is for me an extremely pleasant duty to be able to express and convey to you the feelings which inspire the professors and students of the University of Louvain towards the University of Rochester at the moment when we hang in its place in the big reading-room of this library, which we owe to the proverbial generosity of your great nation, the silk flag which you had the kindness to send us. And foremost among these feelings there is one of deep gratitude for the manner in which once more you have wanted to show your sympathy for a small country, who knew already long ago and admired men and educational institutions of beyond the ocean, but who had learned during the dark and tragic days of war to hail and salute the Stars and Stripes as a dawning of comfort and hope.

· The young men who prepare themselves at the University of Louvain to a scientific career, or intend to occupy a prominent place in the ranks of the leading society of their country, are stimulated at the thought that beyond the seas other men, young like themselves and like them full of enthusiasm for the ideal which is their ultimate purpose are working, and that a day will come when the results which they have obtained in the various branches of science, and the experience which they will have acquired in political, social, or economic life will mutually help them for the great benefit of humanity.

All these reasons taken into consideration urge me to tell you how very much we have appreciated the friendly token which it has been our good luck to receive from you, the memory of which will remain fresh through the successive generations, and to assure you once more of our entire gratitude.

Ten years later, when Rhees of Rochester was in his grave and his soul was marching on, the rebuilt Louvain Library lay in ruins, wrecked again by German madness. The building, the books, and the flags which were the gift of the free to the free went up in flames. But already books, friendship, and freedom are coming back in the Low Countries. Those values cannot be destroyed. Other young men will save them. Other old men like those two university presidents sending to each other hope overseas will stand with youth for the rights of man. If Rochester should send Louvain another flag, it might have a phoenix on it.

That the United States must ultimately take its place as a real world power, not only in demands but in responsibilities, was Rush Rhees's profound conviction. Having survived one World War, destiny allowed him to die before the other. It was better then to leave the world than to endure it. An eightieth year would have been only labor and sorrow.

As a citizen he had done what he could. Like Washington he had "raised a standard to which the wise and the honest can repair" and left "the event in the hand of God." But looking back on a generation of public service he may have felt that the greatest dangers of democracy are the strength of ignorance and the weakness of the wise.

VIII

CO-ORDINATION

In omnibus fere minus valent praecepta quam experimenta.—Quintilian

〰〰〰〰〰〰〰〰〰〰〰〰〰〰〰〰〰〰〰〰〰〰〰〰〰〰〰〰〰〰〰

WOMAN in search of education is neither uncertain nor coy, but may be hard to please. Why she should ever suppose that men could educate her better than she could teach herself is still a riddle. Since men hardly understand themselves and are slow to learn even from their own experience, how can they help girls grow up?

Yet to go to a men's college has been the steadfast hope of many ambitious young women, and of their feminine relatives for them, during at least a hundred years. Since Oberlin opened its doors to women in 1841, female seminaries and finishing schools were no longer enough. A real college it must be, taught by men, with men's standards and men's rewards. Women generally get what they want sooner or later. Just how they do it is not always clear, but this chapter tells one way— money and persistence, a little money and much persistence.

In Rochester it was not Susan B. Anthony who started the movement for a women's college. It was that learned old archaeologist, anthropologist, ethnologist, friend of Indians and beavers, Lewis Henry Morgan. As far back as the early seventies he and Dr. Edward Mott Moore tried to raise a subscription fund for women's higher education. They failed. The author of *Ancient Society* and *The League of the Iroquois* could not convince his well-to-do fellow citizens that their daughters needed more learning than could be acquired at Livingston Park Seminary. In 1878 "Dr. Moore presented the subject of female education to the Executive Committee for

discussion." Nothing came of it. When Lewis Henry Morgan
made his will he left his entire residuary estate to the university
for that purpose. His language was as follows:

> I desire to use my estate for the purpose of female education of high
> grade in the city of Rochester and under the management of the Trustees
> of the University of Rochester, the said institution to be made a part of
> said University if the Trustees choose to make it such, or to be kept
> independent and subject to their management and control.

It is said that the death of his two daughters in childhood
led a rather austere man to make this gift for other girls then
unborn, in a Rochester which he could not foresee. He died in
1881, but since the estate was subject to life annuities, and
since the will was contested after the death of the last direct
heir in 1905, it was not until 1909 that the Morgan Fund, including his wife's estate, became available. It amounted to
about $80,000, in addition to the Morgan library, manuscripts,
bookcases, and museum collections in natural history and
archaeology.

About 1890 Miss Susan B. Anthony, Mrs. Mary T. L. Gan-
nett, Mrs. Helen B. Montgomery, and others began agitating
for admission of women to the university. They met at first
with little encouragement from the trustees, who were always
trying to pay deficits and wanted no more expenses. For some
years on Saturday mornings a few professors had been meeting
small classes of women in literature and other subjects, but
these were mostly teachers, few if any of undergraduate age.
No academic credit was given for attendance at such classes;
they were merely allowed to use classrooms in Anderson Hall.
Nevertheless, it was an entering wedge; and where there's a
wedge there's a way.

President Hill was by no means cordial toward the proposal
for admitting women as candidates for degrees. He had
troubles enough without that. After his resignation in 1896,
under the interim administrations of Acting Presidents Lattimore and Burton, the overtures from the women's committee
were renewed. They were soliciting subscriptions from friends

of coeducation, mostly women, and from business houses and social organizations. On June 14, 1898, the trustees voted that

It is the sense of the Board of Trustees of the University of Rochester that women should be admitted to this institution upon the same terms and under the same conditions as men; that this policy be put into effect when the women of Rochester shall raise the necessary funds for the use of the University, estimated at $100,000, and under such conditions as may be decided upon by the Executive Committee of the Board.

The vote was not unanimous. It was at this same meeting that a committee of three was appointed to select a new president. A year later, on June 20, 1899, a communication from the women's committee to the trustees proposed:

That the Trustees accept the pledges and cash contributions already received by the committee, aggregating more than $29,000, and that the Trustees proceed to erect a new science building for the use of the Departments of Biology and Physics, which they understand can be built for the sum of $29,000 or less, and as such a building would relieve eleven classrooms in Anderson Hall, that the University Trustees admit the coming fall a limited number of girl students to the University, say ten to twenty-five. Such action would be taken by the Trustees on the condition that the committee continue the work of raising the balance of the $100,000 fund.

The trustees voted "that we deem it inexpedient at the present time to grant the request of the Women's Educational Association, but at the same time expressing our appreciation of their efforts." It will be remembered that during the year following his election to the Rochester presidency Rush Rhees remained at Newton Centre, finishing his teaching and his book. He was therefore not present at the next annual meeting of the trustees on June 12, 1900, when coeducation came up again. The women's committee reported:

That they had secured in pledges and subscriptions $40,000. We believe that this amount may possibly be increased to $50,000, but we do not see any probability of our being able to raise the remainder of the $100,000 in this locality. We have done our best. We regret that it is no better. If the Board of Trustees can suggest any method by which we can secure the entire amount, we will gladly continue the work according to their instructions.

This time the trustees relented. They voted, though not unanimously, to admit women in the following September, provided $50,000 was secured by that time. They were aware that the income on $50,000 would not really pay the additional cost of admitting women; but most of them believed in the principle of providing higher education for Rochester women who could not afford to go away to college. The financial problem, while difficult, would not be insurmountable. The minimum figure finally adopted was a token of good faith to be pledged by the women, and the trustees of course expected to keep faith on their part if the condition should be fulfilled. Perhaps they did not really expect that it would. As the summer passed it seemed unlikely that the effort could succeed by September.

When the new president arrived, it was not without knowledge that coeducation was a future possibility, rather remote, but without any expectation or warning that it might come next week. Yet that was what happened. On September 8, 1900, at a special meeting of the Executive Committee, the women's committee announced that the conditions had been met, and presented their subscription rolls as proof. The Executive Committee, in fulfillment of the promise made in July, voted to admit women as agreed.

It was therefore necessary on a few days' notice for the President to make arrangements for thirty-three young women who had already applied for admission. Of these fifteen were freshmen, three sophomores, one junior, one senior, one graduate, and twelve special students. In the President's report at the end of that first year he was able to state that "these young women have proved to be good students and sensible women, and have conducted themselves with propriety and good taste." He had not yet learned so well as he did later to expect the unexpected and "co-operate with the inevitable," but he rose to the situation. Yet the new policy, hastily and informally adopted just as a new executive was arriving, had complications. Rooms must be made ready, principles must be adopted concerning the women's right to enter classes in which perhaps they might not be welcome. Trouble might be expected from a few unruly men students, which must be anticipated and suppressed. But it was all in the day's work. The trustees had acted, and he took steps accordingly. He had promised not to shirk any duty of his new office. This was just one more duty, and he took it in his stride. Whether he liked it or not he was not asked and did not say.

He had to consider future developments. Precedents grow fast in the first year of any enterprise. A false step at the beginning might block future change. He reported to the trustees:

In the coeducation of men and women there are three different methods in vogue. Each has its advantages and drawbacks. In the western states it is common to teach the men and women together in the same classes. In the eastern states, where coeducation exists at all, it is more commonly under what is known as the "annex" system, two virtually distinct institutions being maintained under practically the same government and with much the same corps of instructors.

Besides these two there is a third system which may be described as "co-ordinate education," in which the women are members of the same college, have the same instructors, take most of the lectures and laboratory work in the same classes with the men, but in all or a part of their recitation work are taught in separate classes. This third method has certain advantages which commend it to the judgment of the faculty, among which are:

1. It makes it possible in some subjects, such as literature on the one hand and physiology and hygiene on the other, to give full and frank consideration to all phases of the matter under discussion without such omissions as would be well-nigh inevitable in mixed classes of college grade.

2. It makes it possible to cultivate a feeling of social unity among the women of the college out of which may develop here some of those social advantages which constitute in no small measure the attraction of the separate college for women.

Five years later the President wrote:

The University has not committed itself to any other theory in this admission of the women as students except that they should be received into the college on the basis of the same requirements, to be given the same grade and varieties of instruction, and to be awarded the same degrees as the men. I add this last statement for its possible bearing on the suggestion in Mr. Morgan's will that the Trustees should organize a separate institution for women. No step that has been taken by us will have to be retraced if circumstances or policy suggest the wisdom of segregating the women into a co-ordinate institution under the same administration as the men . . . The present status of the women is consistent either with their permanent identification with the men as students in the same institution or their partial segregation as students under the same faculty but in separate classes.

During the early years there were occasional incidents indicating a lack of cordiality on the part of a few of the men students toward mixed classes. There were also some zealous older feminine champions of the women students who resented these demonstrations, and thought the President should forcibly suppress them. He seldom allowed trivialities to be magnified, trusting more to time and common sense than to discipline. Sometimes in his absence attempts were made to reopen the whole question, which he promptly rejected, as in the following extract from a letter which he wrote to the student newspaper from Florence on March 26, 1909:

The several legal obligations assumed by the University in connection with the higher education of women differentiate our situation from that of many other institutions, and assure the continuance of the policy of receiving more women as students at Rochester. That which may chiefly distinguish our life at Rochester may be our frank recognition of two bodies of students with co-ordinate rights and separate interests and traditions, and such courtesy on the part of one body of the students towards the other as is in accord with the established traditions of Rochester.

The President and trustees were responsible to the community and to the donors of funds for women's education. They could not admit the right of students or alumni to run the college, and they never did. President Rhees knew just when and how to put people in their place without making enemies. He had simply to remind them of facts which they knew as well as he, and to appeal to their co-operation. It generally worked.

During the first ten years many questions arose concerning the nonacademic and social life of the women students and the development of their customs and traditions, in which the friendly counsel of Mrs. Rhees and other ladies of the university circle was helpful. As the number and variety of such questions increased, and the necessity of frequent conferences with women students as to their studies became more evident, the President with the approval of the trustees appointed a dean of women, Miss Annette Gardner Munro, who assumed office on January 2, 1910. In the absence of women's dormitories, and with strict rules concerning residence for women students not living with their families, no attempt was made to encourage applications from candidates outside the Rochester area. The President wrote in 1910:

The admission of women to the University of Rochester was granted by the Trustees with the specific regard for those young women in Rochester and in the immediate neighborhood who but for this concession would be virtually unable to secure a college education. The step was taken in spite of the fact that the funds necessary to carry the new department to a successful issue were not in sight, simply as a recognition of the reasonable obligation which we owe to our immediate community. We do not feel any similar obligation with reference to young women at a greater distance from us, for the reason that there are many other colleges to which they may go quite as easily as to Rochester. We have a few women from a distance, who come for one or another reason, generally because of some family connection with Rochester.

One more quotation from a letter of that early period will give a sufficient impression of his attitude on the question of coeducation:

My interest in coeducation is exclusively practical, and not theoretical. We believe in it here in Rochester as a means of offering higher education to the young women in our neighborhood who are unable to go to the women's colleges. Their admission to the University of Rochester is not in any sense consequent upon a theoretical prejudice for or against the abstract idea of coeducation.

Nevertheless, in 1910 the administration began planning for partial separation of men's and women's classes in prescribed courses. Friends of Susan B. Anthony began raising funds for a women's building, the Anthony Memorial. Until this enterprise and the erection of another women's building, Catharine

Strong Hall, were completed in 1913-1914, the actual separation of the two groups could not be accomplished. But in 1912 the President's report included the following significant statement:

Twelve years ago women were admitted as students in the University. During these twelve years the Trustees have been studying with an open mind the problem of the best method of providing for their interests and the interests of the men students. They have reached the conviction that the organization of a co-ordinate college in the University for women is clearly advisable. As soon as this new policy can be put into effect there will be two colleges in the University, one for men and one for women. In educational privileges and in dignity they will be strictly co-ordinate. The organization of the two colleges will make it possible to provide more adequately and exactly for the needs and the interests of the men in their college and of the women in theirs. This new college for women will need its own equipment. Already land has been promised for it adjacent to the campus, and also money for two new buildings—an academic building for lecture and recitation rooms and administrative offices, and a women's gymnasium and student building.

The year 1912 was a momentous one in Rush Rhees's life. His successful career at Rochester had led his own college, Amherst, to consider him favorably for its presidency. There was no formal election, but such negotiations as precede an election. The opportunity was attractive. Amherst was a nationally known institution with a long and distinguished history and an impressive body of eminent alumni. Many of his best friends were Amherst men. Many of the educational principles in which he believed were already established at Amherst, whereas at Rochester their development was still in the future. Amherst had a complete plant, a considerable endowment, and no acute financial problems. It was not coeducational, and was not likely to be. It was not dependent on local patronage for its students. It could afford to pay its teachers living salaries. It was in many ways a better college than Rochester. At that time it seemed a better place for a lifetime career. The informal offer of such a position appealed strongly to Rush Rhees—not to his vanity, for he had none, but to his natural desire to use his remaining years before retirement in the largest task of which he was capable. To one of the Rochester trustees he wrote as follows:

Any alumnus finds the highest honor in the serious consideration of his name in connection with the presidency of his own college. Amherst College rates as one of the very first of the smaller colleges of the country in dignity, in eminence, and in equipment. It is supplied with all of the buildings which are necessary to its work. It has invested funds amounting to $2,600,000, with considerable increase of those funds in sight. It pays its professors $3,500 a year, against our $2,500. It is backed by a wealthy and enthusiastic body of alumni. I do not hesitate to say that if I were elsewhere than in Rochester, and the presidency of Amherst and Rochester were offered to me at the same time, there would be no hesitancy in my mind concerning which to accept.

But I am in Rochester, have put twelve years of my life into the work here, see that some things have been accomplished, that others of great importance await accomplishment. No man could have a more loyal and responsive Board of Trustees to work with than has the President of Rochester at present; no man could have a more loyal and responsive faculty to work with than has the President of Rochester at present. Moreover, Rochester offers an opportunity for educational accomplishment that I believe is of unique interest, provided certain things can be realized in the not distant future. Notwithstanding the strong attraction of Amherst, if after fifteen more years of active work I could look back upon twenty-five years spent in Rochester with the resultant accomplishment in some measure of attainment of my ideal for this place, I cannot escape the conviction that such an accomplishment would yield more satisfaction than would be derivable from the completion of fifteen years devoted to maintaining Amherst College at its present high level. But if I am to make any change in my work, I ought to do it before many years have passed over my head; hence the seriousness of the problem.

As I viewed the situation there appeared to be two things of urgent necessity for accomplishment at Rochester:

1. Provision for some increase in the faculty, and for definite increase in the scale of salaries paid to professors and assistant professors.

2. We ought to take immediate steps to establish our work for women on a co-ordinate basis. The fact that Amherst College is not coeducational constitutes another strong attraction to a man of my convictions.

I told my friends here that I was quite ready to believe that after careful consideration they might deem the first of these needs impracticable of realization and the second of them undesirable; that if this should be their judgment, I feel it my duty to reply that if Amherst wants me I will accept.

If, on the contrary, it should be the judgment of the Trustees of Rochester that it is both desirable and practicable to undertake the realization of these two ends in the quite near future, I shall be convinced thereby that duty and inclination combine to dictate a negative reply to my correspondent's letter. That the response of my friends was loyal and friendly you do not need to be told; that it was candid and appreciative of my problem you also do not need to be told.

This letter reveals much of Rush Rhees's character and convictions. It shows that he did not believe in complete coeducation. That he had endured it as long as he had, meeting much friction among alumni and some among undergraduates, was evidence of his patience and power of detachment. As long as it was a university policy, dictated by the trustees before he came, he would not shirk his duty of administering it; but the moment he could change it he would. Although women students had "conducted themselves with propriety and good taste," their mere presence in the crowded rooms and corridors of Anderson Hall and the Sibley Library conduced, in the minds of some hostile critics, to a "high school atmosphere," and hindered both study and college spirit. The opposite opinion was stoutly maintained by many students and teachers; but argument on such questions, based rather on prejudice than on reason, does not raise higher education any higher.

Rush Rhees had had about enough of it. Now there was a way out. Unless correction of several major defects at Rochester could be guaranteed, his decision would be for accepting the Amherst offer, which, as he admitted in a letter to a classmate, was "the highest compliment I have ever received." This was not the only time that overtures and inquiries had come to him from other institutions, but it was the most alluring.

The supporters of the university met the challenge promptly and generously. George Eastman offered to give $500,000 if an equal sum were raised by others. The General Education Board pledged $200,000 for endowment on condition that the remaining $300,000 should be raised by others. It took time to complete the fund, but its success was practically assured when Rush Rhees wrote to a friend:

If it should prove that the problem which has been presented to me has turned out to be the occasion for the establishment of the University of Rochester on a surer foundation for adequate work, we shall be

profoundly grateful, for I can think of no task which life could present
to us more fascinating and delightful than living amongst our friends in
Rochester and carrying through to measurable realization our ideals of the
work of building up this institution as an integral part of the life of this
community, as well as a significant factor in the educational enterprises
of the country.

To one of the many alumni in other parts of the country
who had been complaining for years of the complications of
coeducation in their old college, the President wrote in 1912:

From the beginning I have recognized the possibility that the time
might come when we would feel justified in making a different arrangement for the women students in the University, and I will acknowledge
no little satisfaction that that time seems now to be very near at hand.

In fulfillment of the trustees' pledge that a co-ordinate college for women would be established so soon as the buildings
were completed and the funds subscribed, the Executive Committee on April 9, 1912, adopted the following resolution:

Whereas the experience of the last twelve years has convinced us that
in the interests of the most satisfactory college life and successful college
training for our women students it is desirable to provide for their more
distinct recognition in the organization of the University by the creation
of a College for Women within the University;

Therefore be it resolved, that the Executive Committee of the Trustees
recommend to the Board of Trustees that such a College for Women be
created in this University, so soon as it is possible to add to our funds
for this purpose a sum not less than $250,000; $100,000 of which should
be applied to the erection of an academic building for women to provide
recitation and lecture rooms.

And be it further resolved, that this College for Women be maintained
as a department of the University on a basis of perfect parity with the
College for Men in the University in respect of standards of admission,
grade and range of instruction, and requirements for a degree, the students of the College for Women being thus received by the University of
Rochester on the same terms and conditions as the men.

Anthony Memorial Hall, containing a gymnasium and social
rooms, was completed in 1914 at a cost of $58,763.53, of which
the women's committee collected $27,475.01, the balance being
taken from the Women's Education Fund of 1900. Catharine
Strong Hall, named for the mother of Henry A. Strong, who
gave $100,000 for its construction, was finished in the same

year. In September, 1914, just after the beginning of World War I, freshman and sophomore women's classes in required subjects and a few of the larger women's sections of elective courses were transferred to Catharine Strong Hall. The women students, who had been taking their physical exercise at the Young Women's Christian Association, occupied the gymnasium in Anthony Memorial Hall.

Complete separation of women from men students in all classes, whether it was desired or not, was never even contemplated so long as the college remained at Prince Street. It could not be. But in 1925, when a ten-million-dollar campaign was undertaken for development of a separate College for Men at the River Campus, it was assumed by some people that at last adequate funds would be assured for the complete equipment of a separate College for Women on the old site. Whether this was or was not the expectation of the administration at that time, it has never been completely realized. Not from any lack of funds, after the later magnificent gifts of George Eastman and James G. Cutler specifically for women's education, but from other considerations not easy to analyze, a degree of coeducation in mixed classes continues on both campuses. The Rochester method of educating women is therefore a mixture or compromise of the separate college and the coeducational college. It is "co-ordinate" in the sense that the instruction offered to both groups is of equal grade and that social events, class and alumni organizations are separate. Whether the problem has yet been worked out on any consistent plan, worthy of the time and thought that Rush Rhees gave to it, and the large sums of money which others gave for it, is still an open question.

On one point, vital to the understanding of Rush Rhees as an executive, emphatic denial should be made of the charge sometimes heard in early days that he discriminated against women students. It was not true. He did nothing of the sort. He met not only their just demands but their reasonable requests with complete equity and courtesy. Rush Rhees was

CUTLER UNION, COLLEGE FOR WOMEN

never unfair. Those who thought he was did not know all the facts, which were not always made public. That is also true of other matters besides coeducation.

Sometimes a woman student would think herself ill used if she could not get a scholarship, when the fact was that at first few scholarships were available for women, because most of the bequests for that purpose had been made long before there were any women in the college. If a girl who did hold a scholarship fell below the minimum grade in her studies and lost the privilege, again there might be a feeling of grievance, though the policy was impartially applied. But quietly such persons were often helped by special gifts or loans provided by members of the Board of Trustees or other friends of the university. Probably it can be said that no woman student of high intellectual ability was ever obliged to leave college solely because of poverty.

When Rush Rhees, in the later and more prosperous years of his administration, was able to announce to women students or alumnae any new provision for their intellectual, physical, or social advantage, he always did so with genuine pleasure. He appreciated the fact that many of them had made sacrifices in order to get an education, that most of them came to college because of intellectual ambition, and met them on that high level of respect and confidence. Sometimes the level seemed to them so high that the atmosphere felt a little chilly from the altitude. That was because he never got over a certain shyness and formality before a feminine audience, rather incredible in a man of his age, but wholly disarming when one perceived it. Women who did, adored him.

He knew that college girls were young, and that at the right time and place gaiety is good for the young. With all his dignity he could relax, and wish them good luck and happy holidays. But this was not his forte. Unlike some popular presidents of women's colleges, beloved by their students like favorite uncles, he will not be remembered by alumnae as a genial or jovial chief. He was nobody's confidant or father

confessor, and did not care to be. Rather they will remember—
if they ever realized it—that it was his favorable letter or his
kind word that got them a job, his advice that saved them
from a blunder, his consolation that surprised them in sorrow,
his congratulations that crowned their first success. Such things
count as one looks back. Women who were in college when
he was learned not to be afraid of him. He always wished
them well. Now when they look at his rather too solemn portrait in Cutler Union, they may revere him for what he was
and is—their distant friend.

Even the younger generation of college women, who since
his time have enjoyed the luxuries of Cutler Union, the beauty
of the Memorial Art Gallery, the music of Eastman, may come
to know that these delights of life at Rochester were all due in
their origins to Rush Rhees. There were no amenities for the
first women students. In their crowded quarters in Anderson
Hall there was no room for grace, no time for beauty, no invitation to happiness, save what they brought with them. All this
has changed; he changed it. He resolved on September 8, 1900,
to do his duty by the women. He never ceased to work for
their interests, mostly behind the scenes. It was wholly because
of his influence that George Eastman and James G. Cutler and
Mr. and Mrs. Watson and other rich and generous men and
women, without his solicitation, have made Prince Street
worthy of its name.

If it should come to pass, as some predict, that the Prince
Street Campus will gradually become the last refuge of the
humanities, as contrasted with a preponderance of scientific
and vocational studies on the River Campus, then the future
daughters of the College for Women and of the Eastman
School of Music will have in their keeping a great tradition.
Women are less creators than preservers of the arts of life.
They guard beauty which they did not make. But they cannot
keep it for themselves alone; it belongs to the future.

IX

EDUCATOR

The aim of liberal education is the
emancipation of the mind of youth
from the shackles of ignorance; of
prejudice, which is something other
than ignorance; of superficial judgment; and of narrowness of outlook
in life.—Rush Rhees

TEACHING preachers was Rush Rhees's profession at
Newton. At Rochester he might have preached to teachers,
but never did. Instead he led them in a common search for
better teaching. An educator must be a good teacher to begin
with, but that is not enough. An educator, supervising the
work of other teachers in a school or college, can easily become
a dogmatist, either of the right or of the left wing. That is, he
can either lapse into repeating conservative platitudes learned
when he was young, or he can satisfy himself by perennial
protest against current opinion. Many an academic reputation
was won by the former method in days gone by. More recently
certain educational iconoclasts have flourished by reckless
overstatement. Good educators see both sides, and avoid the
attempt to advocate progress by exaggeration.

Rush Rhees was neither a complete defender nor an un-
friendly critic of the American college as it was fifty or sixty
years ago. He saw its merits and its defects, not only by recalling his own years at Amherst but by observing the limitations
of men trained in that system. Among its advantages were
mathematical training for all; acquaintance with some literary
masterpieces and some landmarks in the history of philosophy;

considerable practice in written and oral expression; the discipline of accurate and idiomatic translation; a general though rather superficial knowledge of the evolutionary theory of nature. Among its defects were lack of exact scientific experimentation; ignorance of recent history; inability to detect erroneous reasoning due to inadequate premises; and reluctance to correlate facts derived from many sources in facing a specific problem. In his judgment the test which men should meet in college, as they must after graduation, was not mere possession of knowledge but use of knowledge in new situations. He himself had to do that every day, but saw not only his students but some of their teachers unable or unwilling to attempt it.

He did not begin by trying to change the Rochester curriculum. Coming into a group of professors older than himself, more experienced and better known as teachers, he did not at once challenge them to self-criticism of either objectives or methods. Rather he undertook first to see his own task in the larger perspective of the community and of the state. His earliest educational contacts with schoolmasters and secondary schools were stimulating; his first relations with other college and university presidents were enlightening; and for a few years his impressions of the state educational controls were somewhat apprehensive.

These three contacts—with schools, with colleges, and with Albany—may be considered before turning to the development of his own program for Rochester. Through them he learned what was to be done, though not how to do it. In speaking to teachers on "New Ideals in Education" he said:

I desire to record my growing conviction that education is one; that, however for purposes of convenience we may separate it into primary and secondary and higher and professional, we mistake if we expect to find any clear differentiation in the problems which present themselves in the different stages for convenience set apart.

Enlarging upon this point, he expressed the opinion that many of the difficult educational problems are borderline problems—on the borders between elementary and secondary levels, between preparatory schools and colleges, between colleges and graduate or professional schools. Whereas critics in each of these groups have often blamed the inefficiency of the next lower group or the excessive demands of the next higher, he held that fixing blame for defects has little to do with correcting them. Rhees was not a blamer. Faults are complex, and responsibility for curing them must be shared. Only by mutual understanding and co-operation, based on common admission of imperfection, can progress be achieved.

On this basis of diagnosis before prescription, he usually attended the annual conventions of the Association of Colleges and Preparatory Schools of the Middle States and Maryland, addressed them when invited, and served on committees. He was president of that association for several years, and thus became acquainted with educators both secondary and collegiate throughout the district. Meetings of the officers and committees were often held in New York or Philadelphia, and afforded opportunities for other contacts. He was a great traveler, visiting high schools, addressing teachers' conventions, getting acquainted not only with persons who might send students to Rochester, but with many others from whom he could expect only friendly comparison of experience, sharing of problems, and mutual encouragement. Educators may welcome even a keen competitor, but talk more freely with those who have no designs upon them.

During those first few years much of his time and strength were spent on the road. In order to accept invitations to speak in small towns and villages, he rode on slow trains, waited on station platforms, ate at lunch counters, walked through rain and snow. He got up early and went to bed tired. He worked harder than any of his faculty to put the college before the people. It was pioneer work, with rewards slow and indirect.

But now and then a freckled boy in a country school, listening to one of his scholarly Commencement addresses in a village hall, crowded with proud mothers, crying babies, and whispering girls, would suddenly realize that on the platform was a first-rate man, a man who was working in Rochester to give boys like him a chance. That boy would come to Rochester with little money but a big ambition, struggle through freshman year, get a scholarship or a loan, and make his way. Sooner or later he might be a teacher himself, or perhaps a bank president; incidentally, a loyal alumnus. That is how a small college grows—by winning big boys. An educator in those days would get nowhere by sitting in his office, thinking great thoughts, and looking out the window. He had to be up and coming or soon he would be going. Rush Rhees knew books; he had to know people, and before long he did—knew them often better than they knew themselves.

From numerous addresses at educational meetings during the first decade it is possible to detect on what themes he was concentrating his attention. One was the tendency spreading among some colleges and schools toward wider latitude of elective studies. In one of his first speeches before the Middle States Association he attacked excessive "enrichment" of the secondary curriculum by introduction of social and economic studies at an adolescent level where more thorough grounding in fundamentals would be more profitable. Yet for every doubt concerning secondary studies he raised another as to the collegiate system, thereby avoiding any appearance of condescension. In a letter of 1910 he wrote:

I question the practicability of drawing any exact line of demarcation between college and secondary subjects. That impracticability is shown by the necessity of teaching elementary foreign languages in college, although instruction in these subjects may be had in all well equipped high schools. Many students prefer not to begin their modern languages in the high school, and if they are to take them at all must have them in the college; and an increasing number of students who have for one or another reason neglected Greek in the high school are welcoming the opportunity to begin it in college. I personally find the conviction growing that young people who expect to study sciences in college would do better to spend their energies in the secondary schools upon other subjects, so as to come to the college study of science with a fresh interest; but it would manifestly be impossible to persuade high schools to leave the teaching of physics and chemistry entirely to the college, nor would it be fair to the large number of students who never expect to enter college.

This last sentence illustrates his recognition of one fact about high-school teaching alleged to be ignored by some college presidents and professors—the fact that public high schools are not and cannot be primarily preparatory schools for colleges. Only a minority of their graduates will attend college, and even in a large school it is obviously improper to shape the whole curriculum for that minority. That public high schools must give "terminal education" to more than half their pupils is not, however, a reason for slighting fundamental training in subjects needed by all.

In numerous addresses to teachers Rush Rhees emphasized the vital importance of the secondary school in the formation of intellectual habits and moral character. Neither can be well begun in college. It is almost too late to attempt at eighteen what should have been done years before. If a freshman does not really know how to read, in the sense of grasping the meaning of a whole paragraph just read, because he reads only words, college cannot teach him. He ought not to be in college at all.

On the other hand, in cases of prolonged adolescence and intellectual immaturity, especially among the products of soft schooling, college should bring a great awakening. To this end President Rhees deplored all features of freshman and sophomore college teaching which seem to students a mere continuation of high-school methods. This criticism included undue dependence on textbooks, tests chiefly or wholly of memory, routine methods of grading papers with no allowance for individuality, undue emphasis on form at the expense of substance, shallow generalizations and overstatements in lectures, and especially lack of proportion in distinguishing fundamentals from trivial details. He used to tell a story of a faculty member in another college who disapproved of routine grading:

He became troubled by the habit which seemed ingrained in his colleagues to require stereotyped answers to quiz questions, conforming to the way in which matters had been presented in the lectures. He managed to get hold of a set of the questions for the next test, answered them himself in ways that he knew to be correct but quite unconventional, signed an assumed name to the paper and turned it in. It was rated "failed." Then he had a merry time with his colleagues proving to them that the answers were correct, and that their reading of the paper had been so perfunctory that they had not recognized the truth in unfamiliar phrasing.

All such grading he regarded as foreign to real education. There is a good deal of it still, which does little to increase the intellectual maturity of freshmen or of their instructors, equally unable to "recognize the truth in unfamiliar phrasing." A "true-false" test in which neither alternative answer to some questions is wholly true, or a "multiple-choice" test in which two out of five answers are equally correct, does not raise the respect of a student for his teachers. Truth is not simple to learn, to teach, or to grade.

According to Rush Rhees, no student should be allowed to be satisfied until he can say exactly what he means. Careless hit-or-miss recitations annoyed him. He said once to teachers:

I had a rare and merciless teacher once who would listen to a student's floundering efforts to put a Greek clause into English, and when he had struggled long enough to have discovered his own ignorance the teacher was wont to remark with a twinkle in his eye: "You have the tail-feathers of that idea, but the bird got away from you." We do not know what we think until we try to tell it. We only discover some of our own absurdities when we state them in order to defend them.

Between high-school and college teaching there is often supposed to be the difference that the high school teaches boys and the college teaches subjects. This distinction he denied. In an address before the Middle States Association in 1903 he said:

The college teacher does not deserve his chair if he is supremely absorbed in his subject. His business is to open the doors of a larger life to the students before him, to introduce them to the broad field of knowledge, and thus to introduce them to themselves. Now the teacher that has this interest in his students will teach unconsciously and inevitably with a different spirit in a different way from the man whose supreme interest is in the investigation of some corner of the field of

EDUCATOR 121

knowledge to which he is devoted. The teacher in the college ought to
be investigating some such corner of the field of knowledge; but his
supreme interest should be fixed on awakening in the group of students
whom he meets day by day some consciousness of what knowledge truly
is, and of their own power to enter into the heritage of knowledge in
order that they may be better adapted not to pursue the same investigation that the teacher may be following, but to pursue whatever line
of activity their own lives finally may open out before them.

Enthusiasm for the subject and enthusiasm for the class are
not always found in the same man, as he well knew, the rare
combination of a first-rate scholar and a first-rate teacher being
none too common in any faculty. But what he objected to in
college teaching was the graduate-school attitude applied to
freshmen or sophomores, with wholly negative results. He tried
to avoid both extremes—the drillmaster, accustomed to controlling adolescents in a high school by exerting authority and,
on the other hand, the new Ph.D. fresh from graduate school
who cannot forget his specialized interests and technical vocabulary long enough to remember how little freshmen know.

In his relations with the heads of other institutions he had
the advantage of not claiming too much or too little for his
own. Now and then in the earlier years someone would ask
him why he called his college a university. His reply always
informed them that the name was merely a historic relic of the
founders' ambitions, that trustees and faculty were well aware
that it had at that time none of the qualities of a university,
but preferred not to change the traditional title. To one such
inquiry in 1915 he replied:

The University of Rochester is strictly a college of liberal arts, and
for fifteen years that definition has been carried on the title page of our
catalogue as an indication of our understanding of our own category.
Our understanding of our own correct classification as a college is also
set forth in the preliminary statement concerning the organization of
the institution. It has seemed better to the Trustees to make their
position clear in this way rather than to disturb the memory and traditions of older graduates by undertaking to change the name of
the institution. At the time Rochester was founded the term probably
implied in the minds of most thinkers in America a group of schools
of higher learning, and the notion may have prevailed that an affiliation
between a college and a school of law or medicine or theology would

by that process of addition make a university, without respect to the graduate character of the professional schools. That conception prevails in the minds of not a few today. It is not, however, accepted by careful students of education.

Such frankness concerning the strictly limited aim of his institution—to make a good college and nothing more, until means for legitimate growth should appear—commended Rush Rhees to the friendly attention of his university colleagues. Almost from the beginning his annual contacts with other presidents in the Middle States Association and the Association of Colleges of the State of New York led to correspondence on matters of common interest. More especially, presidents within the state were drawn together by joint protests against some rulings of the State Department of Education, by some of the entrance requirements favored in certain colleges outside the state, and by attempts of the state legislature to tax educational endowments. Presidents of large and small colleges, differing in many ways on internal policies, agreed in opposing measures harmful to all.

When, as occasionally happened, the Rochester president was urged to take sides secretly against some other institution, on such questions as financial aid to athletes or state appropriations, he never swallowed the bait. He could satisfy an academic correspondent with a few complex and polysyllabic sentences that did not mean much except that he would not play that game. He could say much in few words or little in many, according to circumstances. No one succeeded in pinning him down with the command "Answer yes or no." But he himself could write such posers as the following, sent to a colleague after an inconclusive presidential debate:

Why may not the same institution carry on both "education" and "training" if it is awake to the significance of what it is doing? Don't answer; wait till you can tell me.

His pleasant contacts with secondary-school people and with college presidents prepared him for much more delicate relations with officials at Albany. In 1904, when a bill was pending in the legislature for reorganization and unification of the state's control of education, he protested against some features of that bill. There was at that time a Department of Public Instruction in charge of public schools throughout the state, exercising great power over appropriations and regulations, not without political complications; and there was the Board of Regents, also controlling education by means of its examinations, certificates, and rules for college and professional degrees. It was in order to unite these overlapping and partly competing bodies that the new act was drafted. But owing to political pressure the election of the first commissioner of education under the new order for a term of six years was left to the legislature instead of to the Board of Regents. With this and other defects, the new Education Law at least put an end to divided powers. In the new Education Building at Albany, erected in 1909, bureaus multiplied in number and prerogatives. Their powers reached out to every city and hamlet, to every college and university and professional school in the state. No college could do business without learning how to get along with Albany.

All the varied activities of supervision and control are under one head, the commissioner of education, who is also president of the University of the State of New York, together with several assistant commissioners. This control is subject to the constant vigilance of the twelve members of the Board of Regents, elected by the legislature for twelve-year terms, one member retiring each year. When the commissioner is a wise and experienced officer, acquainted with the problems of higher as well as of secondary and primary education, and disposed to use his great powers discreetly, all goes well. With some of the assistant commissioners President Rhees had arguments from time to time over their interpretation of rules, but on the whole maintained amicable relations with the department.

He regularly attended the October Convocations at Albany, and addressed them on many occasions. As a member of various committees of the Department of Education he had much to do with the state regulation of secondary education and with the

Regents' examinations. Although the University of Rochester was for many years a member of the College Entrance Examination Board, and President Rhees served also on its committees, few Rochester freshmen entered on the basis of those interstate examinations, but came generally on the basis of their school records. The President's active share in the improvement of secondary education through both agencies was not confined to the direct interests of his own institution. He saw this and all problems broadly.

Less autonomy is left to a New York college than might be supposed. Rochester has sometimes been called to account by Albany for alleged infringement of state regulations. These generally centered about quantitative standards set up by the state for the length of a college year. No college could grant a bachelor's degree except for a minimum of so many hours of credit "or their equivalent." The length of the college course was therefore rigidly fixed. Every attempt of the Rochester faculty and administration over a long period of years to render more flexible these "adding-machine" requirements, as Rush Rhees used to call them, caused complaints from Albany. The State Department of Education went so far in a few cases as to question for admission to professional schools certain Rochester degrees of honor graduates whose standing was so high that their grades were mostly A's, reducing under the "credit-point" system the number of months spent in residence. By reasonable interpretation of the phrase "or their equivalent" such cases would not have been questioned. Penalizing the best students by forbidding them to graduate until they had sat so many hours in so many rooms was the sort of thing that brought Rush Rhees near the brink of indignation. He scorned exaltation of means above ends, and of rules above the purpose for which rules are made. Some of these matters of friction have since been adjusted. Perhaps in their adjustment the stout independence of Rush Rhees may have helped.

For governmental control of higher education in so far as it had to do with raising quality he had great respect; for red tape and rigidity, great impatience. Having seen what state regulation could do in this latter direction, he was unalterably opposed to federal subsidies and dictation from Washington. Time after time when bills came up in Congress for a federal Department of Education with greatly increased powers he protested with all the force at his command. In his opinion

Federal authorities by virtue of the power to distribute subsidies acquire a virtual control over the educational activities of states and local communities, out of all proportion to the share which the Federal Government takes in the cost of these activities, apart entirely from the consideration of the wisdom of such virtual control. I believe that Federal control of education is in itself unwise. The highly centralized educational systems of France and Germany have not appealed to me. They take away from local communities the sense of responsibility, and responsibility for public work cannot well afford to be lessened, but needs rather in my judgment to be greatly increased.

The earlier part of Rush Rhees's career as an educator has been presented from the point of view of his growing contacts with outside agencies that affected his task—with schools and schoolmen, with heads of other colleges, with state officers and bureaus. But after all, an educational policy is not chiefly a contest against restraining forces or an adaptation of what is being done elsewhere. It must develop from the inside out. It must arise from study of goals to be sought, obstacles to be overcome, and methods most likely to yield definite results.

Educational reform must be gradual. Wholesale overturning of a college curriculum and of the principles on which it rests yields only confusion. There have been recent examples of this confusion in several colleges and universities. Rush Rhees never made that mistake. He was deliberate. Some thought he did not move fast enough, that several successive revisions of the curriculum might have been combined. Some may have thought Rochester was merely experimenting. Nevertheless, the major steps in the educational transformation wrought during his administration show orderly progress. Among these major steps were:

(1) The group system, regulating the student's choice, under

advice, of courses for his three later years. There must be distribution, ensuring a minimum of study in each of four fields—literature and other arts, social sciences, biological sciences, and physical sciences. There must also be concentration during junior and senior years in one or two fields.

(2) The credit-point system, designed to reduce mediocre work, putting a premium on high grades and a penalty on those which are barely passable.

(3) The comprehensive examination required for graduation, covering all of the student's work in the field of concentration, requiring correlation of knowledge, and emphasizing ability to use knowledge in dealing with new situations involving judgment and initiative.

There were other innovations, including elaborate investigations of examinations and grades, to lessen divergence of judgment among teachers upon a student's performance, and increased attention to personal counseling of undergraduates. All these steps were taken by vote of the faculty after prolonged investigation and discussion by special committees. They were agreed upon in principle, though not always in details, by practically the entire faculty. It might have seemed to an observer that the initiative came wholly from the teachers rather than from the administration. Yet those most fully acquainted with the origins of these changes were aware that the President had been thinking about them and conferring with the more progressive members of the faculty long before committees were appointed. These committees were provided with information which he had collected, but were expected to look at all sides and draw their own conclusions.

There was never any disposition on his part to submit a program and ask to have it recommended to the faculty as if it had come from their own ranks. Nevertheless, in the long run, the changes that were finally brought about represented a policy which he had desired almost from the beginning. He got what he wanted by leading others to want it too. He educated his faculty without letting them know it. Even the

best of them did not fully realize till afterward that the transformation of the college was largely his achievement. They
thought they had done it themselves—which is the best leadership.

He had broad conceptions and ideals of what four years spent
in self-discipline might do for the young men and women who
really want it. But he had no illusions as to the gap between
ideals and reality. To meet the practical conditions of a small
college, attempting with limited means to open wide vistas for
all, he sought patiently for ways and means of improving the
machine. He always knew that it was a machine, with all its
paraphernalia of courses and hours and grades and tests, its
daily assignments and penalties for irregularity. He knew that
college could do nothing for a dunce and little for a genius.
But by keeping the ultimate aims always in view, by insisting
on quality rather than quantity, by leading good men to do
better and better men to do their best, it could raise the general
level.

Fewer courses better taught were his program. He resisted
the tendency of departments to multiply new electives in their
desire for completeness. "We lack the courage to acknowledge
that fewer courses with freer opportunity to develop initiative
and intelligent thought would result in an increase of intellectual power, far more valuable than the scattered courses
sacrificed for such leisurely study could possibly afford." That
phrase "increase of intellectual power," is the clue to his whole
program of college education. What should be studied was of
less consequence than how it was studied; yet there must be
reasonable balance and distribution of effort in order to avoid
narrowness. In 1910 he wrote:

If it is true that college students are losing respect for scholarship,
if the training of the college is no longer begetting a love for letters
and a delight in the intellectual life as such, the situation for higher
learning in this country is serious. We do well to emphasize the social
value of college fellowship, and we do well to ask that college training
have as close a bearing as may be upon the work which will engage
the graduate's attention in after life; but it still remains true that the

proper product of a college is scholars—scholars enriched by the broadening influence of college fellowship, scholars made efficient for after life by the adaptation of their training to maturer tasks, but first and finally men of exultant joy in the intellectual life, and of as full familiarity as may be with the attainment of the human mind throughout the ages.

By saying that "the proper product of a college is scholars" he threw down a challenge to those who maintain that "joy in the intellectual life" is for the few. He held that cultivation of the intellectual life was the main task of the college. If it failed in that, its use of the four best years of youth could not be justified. Separate bits of knowledge collected during those years, though they might be turned to some useful purpose later on, would not be worth the time and effort, unless thought itself had become habitual, obligatory, concentrated, and sound.

As an example of the way in which he defended the so-called cultural studies against the charge of uselessness may be cited his approach to the teaching of foreign languages. In the case of Greek and Latin, the right kind of classical study should make it possible for men of today to understand the past. By mastery of a modern language sufficient to gain more than a superficial knowledge of a modern literature, a student is in some degree prepared to comprehend the differences that separate nations and the underlying sympathies that can reunite them. In an ingenious and unusual plea for translation as a valuable intellectual discipline he wrote:

There is one aspect in which the study of Latin or Greek or both has peculiar advantages for the development of exact intellectual habit. The study of language is the study of the medium of communicating thought. A sentence or a paragraph presents to the student a compact problem for the mind to deal with; the problem is by means of translation of words and understanding of syntax to reproduce in his own mind and speech the thought of an author strange to him. The fact that the problem is confined to the sentence or the paragraph gives that limitation to the task which makes it manageable for the mind of the growing boy or girl, and therefore a means for training in exactness of analysis, clearness of thought, and accuracy of statement. In these particulars an ancient language is superior to any modern language, for the reason that the syntax is more exact in its relations, and that the thought by its very strangeness presents a more definite problem to the student's mind, one at the solution of which he can less easily jump by guesswork. . . .

The supreme problems of our modern life are the problems of human relations. Nine-tenths of the various controversies and misunderstandings that arise between individuals or groups of men result from failure on the part of men to understand each what the other means by what he says. The study of any foreign language is of very great value in the development of that power of mind whereby unfamiliar words and constructions are understood to be a means of the communication of thought. In this particular the very removal of Greek and Latin from our modern life, and the distance between us and the intellectual interests of the Greeks and Romans, give to the study of classical literature a value for the development of quick human understanding which is superior.

In another context, speaking of translation from modern languages, he extended this line of reasoning to include all human intercourse by means of language, even in the mother tongue:

It is a mistake to think that translation is necessary only for the understanding of writings in a foreign tongue. All language has to be translated if it is understood. When I talk to my neighbor, I do not hear his thought, but only words more or less familiar in relations more or less exact. Unless I am intent on knowing what he is actually thinking, the words may mean to me something different from what he has in his mind. It is only when my imagination, intent on recovering in my mind the thought which was in his, takes his words, and, connecting them with all that I know about him, creates out of them a thought, that I have understood him. Moreover, I have no ground for confidence that I have understood him until I can choose for myself other words to express my understanding of his meaning. Then the translation is complete; words have been transmitted into thought, and then back again into other words.

This is about the most important thing men ever do in their relations with each other, whether as salesmen, as teachers, as lawyers, as politicians, or as engineers. Very few college men use Greek or Latin, or for that matter French or German, in the occupations of their later life. Every man, college bred or otherwise, is forced every day to translate for himself the words and actions of other men, and on his success in such translation most vital issues oftentimes depend.

He was really talking about what it is now the fashion to call semantics, as if it were a new discovery. It is really a process known to all trained minds since the days of Plato—known, but not much used. Upon the meanings attached to the words "liberty," "democracy," and "sovereignty" may depend the peace of the world. The bearing on liberal education of a kind of language study that encourages the discovery of ambiguities in terms and fallacies in definitions becomes clearer by such an analysis. Literature, philosophy, and even history become in part a transmission not of words but of meanings from minds now vanished out of the world into minds still capable of altering the world. Education is largely understanding what the dead meant when they wrote and what the living mean when they talk. Neither is self-evident, for language is not transparent. Even the verb "to be" conceals a mystery. The meaning of the adverb "now" can be reduced to an instant, brief beyond imagination. "Now" is gone before we finish saying it; the present is past. Thus words delude us into pretending to conceive the inconceivable. If we thought more we might talk less. If we thought enough, sometimes we need not talk at all.

He was never too much concerned with demonstrating the direct utility of liberal studies. They demonstrate their own value in the lives of those who have arduously pursued them. The following words from one of his later academic addresses best sum up his ideal of what a college education may do for a young man if he is capable of seeing, while still at a center of learning, what it may mean to him when he is far away:

Sanity of judgment and versatility of adjustment to new circumstances grow out of intellectual life lived with the broad horizon of a varied knowledge of truth. As the man looks abroad over his intellectual world he has a sense of being everywhere more or less at home, of being ready for work in any part of it.

So high an ideal of college education called for teachers of breadth and depth of culture as well as of special competence in a particular field. They are not numerous. President Rhees regretted the increasing tendency to turn freshmen over to the least experienced instructors. Yet, on the other hand, he recognized the importance of research for professors, and time for research implies a minimum of elementary teaching. To permanent members of his faculty who showed special aptitude for research many opportunities were given in the way of leaves of absence and reduced schedules. Every teacher, in his judgment, should be constantly enlarging the range of his own knowledge, but not all could contribute to learning. Writing textbooks and book reviews he did not regard as research. How to keep teachers of undergraduates from settling down to a mere routine, without giving them time for something more, was a puzzle he never solved.

Mere possession of a Ph.D. degree was not for him a proof of a growing mind. He had doubts about the conventional view that no one can be a full professor without it. To another college president, who inquired about the Rochester practice in this respect, he wrote:

I have never been a fetish worshiper in the matter of graduate degrees, although very much concerned in the matter of graduate study. I would like to quote the answer which Professor Kittredge of Harvard gave to a youth who asked him whether he was a Doctor of Philosophy. He replied, "No, but I make them."

Some years ago there was a good deal of agitation in teachers' colleges and centers of pedagogy on the subject of requiring college instructors to have graduate courses in teaching methods, as all high-school teachers must. To an inquirer on this subject he wrote:

No amount or kind of preparation will make a good teacher. It can only furnish the necessary basis of information and discipline for a good teacher. The indispensable qualification of a teacher of English is that he shall have some power of awakening in his students a love of reading for the joy of it. In so far as the work prescribed by the graduate school for the doctor's degree in English directs the candidate's attention to some little known corner of the field of English literature, and occupies his energies with questions of form and method and idiosyncrasy, those requirements may beget in a man of shallow insight a desire to impose upon undergraduate students similar recondite undertakings; but if a university graduate yields to this temptation, he simply by that fact demonstrates his lack of the fundamental qualification for a college teacher, which is ability to judge sanely concerning the task which he personally has to perform, and controlling interest in developing in his students that kind of intellectual growth which is suitable and desirable for them.

His final judgment on the relation of research to college teaching, as distinguished from university teaching, is perhaps that found in his annual report for 1933-1934, in the course of which he said:

I heartily concur in the unanimous opinion of the committee which prepared the report on the ten-year plan "that the undergraduate work of the college is our major concern." It is in the interests of that major concern that any undertaking we may make in graduate teaching should be considered. We are well aware that much that goes by the name of research has little if any significance. And an institution which measures a teacher's success by the number and size of his "research" projects misses the most vital element in any success which is of any importance for the service which a college may render to its students. The great teacher is the largest asset of any college. A great teacher must be one who is constantly deepening the wells of his knowledge, and there is no way of so enriching and refreshing a teacher's power comparable with the serious study of a problem or set of problems which challenge him to put forth his full intellectual power. Of course, if such problems divert his interest from the guidance of his students—especially his beginning students—he ceases to be a good teacher, however marked may be his success as an investigator. The investigator who cannot teach may have an important place in a large university or a research institute, but he is a heavy load for a college of the arts and sciences to carry. However, an instructor who does not constantly enlarge his own range of knowledge of his subject is in danger of losing his power to stimulate his students to intellectual eagerness and curiosity. It should be clearly acknowledged that such necessary enlargement of the teacher's own range of knowledge may be secured and maintained by forms of study that do not issue in publication. We have all known such teachers. But they were students all the time. The burden resting on the shoulders of the teacher who is not a "productive scholar" is to satisfy his own conscience that he is a student all the time, and not a drill-master of boys.

Graduate instruction, leading to the master's degree only, was carried on for many years at Rochester in small classes or by individual instruction, to meet special needs of teachers and others who could not go away to a graduate school. Not until great increase in endowment accompanied the expansion movement of the twenties, with a sudden rapid increase in graduate work in science, was work for the doctorate undertaken; and then only in such departments as were able to provide the laboratory and library equipment necessary for advanced research. His principle was to undertake nothing that could not be well done. The college refused to grant masters' degrees for work done even partly in absence from the campus, steadily raised the quality of work required for graduate degrees, and merely met reasonable demands of the local community, as it was bound to do. Later enlargement of graduate instruction, especially in the field of the sciences, does not belong to this biography.

In University Extension, also, his policy was never to spread out too thin. Evening classes for teachers and other employed adults were conducted for many years. This branch of the university has recently expanded into the University School of Liberal and Applied Studies, with larger facilities for meeting any legitimate demand for adult education not already available elsewhere. In general, it was President Rhees's policy to respond so far as possible to all needs of the community for higher education, in so far as they did not involve additional costs beyond those covered by tuition fees, and did not unduly divert the attention of the faculty from its major duty toward candidates for degrees.

That no door should be shut to ambition with merit, no door open to the aimless or the idle, was his principle in admission and retention of students. At one time when it became necessary to limit the size of entering classes, he spent much time in considering with deans and faculty committees the basis on which selection should be made. School records were not always sufficient; brief personal interviews were sometimes misleading. Before the Association of American Colleges in 1923, speaking of limitation of numbers, he said:

How are we going to make the selection? The most obvious suggestion is to select those whose entrance credentials by examination or school record are high; but then we are troubled by memory. We think of this one and that one and another one who entered college with very unpromising preparation, and after a little time demonstrated the possession of power that gave ultimately very distinctly superior attainment and the accomplishment of a genuine leadership.

Psychological tests and intelligence tests of all sorts, highly valued by pedagogical experts, he viewed with mixed feelings, knowing that they show some things about candidates with unerring certainty and conceal some other things with equal frequency. In another address he said:

When we come to the consideration of these psychological tests, there are some of us, either because of innate perversity or obtuseness of mind, that are not entirely convinced. I have in mind a man who entered our freshman class this year. We applied the Thorndike tests to our freshmen. This man was rated by those tests almost exactly at the middle of the class. At the end of the first half-term this youngster was one of the first two in accomplishment. Now what is the matter? There were fifty or sixty men superior to him according to the psychological rating. When we took the trouble to investigate, we found out one or two things. In the first place, the young man was abnormally industrious; and in the second place, he was abnormally ambitious; but that quality of industry and that quality of ambition were not detected by the psychological tests.

Since he was always on the lookout for intellectual superiority, it might be supposed that he had little use for the "common run" of undergraduates. These are the C men, who just "make the grade," but are often leaders in athletics, fraternities, journalism, and the like. Any college president—and almost any professor—has to talk that way sometimes just to keep up his courage. But they all know that some of the most loyal alumni and best citizens ever turned out by Rochester or any other college never got an A. Many of these boys do the best they can, which is not very well, because they are so busy doing a dozen other things. Some do not really do their best even as seniors, because, as Woodrow Wilson once said of sophomores, "the sap of manhood is rising, but it has not yet reached their heads."

Yet by some mysterious Providence, before they leave college some such men have not only raised its morale and cheered its

low spirits, but have absorbed at least a suspicion of what it
is all about. They become bachelors of arts because they have
not yet married the arts—but in time they may. Those were the
boys Rush Rhees liked, though he did not always show it. He
asked their opinions and sometimes followed their advice. Years
afterward they came to like him, when they had ceased to be
afraid of him.

No college can do without those average men. No campus
would be quite the same. Some of them have gone out to die in
the wars, some to live just as bravely through what is called
peace. Not to have tried to educate them would have been
ungenerous. Not to have entirely succeeded would have been
a regrettable though not unexpected misfortune. He was
"Prexy" to them all, preached them into college and out again,
remembered their faces and even some of their names. Perhaps
he carried with him out of the world some of the unspoken
respect and affection with which they watched him grow old
and mellow and ready for the great change. During his thirty-
five years there were more than seven thousand men and
women on whom he conferred at Commencement not only
degrees but "all the rights and privileges" that go with them.
Some of those graduates may claim even now the right and
privilege of remembering him as a great chief of their vanished
youth.

X

ADMINISTRATOR

On fait presque toujours les grandes choses
sans savoir comment on les fait.—Fontenelle

Order consists mainly in digressions on each
point which may illustrate the main end, and
keep it ever in view.—Pascal

Before making a promise think of what you are
doing, of what you say you will do; and in
the next place, do it.—Theodore Roosevelt,
at the Rochester Semicentennial, 1900

RESPONSIBILITY was the key to Rush Rhees's success.
He never let things slide; he never let Rochester down.
Day or night, winter or summer, at home or abroad, the university was always on his mind. He could not forget it, even
if he had wanted to do so. In July, 1899, he had married a wife
and a new job, for better or worse, for richer or poorer, in sickness or in health, and kept both promises. Having agreed to raise
a small college out of a rut, he kept at it until he was old and
tired. He never let go or shifted to something easier, as he
could have done before the tide turned in his favor. By his own
high standards he made it respected among educators when it
was still small, and kept it respected for more than money when
fortune at last surprised it.

To whom was he responsible? To the trustees who elected
him, of course; to supporters who gave money for education;
to the alumni, the community, the state; in some degree to the
faculty, because they were responsible to him and responsibility
is mutual; but most of all, responsible to the students, present

136

and future. They were the ones who all their lives would gain or lose by the kind of education received under his direction. Four of their best years were partly his to make or mar—in so far as anybody can make or mar a man except himself. They little knew, when they came to him with petty claims or protests about this or that privilege or grievance, that he held himself accountable, not for little things which they would soon forget, but for great things which they would never know. A college president's responsibility includes quiet settlement of many grave matters never reported to the world. Only conspicuous successes and obvious failures are talked about. The best of many a man is off the record.

Obligation is not the same as necessity. A man or a corporation is obliged to pay debts or become insolvent. But each has other obligations not legal but moral, arising not from honesty but from honor. For a gentleman and a scholar these are no less binding—even more, because never written down. Rush Rhees had a code which forbade him ever to take unfair advantage of his position for private or even for institutional gain. When others falsely accused him of violating that code, he came as near anger as his religion allowed. It will not be amiss, after this lapse of time, to illustrate the point by recalling an unpleasant episode which showed his inflexible side.

Having been almost from his arrival in Rochester a trustee of the Reynolds Library, a privately endowed institution now merged with the Rochester Public Library, he was under obligation to consider the business affairs of that corporation with impartiality and detachment. He did. After 1911, when the mayor appointed him a member of the Public Library Board, it became also his public obligation to advance the interests of that new institution for the good of the city. He did. Then the Reynolds trustees, aware that their endowment, consisting chiefly of a business block in the downtown district, was insufficient to maintain permanently an adequate reference library, negotiated with the city for terms of a joint contract by which both would profit and the donor's intent would be carried out.

Here was a double relation, hazardous for any citizen except one universally respected. Rush Rhees knew that, and would gladly have withdrawn from one board or the other except for his sense of public duty. Prolonged negotiations finally reached an impasse. Nothing seemed less likely than that the city would accept the Reynolds terms, made rather excessive by a conservative element in the board. All this time Rush Rhees was seeing both sides and trying to bring them together.

Then, when the whole thing seemed likely to fall through, it was proposed that the Reynolds Library should be merged with the University Library, of course with proper legal safeguards. This was contrary to the judgment of a committee of experts from New York who had studied the whole problem and recommended a merger with the Public Library. In this situation, which came to a head in December, 1930, the university was accused in the newspapers of attempting to capture the Reynolds books and endowment against the public interest. In this agitation certain women's clubs and ministers of the city, as well as irresponsible letter writers wishing to stir up trouble, unhappily joined.

The President's good faith was involved. The implication was that he had promoted the proposal for sending the Reynolds books to the River Campus. The whole unfortunate affair was amicably settled long ago; but Rush Rhees's reaction is what interests us here. He immediately wrote to the city manager:

The long continued and persistent misrepresentation of the attitude of the University toward the proposals for a combination of the Reynolds Library with the Public Library has now reached a point at which my self-respect makes it impossible for me to continue as a member of the Public Library Board. I have reached this conclusion with regret, because it has been a pleasure to render any service in my power to the city government.

To the press he sent the following statement:

The University of Rochester harbors no desire for or expectation of a union of the Reynolds Library with the library of the University. The new library building on the River Campus makes no provision for such a union. The University resents intensely the persistent implication to it of bad faith in some current discussions of the relations of the Reynolds Library and the Rochester Public Library.

Responsibility in that case for the university's good name and his own led him to a prompt but not impulsive decision which showed him to be as strong as he was sensitive. He would listen to no further argument on the subject; it was closed.

This was not the only time he took a bold stand against public criticism. In another case, during the earlier days of the Eastman Theatre in 1922, ministerial critics in the local Federation of Churches received a sharp reply to their official protest against Sunday evening concerts. After consulting the Board of Trustees, he wrote to the president of the federation:

When Mr. Eastman submitted to the University his proposal to make his great gift for musical education including provision for the large hall to be used for music and motion pictures, he stipulated and the University agreed "that the University will not object to such use of the same on Sundays as well as on weekdays, provided such use be legal and orderly."

In conversation with Mr. Eastman it developed that he had strong convictions that the policy he proposed was in the best interests of the public. His whole purpose in establishing the School of Music was to raise the standards of the community along the lines of music, believing that such raising of standards would work for the moral betterment of Rochester. . . .

We cannot agree with you in your fear that our action in accepting Mr. Eastman's gift, subject to the condition mentioned above, will contribute to an increasing "commercialization of the Sabbath," for the reason as stated above that the object for which a charge will be made for admission to the Eastman Theatre is not the making of money but the increasing of opportunity for wholesome and innocent recreation for multitudes of the people. . . .

It is true, as you say, that there have been many changes of belief as to the proper observance of Sunday, and the process of change is probably not yet completed. I firmly believe that Sabbatarian hostility to harmless recreation provided on Sunday for the public will do more to develop an irreligious indifference in our time than the offering of such harmless recreation under the conditions contemplated for the Eastman Theatre can possibly do. . . .

As Christian men deeply interested in community welfare we venture to hope that the sincere and earnest men who have launched with us this protest will wait and observe the actual workings of the policy to which we are committed, rather than inaugurate a controversy over a policy to which in all good faith we are committed.

The letter was stronger than that before he toned it down. The ministers subsided. The President was not too pious to resent misguided zeal. You could do much with him by persuasion but you could not force him. His responsibility was vertebral as well as cerebral—backbone and brains. He sent a copy of the federation's protest to George Eastman with a copy of his answer. Mr. Eastman replied:

If the University had not been willing to accept that condition, I would not have transferred the title of the Theatre to it; so the University has not in any way contributed to or caused the use of the Theatre on Sunday nights. By agreeing not to object to such use it insured the advantage of an unbroken connection and co-operation with the Music School.

Responsibility led him to take the leadership in the earlier money-raising enterprises of the university, not because he liked it, but because he would not ask others to do what he was unwilling to do. If all the begging letters he wrote before 1920 could be brought together for the consolation or encouragement of other reluctant scholars in presidential chairs, they would add point to the following warning, addressed by him to a fellow clergyman considering an academic office:

You should not blink the fact that the responsibility for raising money for the college will rest on your shoulders. Some presidents try to pass that responsibility to their board of trustees. That simply will not work. People who give the college money wish to have contact with the man who is going to use that money.

Bearing of this on Mr. Eastman's often quoted remark that "Dr. Rhees never asked me for a dollar" and of the details of that great benefactor's personal dealings with the President, must be postponed to a later chapter devoted entirely to them. But, with the notable exceptions of Mr. Eastman's gifts after 1904, and of the ten-million-dollar campaign of 1924 headed by George W. Todd and his associates, most of the other large additions to the university's funds were solicited. The trustees did much of the work, but the President supervised it, and undertook to see that it should succeed.

That word "undertake" was his word for administrative

responsibility. In commenting on an academic announcement submitted to him before publication, he wrote:

I have only one suggestion to make, and that is that in the second line of your second paragraph you substitute the word "undertaken" for "endeavored." I may be supersensitive, but the word "endeavored" rather suggests skepticism as to our success. If we have such skepticism, the course for us to pursue is to modify our program in order to insure success.

In his historic letter of July 4, 1899, to Rufus A. Sibley, chairman of the committee that chose him president, he said: "If I accept the presidency of Rochester, I shall not try to shirk any duty belonging to that office." He did not say, "I shall try not to shirk." Either he would or he would not: there was no guesswork about it. If he "undertook" anything, he did it. The rare exceptions were due to causes beyond his control. He was not good at making excuses for himself, and seldom had to do so. His excuses were for other people, and they were generous. Toward himself he was severe. His sense of duty and propriety led him, for example, to attend all public functions of the college, including social events and student dinners and entertainments, even when most men would have preferred to spend the evening at home.

His responsibility for the good name of the university made it hard for him to condone the irresponsibilities of youth. When students off the campus in the course of a celebration or a class contest smashed furniture or disturbed the neighbors, he did not scold them, but made them pay and apologize. "Boys will be boys" did not appeal to him as adequate compensation. Students will not become responsible for their own misbehavior so long as somebody else pays the bill or the bail.

Neither will students accept responsibility for the misbehavior of others. They resent outside policing but will not do their own. Rochester made many attempts to conduct honest examinations without proctors, depending on honest men to report dishonest ones. That never worked. A so-called "honor system" which received its only reports of violations not from students but from suspicious teachers became a farce. President Rhees reluctantly gave up this hopeless attempt at student self-government.

In general, as an administrator, whenever after thorough trial of a plan he became convinced that it was a failure, he dropped it. He was realistic enough for that. Daily chapel with compulsory attendance prevailed during his early years, subject to excused absences of students who had religious scruples against a Protestant service. He believed in the value of an assembly of all or most of the students, apart from any religious influence it might have. But gradually, as the growth of the college and other causes made a daily meeting impracticable, it was reduced in 1911 to twice a week, then to once a week, with a nonreligious assembly on the alternate day, and attendance was made voluntary. This was contrary to the President's personal conviction, but he accepted it. Faculty and students alike were opposed to compulsion. Near the close of his administration he wrote to a correspondent who asked for his final judgment on the subject:

My experience both as an undergraduate student in college and as an observer at Amherst, my Alma Mater, and in Rochester, convinces me that so far as religious influence is concerned, compulsion is a distinct detriment. There are many arguments in favor of compulsory chapel as a means of assembling the whole student body from time to time; but that is not an effective contribution to religious influence or religious atmosphere so far as student reaction is concerned. However, it would be a source of great satisfaction if some means could be found to bring a large student body together in a respectful and reverent attitude.

Another aspect of administrative responsibility is concerned with the proper use of specific trust funds. People who want to give a little money to an educational institution often prefer to do so by founding a new prize. They suppose that each new annual award for this or that intellectual competition is a great help to the college. Perhaps it used to be so, but is no longer. Every year it becomes harder to induce students to write special essays, make speeches, organize debates, for the sake of possibly winning a few dollars. They are frankly not interested, unless assured that the number of contestants will be so small that they have practically a sure thing. Funds left for such purposes in the past have to be administered, in so far as possible, according to the intent of the donor, unless by some legal procedure the college is allowed to divert the income to some more useful object. Only those awards made for excellence in regular work, without a registered competition, have much educational value.

Likewise in the case of scholarships, the natural desire of donors to perpetuate their names for a relatively small capital sum often leads to the multiplication of small individual grants. Any college administrator who could induce well-wishers to leave their bequests to general scholarship or loan funds, to be divided according to the discretion of a dean or committee, would be a public benefactor. But when a will is probated it is too late; the President's responsibility for administering one more restricted bequest must be maintained.

Several philanthropists and educational foundations have recently tried to interest rich people in making undesignated bequests. Whenever a fortune is tied up by narrow specifications, intended to safeguard its use in perpetuity, the chances are that within fifty years the gift will be obsolete. Unrestricted income may indeed be unwisely spent by incompetent trustees. But givers must trust the future. There will always be good trustees to use money for good ends. Some wise men have even permitted the use of capital as well as income after a suitable interval. Endowed institutions in the future cannot live wholly on the hoards of the past. Other means must and will be found; what, no one knows.

Some of these restricted gifts or bequests are lecture funds. Rush Rhees had frequent occasion to arrange lectures and other public functions chiefly because there was money that could be spent for nothing else. Lectures are supposed by many rich men to be eagerly welcomed by ambitious youths, bored by classroom routine. They are expected to fill cultural gaps in the undergraduate program, and to keep the campus in touch with the great world. Authors, statesmen, publicists, experts of all sorts, are invited to address a theoretically academic audience.

Doubtless a college owes something to the community in the way of providing free entertainment and information for a general audience. But as for students, with rare exceptions they never voluntarily attend public lectures. Most of them, even though living in dormitories within a hundred yards of the lecture hall, will not venture within its doors. They seem to be afraid of learning something outside union hours, without college credit. This indifference of undergraduates to extra-curricular education was as incomprehensible to Rush Rhees as to other intelligent people, but he went right on doing his duty. The lectures had to be held. Letters had to be written, announcements prepared, trains met, lecturers entertained, and the small attendance had to be explained to them either by bad weather or by conflicting dates. This is an old story. Probably nothing can be done about it, as long as the funds hold out. But sometimes it must be a strain on the few people who do all the work and make all the apologies.

One lecture series, founded by James G. Cutler in 1920, has been in some degree an exception to this rule. The Cutler lectures, always on some aspect of the Constitution and constitutional government, have generally been well attended by students of history and government, possibly not without some missionary work by the department. They have also attracted substantial citizens, lawyers, and other professional men, drawn by the eminence of the lecturers and the timeliness of the subjects. Mr. Cutler was a conservative, but in the terms of his endowment he specified that the lectures should deal not only with the principles of the Constitution but with "its historical development as illustrating the application of it to and under changing conditions."

President Rhees in 1925, writing to a Cutler lecturer, explaining the nature of the foundation, added the following significant comment, pertinent not only to the Constitution but to his own policy as an administrator:

I must confess to some disturbance of mind caused by some of the ardent advocates of the Constitution who in my opinion overlook the futility of commending it to the interest of the present generation solely on the basis of its past services. Whatever may be our judgment of the folly of the present generation, it is futile to ignore the fact that it is extremely restive under anything like the control of the dead hand; and I believe that unless we can convince this generation that the Constitution is a precious guard of interests recognized as vital, or which should be recognized as vital, for our present and future life, reverence for antiquity will be insufficient to secure either that respect for the Constitution which we feel to be essential, or the instinctive understanding of its function which will protect our people from its insidious destruction by amendments foreign to its purpose.

Administrative responsibility also obliged Rush Rhees to continue throughout his entire term of office the custom of granting honorary degrees, in which he did not wholly believe. The award of such degrees, as a spontaneous recognition of genuine scholarship or high public service, carefully guarded against cheapening by excess or by open or secret solicitation, he regarded as a legitimate academic function. But when a function becomes perfunctory perhaps it should be defunct. He soon became so disgusted by attempts of ministers to get D.D.'s for themselves or their friends that he secretly rebelled. In 1902 he wrote to a trustee: "In the present situation the whole honorary degree business seems to me a necessary evil." A little later:

Perhaps I may be permitted to confess that I wish this whole business of honorary degrees could be abolished and forgotten, but that I suppose at present is out of the question. I can only rely upon the loyal good sense of our alumni to recognize that active interest in their careers may be real and warm notwithstanding the fact that many forms of faithful, useful, and effective work fail to fall within the scope which academic usage defines for honorary degrees.

One more outburst will suffice to show how he felt:

It might be well if the whole business of honorary degrees were sunk to the bottom of the sea. I often envy an institution like Cornell, whose policy practically prohibits the award of such degrees. On the other hand, it is a source of gratification to be able now and then to recognize distinction. The difficulty with the honorary degree business is that in the minds of many people such degrees are regarded as a means of conferring distinction rather than recognizing it.

Responsibility for prizes and lectures and honorary degrees is of far less consequence than responsibility for the main business of the college, which is education. Rush Rhees's deep interest in liberal education and his policy in promoting it were the subject of the previous chapter. In that same field, the executive functions of appointment and promotion of teachers are vital to efficiency. Rush Rhees took seriously his duties toward faculty changes. His recommendations to the Board of Trustees were always approved, and in reality the decision in such matters was his, always in consultation with the department and with the deans. In the case of instructors on temporary appointments, the preliminary screening of candidates was done by the department, which selected the more promising men to be interviewed by the President. He always required a personal interview with candidates above the rank of instructor. The university paid traveling expenses. It cost a lot of money but saved more. A mistake a year long is worse than any round-trip fare. Sometimes one look was enough; sometimes too much.

Rush Rhees was not a particularly good judge of men. He made mistakes, perhaps not so many as those of his deans or professors, but not less embarrassing. He once wrote: "I know only too well how misleading some first impressions may be. I know also that some men carry most of their goods in their show-windows, and we do not need such men."

His method in interviewing candidates was first to put them at their ease, if possible, by informal conversation, and then to get them to talk about their specialty. This showed them at their best, if good, and at their worst, if not; but it did not show everything. When he was looking for a sociologist, for example —and he generally was—he would allow all the candidates one after another, at half-hour intervals, to expound their pet theories, largely without comment. Then he would ask them a few searching questions about other more or less remote branches of the subject. Whether he had just read up on them one could never tell, but on almost any topic in the social sciences or in literature he could raise questions that showed up ignorance or prejudice. His favorite inquiry, "Just what do you mean by so-and-so?" led to discussion of definitions and technical terms, frequently revealing nebulous thinking.

He never thought the less of a man for saying "I don't know," but one should not say it too often in the wrong places. Cross-examination, however, was not the main feature of his method. He wished to find out if the candidate was of an unstable temperament, likely to go to pieces under strain; or of unsound character, or definitely antireligious opinions. He set great store by something he called "reverence," not much known in graduate schools.

He did not care too much what church a man belonged to, if any, but a great deal whether he had or had not inner force of character, anything beyond self-seeking ambition. It was one of the major disappointments of his administration that he could never find enough even moderately religious teachers to go around.

Having chosen his teachers, always with the approval of the department—unless it was a department head he was choosing—the President gave them liberty unless they proved themselves unworthy of it. His principle was to get good men and let them alone. If they could not be let alone, they were not good. He did not visit classes, nor even insist that department heads should do so; but was of the opinion that young men in their first years of teaching should be more closely guided than they sometimes are.

Since the college had rules against indefinite tenure for instructors, the time always came when a decision had to be made—retention with a prospect of promotion, or notification that the appointment would not be renewed. This is the most difficult part of educational administration—not the first decision to give a promising man a trial, but the later decision whether he is good enough to stay, with a large factor of contingent liability. President Rhees found it just as hard as less experienced men to make up his mind. To one who confessed to him a tendency to postpone decisions he replied: "I have only to say that final decisions made before the mind has reached a definite judgment are more prolific of trouble and danger than anything I can think of. My own mind acts like this in connection with such matters."

Once his mind was made up, however, he did not vacillate. He would stick to a wrong decision until he was sure it was wrong, and by that time it might be too late to change. A marked reluctance to evade responsibility for his own mistakes, a preference for shouldering blame and taking the consequences, conflicted sometimes with his sense of larger responsibility to the institution. This was true not only of faculty changes but of administrative appointments. He would hope against all probability that there might be a turn for the better. When it failed to appear, there would be an equitable adjustment. In few cases where teachers or administrative officers were released was anything done or said that could be called injustice, unless there be such a thing as injustice by procrastination. He could not bear to hurt people's feelings or lessen their chances for a future career. That they nevertheless often felt hurt was depressing, but he bore it in silence like all other unchangeable facts. Responsibility ruled. You cannot make a good college just by keeping everybody happy.

To the faculty he was not only just but generous. As soon as the 1912 addition to the endowment was assured, salaries were raised. He made it a condition of his staying at Rochester, when offered another position, that the trustees should increase the pay of professors, and would take no more salary for himself until he was sure they would be well taken care of. Furthermore, when in later years the Carnegie Foundation radically reduced the scale of retirement allowances for older professors to a flat $1,000, President Rhees as a member of the Carnegie Board insisted on reconsideration of this unreasonable ruling, and in co-operation with others was influential in having the figure raised. He also arranged that older members of the faculty, who had looked forward to retirement at half salary, should receive a supplement from university funds to meet that expectation. In these and other ways he showed magnanimity. All that he quietly did for others without thanks is not yet known.

Responsibility toward students was not confined to providing for them a good curriculum and competent teaching. The President was conscientious about other implied obligations. When near the time of graduation it is discovered that a student lacks some necessary credits, whose fault is it? In one such case the question was answered thus:

An institution incurs a certain liability for students who register and pursue the course assigned to them in good faith. We need to fill up, so far as practicable, the gaps in their training before they come up as candidates for degrees, but we cannot pass on to their shoulders responsibility for our own failures in the organization of their work.

It was partly because there were so many loose screws in the old machinery for registering students and altering their programs, leading sometimes to the belated discovery of deficient hours for graduation, that an Administrative Committee was set up in 1912. Its function was to act on all cases of interpretation of rules, with authority to correct errors and make exceptions when justified, thus saving the time of the faculty. It worked so well that in later years other standing committees were appointed, such as one on Educational Policy, whose prolonged investigations were reported at suitable intervals and led to many improvements in the curriculum.

As presiding officer at faculty meetings Rush Rhees was fair, good-humored, and impartial. He never made a speech from the chair on one side of a debatable question, though he might correct errors of fact. Accustomed as he was to hearing keen and rapid-fire debates elsewhere, he must often have been bored by rambling talk at some faculty meetings. If the trouble was merely that speakers sometimes forgot the motion before the house, he would remind them. But when sharp dissensions arose, along about six o'clock he would bring forth with a bland smile his familiar remark about the Quaker meeting. "It was when the clerk of the meeting could not report the sense of the meeting that one aged Friend would rise and say, 'Brethren, it appears that we are not of a mind.' The matter will be referred to the committee for further consideration. The chair will entertain a motion to adjourn." Faculty meetings in those days were not really good comedy, for they lacked continuity and climax, but at least they had complication and surprise. Perhaps it rather amused than tired the chairman to see so much unnecessary commotion. It was so unlike his own way of doing big things quietly.

His responsibility to alumni for athletics, political opinions of faculty members, and kindred controversial matters was viewed by Rush Rhees with some reserve. He once replied as follows to an alumni secretary of another university, who inquired, "What should a university expect of its alumni?":

A university is naturally greatly interested in securing the active and intelligent co-operation of its alumni. Such co-operation to be of value must be the natural expression of interest by the alumni in the present work and ideals of the institution. It may advantageously take the form of suggestions for or criticisms of the university's academic program. A university cannot welcome a tendency on the part of its alumni to dictate its policies, but it misses a great asset if it does not use every legitimate means to convince its alumni of the wisdom and significance of its policies and aims. In the matter of contributions to its financial resources a university is justified in appealing to its alumni as presumably its most interested constituents. It is not justified in demanding such financial assistance as a matter of right.

In so far as President Rhees met any considerable criticism or opposition from alumni, it generally centered around athletics, chiefly football. Many of them thought the coaching policy wrong, grew bitter about defeats, and wanted a change. November was always a bad month. President Rhees, like most sane college presidents, saw the game of football in a perspective different from that of undergraduates or sporting alumni. He regretted to see the boys lose games; but he regretted much

more to hear grown men talk as if two hours on Saturday afternoon were much more important than all the rest of the college
week. Athletics for exercise and healthy competition was one
thing; athletics to draw big crowds and big money was another thing, having little or nothing to do with education, but
perhaps another "necessary evil."

When, however, alumni began to complain that athletes
did not have a fair chance in college, that their marks were too
low and their work too hard, that charge was more in his line.
Investigation generally showed that anything like discrimination against athletes was unknown, but that special favors toward them also were unknown, which was probably what the
alumni really meant. From time to time a few discontented
alumni and sports writers have tried to make copy out of athletic
dissensions on the Rochester campus. Except for the unfortunate effect on readers who did not know the facts, the President took little interest in these petty agitations. He was aware
that college enrollment and college reputation do not depend
on football victories. He did not have so many headaches over
athletics as some other people around the institution, who had
to take the hard knocks.

Responsibility was not the only element in Rush Rhees's
success as an administrator. It was the leading one, but among
others were information, co-operation, and courtesy. A good
administrator must have the facts, get people to work together,
and avoid offense. In these respects also Rush Rhees was careful, though he did not always succeed.

Whenever any change of policy was proposed, he usually
wrote to selected presidents or deans of other institutions a
personal letter asking a few specific questions. He did not write
long form letters, and rarely approved sending out elaborate
questionnaires. Disliking himself to answer long lists of detailed
questions from strangers, he never circularized the country in
order to get statistics for a sentence in a speech. But so careful
was he not to be the first or the last to adopt a new method that
he gathered, himself or through a committee, all pertinent

material necessary to a decision. Nothing seemed to him less useful than spinning ideas out of one's own head, with no material except from within. Much information on academic changes came to him as a member of committees of the State Department of Education and of the Middle States Association. From time to time a member of the faculty was released from teaching to visit other colleges and observe the working of new systems, with written reports which the President examined with care. He knew what was going on, especially in colleges of the same class as his own, and worked with others to raise standards.

Co-operation with men of varying shades of opinion was so natural to him that he could not readily tolerate willful lack of it in others. When now and then he received from some department head or subordinate a complaint of lack of team play, his reply was "Co-operation always involves two." Some people mean by co-operation the submission of a whole group to a dominant individual. He did not so understand it. In order to work together there must be some freedom for all, including young teachers, if they are to do their best. Sooner or later, by his standards, if two men cannot co-operate, one must go. Which one?

As for courtesy, he believed in using polite phrases even in difficult situations. He advised tact in denying requests.

It is worth while to notify such people in a manner which will not cause their friends to think that they have been treated without due consideration. There is much wisdom in the word of ancient wisdom, "A soft answer turneth away wrath."

He seemed always to remember that every human being has not only certain rights, but feelings of self-respect and self-esteem which should not be rudely shattered, because they are all some people have to live by. Most men have friends and relatives who idealize them; they may even idealize themselves. To tell anyone, student or teacher or intellectual worker of any sort, that he is a failure and has no future, or even to imply it by a word or a letter that slams the door in his face,

is not only unkind but dangerous. It will make an enemy, and
may cause a mental crisis. Yet false hopes may be read into a
considerate phrase. President Rhees generally took the pre-
caution to put everything in writing, including confirmation of
conversations, after experience had taught him to trust nothing
to his own or others' recollection. After one stormy interview
with a faculty member who produced a letter to support his
contention, the President reported ruefully: "He practically
called me a liar, and what is worse, he proved it." But he was
not often caught in that way. In his efforts to "save the face"
of people out of luck he may have raised expectations which
he never intended and could not fulfill. Courtesy can be misunderstood; consideration may be mistaken for reconsideration.
But when he said no, he meant no. His final decisions were
final; they had to be. Executive vacillation is fatal.

One remaining question in regard to his qualities as administrator is "How did he manage to get so much done?"
Not only was he often obliged to be absent from Rochester on
university business, but he found it necessary in his later years
for reasons of health to take winter vacations. Travel enriched
his experience, and made his work more valuable, but it did
take him away from Rochester during some critical periods.
Something unexpected was likely to happen when he was out
of reach. How did he keep things in hand?

There are two answers. In the first place, in addition to the
deans, he always had, after the earliest years, a confidential
assistant, some young man not long out of college, of quick
mind and good judgment, able to size up a situation and decide
how to handle it. When the President was in residence, his
assistant attended to a multitude of details, collected information, prepared announcements, met visitors, arranged interviews, secured transportation, helped to keep engagements
from conflicting, and performed other secretarial duties beyond
the scope of a stenographer. When the President was in Maine
or in Europe, his assistant became a sort of "trouble shooter,"
to whom people applied for information on small matters, and

who sent important news by mail or telegraph. What Rush
Rhees owed to these alert young men, all of whom after a few
years with him rose to executive positions of importance, it
would be difficult to exaggerate. He was the making of them,
and they kept him from working himself to death. They, his
physicians, and most of all his wife made it possible for him,
with rather poor physical resistance, to accomplish more than
most stronger men.

The other reason why he accomplished so much was that
there was an Executive Committee in the Board of Trustees,
composed of resident businessmen who met whenever occasion
required and could take prompt action. Whether some financial
problem arose, beyond the treasurer's jurisdiction to settle
alone, or whether some matter of building construction needed
decision, or whether a misleading newspaper story had to be
corrected, there was always someone on the spot with sense
enough and power enough to act.

Rush Rhees had a Board of Trustees so loyal, so generous,
so lavish of time and thought in the interest of the university
that without them he could not have been what he was or
have done what he did. He wrote of them in 1924, before the
height of material prosperity had been reached:

> After an experience of twenty-four years with some of these men, and
> with the rest of them during all of the time of their membership in the
> Board, I have never known a group more interested, more keen and
> wise in the conception of business, and more loyal to the affairs of the
> University than this Board of Trustees.

In conclusion it may be repeated, as was suggested earlier,
that few would have expected a man of theological and clerical
experience to develop into an administrator of large affairs.
The power must have been latent half of his life, while he was
apparently content to study and teach Greek grammar and
Pauline theology to small classes of Baptist preachers in a
New England village. Perhaps some light may be thrown on
this problem by a passage from a speech which he made in
1920 in honor of another university president:

We used to be familiar with the professor of philosophy as the chief executive of an academic institution. The custom has gone out of fashion. We can think of few of the eminent executives of the present time who have brought to their task that broad intellectual training. The philosophic mind is not to be confused with the speculative mind, and therefore the impractical mind. The philosophic mind is familiar with human speculation, but it cannot be philosophic unless it is equally familiar with the severest criticism of such speculation, and has become keen in its analysis and criticism of all the projects which man has put forth for solving the riddle of existence. That type of mind is peculiarly well adapted as an equipment for a man who is charged with the administration of a great and influential institution for the education of youth; particularly so because of the fact that such a mind may happily emancipate him from the tyranny of current fashion in educational thinking, and qualify him for calm and unprejudiced and critical judgment of the new projects that year by year are launched upon our long-suffering educational public.

What he described, he had. While the pendulum of educational theory swung left and right, he watched the center of its arc. Observing the stars, he estimated the probable error of the clock. In avoiding extremes he did not, like some apostles of the *via media*, avoid action altogether. But he preferred long views, and reckoned progress by decades.

Perhaps the most characteristic administrative act of his entire career was in 1932, when he had already submitted his resignation but was retaining his office by request until his successor could be found. The university had then come into a good deal of money, as well as a new campus and material equipment. It had also by that time a flourishing School of Music and a School of Medicine, of which more will be said later. Believing, as he always had, that a strong College of Arts and Science is the indispensable foundation of a true university, he requested the college faculty to co-operate in studying proposals for a ten-year plan for future development. He well knew that they could not bind the future, that he would not be the one to carry out such a plan if adopted, nor would he live to see it finished. That was why he wanted to see it begun, like an old man planting an oak. *Felix qui prospicit.* Fortunate is he who looks forward—forward beyond himself.

XI

EASTMAN

I am not interested in education.—George Eastman, 1898

The progress of the world depends almost
entirely upon education. Fortunately the
most permanent institutions of man are
educational. They usually endure even
when governments fall.—George Eastman, 1924

GEORGE EASTMAN had expressed indifference to educational giving before Rush Rhees came to Rochester.
Within five years something changed his mind. It kept on
changing—toward the University of Rochester—until the day
of his death. He began by refusing to give it anything. He
ended by leaving it nearly all he had.

The present chapter, concerned with the personal relations
of Rhees and Eastman and the intellectual effects on both, is
about men—not money. Figures can be found elsewhere. In
1930, suggesting to an employee several radical alterations in
a proposed university announcement for the press, the President wrote:

A less urgent objection is my strong feeling that boasting of one's
wealth is not usual among gentlemen. Acknowledge great gifts with all
gratitude; but why play Jack Horner and cry "What a great boy am I"?

In 1900 George Eastman was an upright, thrifty man and a
good citizen, but rather hard, rather narrow. His early ambitions were centered on money, power, and justice; money
as a means of power to bring about justice for himself and
others. There came a time when he had achieved all three,
but was not satisfied. Before he was sixty he had discovered

that besides money, power, and justice there were other values.
There was mercy, kindness, beauty. There was a chance for
the weak as well as for the strong. There was charity for those
who failed. There was health for the poor, pleasure for the
undeserving, happiness for the obscure. None of these goods
can be bought, but wealth can make them possible. Fortune
can alleviate misfortune. A man cannot give away happiness
which he does not possess, but he can help others find it.

Mr. Eastman had always taken good care of his own employees and loyal business associates. He seldom praised them,
but he paid them well, advanced them, and made their future
secure. The time came when he looked beyond his own circle.
His justice and charity had begun at home, in his own city.
He had given to Rochester hospitals and philanthropies from
the beginning of his success. But when he began to think of
distant distress, when during World War I, with men like
Herbert Hoover, he sought to feed hungry people whom he
had never seen; when after the war, with men like Julius
Rosenwald, he began to give largely for industrial education
of Negroes; when his imagination took in poor children, youthful musical talent, potential skill, undiscovered human material
for leadership and fellowship and social progress—then he
began to be the great man whom Rush Rhees admired. He
began to be the man he was meant to be. He ranks now with
Edison, for those two were bringers of light and shadow and
beautiful sound for all the people and all the future.

Edison and Eastman made the motion picture; one of the
blessings and the curses of mankind, recording with equal
vividness the wonders and the follies of the world. For both
of them life itself was a motion picture, full of change and
color. When all its frames had faded, music was left. That also
they have preserved. Music, whether sounding in the concert
hall or from phonograph records, will repeat till the end of time
men's mortal struggles and immortal peace. When we hear
Brahms or Beethoven, directly from strings and brass or at
home from tracings on black discs, we shall remember this

perennial miracle of beauty returning by the command of the dead for the delight of the living. It has "the form of eternity."

Did Rush Rhees see what was latent in George Eastman when he first met him about 1901? Probably not. But he had a singular power of seeing in men and women more than they knew they had—not something to praise them for, but something fine to expect of them, some hidden talent, some unused capacity for service. This power of discernment explains why he started so many men on a new career, often without their knowing it at the time. By a hint, oftener by a question, he showed wider horizons. His best work of this sort was not done by preaching, but by waiting, watching, and hoping. Though generally disappointed—for men are seldom what they might become—sometimes his faith was justified.

On the afternoon of March 14, 1932, when word came to him that his friend had suddenly gone where no one could find him, his first thought may have been not the riddle of what was done that day, but the spiritual transformation of those many years before. That was the "flash-back" of the film called life, seen by a light that comes only once.

This transformation was all the more wonderful to Rush Rhees because it had been wrought by some other means than the love of God. George Eastman was not a religious man in the ordinary sense. Not only was he not a churchman, but his general attitude toward life was that of the humanist, not of the believer. He did not doubt the existence of a supreme intelligence in the world, and duty was to him more than a word. But he saw no continuity in human destiny beyond natural causes, and did not believe in immortality. A man should serve his time. When his work was done, he might go.

He seems to have regarded discovery of truth, saving of time and enrichment of leisure, lessening pain and increasing innocent pleasure, as sufficient goals. That through these channels of solicitude for human welfare there could flow into the world fresh impulses toward a higher life than he himself knew must have been to his friend a source of great contentment. Rhees

GEORGE EASTMAN

of Rochester was a big enough man to recognize religion outside religion. This devotion to the unknown, this Christless
Christianity of silent service, he had seen also in scientists and
artists, whose only creed was truth or beauty, but whose lives
showed a better gospel. They followed their own best, never
found it here, and went away seeking.

Until George Eastman built the Mechanics Institute building
on Plymouth Avenue in 1900 he had made no large gifts for
education of any sort. Some time before that, two members
of a women's committee soliciting funds for admission of
women to the college called on him and were refused. "I am
not interested in education," he said. At the door one of them
turned and replied, "Mr. Eastman, you may not be interested
in education now, but you are going to be."

Since his business was founded on chemistry, he had great
respect for expert chemists and the training that had made
them. He believed that boys should be taught how to handle
tools. He admired skill in any craft. Being the son of a business-
school proprietor, and having got his start in insurance and
banking, he knew that practical instruction beyond that given
in elementary schools was necessary for success. These were
not what he meant when he said he was not interested in education. He had the self-made man's indifference toward institutions professing to do for the student what he might better
do for himself. Men who wished to read history, biography,
science, or sociology could do so at home, in their evenings or
on Sundays, as he had. They needed no college for that, only
books, brains, and resolution.

By self-help, thrift, persistence, and boundless energy he had
built up a large and growing business. Not only by his own
inventions but by purchasing and improving the inventions of
others, he had made the trade name Kodak known around the
world. As a youth, while still a bank clerk, he had experi-
mented with amateur photography by the old wet-plate
method. Dry plates, already introduced in England, he began

making by his own formula in 1879. The first Kodak camera, a fixed-focus box loaded with a roll of sensitized paper film, with a shutter operated by pushing a button, appeared in 1888. Transparent flexible film was produced in 1889, and motion-picture film in 1896. The growth of the business was rapid. By mass production, economy, lavish advertising, world-wide distribution, catering both to amateurs and professionals, Kodak won supremacy. The story of its growth is told in Carl W. Ackerman's biography, *George Eastman* (1930). By 1900 the company was using silver by the ton and making money by the million.

In 1900 the University of Rochester could almost say to students, like St. Peter, "Silver and gold have I none; but such as I have give I thee; rise up and walk." The most pressing need, apart from increased income to cover annual deficits, was a laboratory building for biology and physics. Prospects for raising $50,000 or more for such a purpose were poor. Alumni were still paying off subscriptions for a recently built gymnasium. Trustees were called on every year to contribute to running expenses. In the summer of 1902 Rush Rhees, then at his summer home in Maine, wrote to Lewis P. Ross, of the Board of Trustees, inquiring about the plans for a laboratory. The reply was not encouraging, being in the following vein:

If you could possibly, instead of designing new plans, discover either a gold mine or a bank-note factory, it would probably accelerate the erection of such a building as we need. Such things seem to be a little scarce in this locality, but you may find them more plentiful in New England.

This plaintive note, not unmixed with sarcasm, showed Rochester as an unlikely place for miracles to happen. But Rush Rhees believed in miracles, also in the right approach to persons able but reluctant to work them. He had already met George Eastman socially, and had some correspondence with him in arranging for a visit to the college by Lord Kelvin, then in Rochester as Mr. Eastman's guest. Lord Kelvin visited the campus with Mr. Eastman on May 1, 1902, and was present at

the student assembly in Anderson Hall. In this and other connections President Rhees had learned that the scientific rather
than the philanthropic appeal was the more likely to succeed
with Mr. Eastman. It took many months for him to get up his
courage to present the appeal. On April 23, 1903, he wrote to
Rufus A. Sibley:

> I am sure you will be gratified to hear that I secured from Mr. George
> Eastman a day or two since his pledge to pay $10,000 to the fund which
> we are seeking to raise. I had two interviews with Mr. Eastman on the
> subject, and found him most cordial and attentive to the matters which
> I had to lay before him. His generous response has given me a good deal
> of encouragement.

The fund to be raised was $150,000, of which $50,000 or
more was the estimated cost of the building and the remainder
an addition to endowment to cover increased costs of maintenance and instruction. During the following year the campaign among alumni and friends of the university for raising
this fund, all pledges being conditional on its completion, made
slow progress. Plans were drawn, however, and estimates obtained from contractors, so that by the spring of 1904 the
President decided to make another call on Mr. Eastman in the
hope of further assistance. Mrs. Rhees tells the story of these
several interviews and their result in an article written by
request of the Rochester Historical Society and published by
it in 1942 on "Rochester at the Turn of the Century":

> As early as 1904 Rush Rhees had gone to George Eastman (with
> genuine trepidation, for this soliciting business was new and the hardest
> thing he had to do) to try to interest him in a building for biology and
> physics at the University. Mr. Eastman was not interested but reluctantly
> promised him five thousand dollars. Then, as Rush Rhees moved towards
> the door, Mr. Eastman looked at him and said, "You're disappointed,
> aren't you? What did you want me to do?" "I hoped," replied Rush
> Rhees in his disarming way, "that you might feel like giving us the whole
> building." "Well," said Mr. Eastman, "I'll think it over." His thoughts
> resulted in a promise of $60,000 before long, and in the end he increased
> it to $77,000 to cover the cost of the completed building. "But this is the
> last I shall do for the University," he declared. "I am not interested in
> education." Rush Rhees enjoyed quoting that remark, after the sums
> given to the University by George Eastman had rolled up into many

millions. This was the only time that Rush Rhees asked George Eastman for money; indeed, Mr. Eastman, forgetting this first shy approach, often declared, "Dr. Rhees never asked me for a cent."

The next stage in this transaction, nearly a year after the first two interviews in 1903, is best represented by the following letter, written by Rush Rhees with his own hand and rather illegibly copied in his letterpress copybook:

March 7, 1904

My dear Mr. Eastman:

Mr. Hubbell has reported to me your characteristically generous addition of $10,000 to the sum you mentioned to me on Saturday, so bringing your final total up to $60,000, the sum I named to you as probably necessary to erect our building. I may be permitted to say that from my first two interviews I came away very cordially taking you at your own measure of interest in my enterprise, and pleased and gratified beyond my words to express—all the more so because you had permitted me to say that before that I had cherished a dream that you might wish to do a larger thing.

Happy in your helpful interest, I set about securing the rest of the $150,000 needful to make your subscription valid, and had succeeded in bringing my total up to between $50,000 and $60,000, with several friends ready to lend a hand who had not named their sums. I did not see where my additional $100,000 was to come from, but believed I should get it by sufficiently persistent work. I believe you can appreciate what a relief it is to me to have that task more than cut in two by your unexpected but most welcome reconsideration of your subscription. Your addition of $50,000 much more than cuts in two my task, for it will be a challenge and encouragement to others. I shall not attempt to express my gratitude in words—rather would I assure you of constant study on my part to keep you well pleased with your generous investment in my enterprise.

As you will remember, you made your initial subscription on our form which provides that the subscription is binding only when $150,000 has been secured. Will you kindly tell me whether you wish me to delay active work on our building until I have completed the $150,000? You may be sure that every consideration alike of honor and of self-interest will impel me to complete that subscription. But I think you have made success certain. Should you not care to stand on the formal condition, I think we should find some advantage in pushing our plans and beginning construction at once, so that we may have our building enclosed at least before snow flies next season. If you should authorize me to go ahead at once, I think it would not reduce my chances of completing my subscription, and it might increase it. However, I most cordially recognize your right to regard the condition as binding, and shall happily

abide by your preference in the matter. Knowing that you will reply to
me quite promptly, I am

Very gratefully,
RUSH RHEES

May I add that Mrs. Rhees shares fully in my own great happiness over
your generous subscription?

The answer was prompt and reassuring, and on April 1, 1904,
came Mr. Eastman's check for $60,000. The building was
begun that year and, though construction was delayed by
various causes, was finished in 1906. Mr. Eastman was shown
over the building before it was completed, consented somewhat reluctantly to have it bear his name, and expressed much
interest in its design and general appearance. He did not approve of spending money for decoration in a building intended
for utility, and was pleased that certain features intended by
the architects for that purpose had been eliminated. He said
to Rush Rhees that he supposed the building had cost more
than the original estimate, as buildings generally do, and asked
to have a detailed statement of costs including extras sent to
him. This amounted to somewhat over $77,000. Since interest
on his original gift of $60,000 had been accumulating for over
two years and had been credited to the account, he wrote the
following letter:

December 13, 1906

My dear Dr. Rhees:

I am in receipt of your letter of the 12th enclosing cost of the laboratory. To make the sum a round amount I hand you my check for
$15,000. I am very glad to send you this without any solicitation on your
part, either direct or indirect, because I am satisfied that the extra
expenditure was unavoidable, and I am so well pleased with the result
of your efforts to get a suitable building without undue expense. With
great regard, I remain,

Yours very truly,
GEORGE EASTMAN

This is the whole story of his first gift to the University of
Rochester, worth telling in detail because it reveals the caution
and deliberateness of both men and their confidence in each
other. George Eastman could no longer say that he was not
interested in education. Probably he meant what he said when

he warned the President that no other contribution would be made to the university. For the next six years nothing more was asked or received from that source. Another science building was needed by that time, for applied science, but as already related that laboratory was financed by a grant of $100,000 from Andrew Carnegie and a subscription of an equal amount from others.

During those six years the acquaintance of Rush Rhees with George Eastman grew more intimate. He and Mrs. Rhees were always at Eastman's home for the Sunday musicales. Common interest in music, public affairs, municipal reform, occasional contacts at the Chamber of Commerce and the Mechanics Institute, and for a time in the Pundit Club, of which Mr. Eastman was a member for a few years, brought the two men much together. Rush Rhees's year abroad in 1908-1909, with his extensive investigation of European technical education and industrial methods, had given him new material for friendly discussion with Mr. Eastman. Rapid advance in the art of photography, followed even by amateur photographers like Rush Rhees, was another topic in common. On business, politics, reform, and local improvement plans, their opinions were much alike. That they differed radically about education and religion made no difference, for both were good at avoiding delicate subjects.

Then in 1912 came the informal overtures to Rush Rhees for the Amherst presidency and his proposal that the Rochester Board of Trustees raise a fund to increase faculty salaries and establish a separate College for Women. The possibility that the city might lose President Rhees's services was one that Mr. Eastman could not accept. He was at that very time secretly negotiating with the president of the Massachusetts Institute of Technology in regard to his subsequent large gifts for the removal of that institution to its new site in Cambridge and the erection of its new buildings. That he was the mysterious "Mr. Smith," whose true identity was not formally revealed until 1920, though suspected long before, was not known to

many in Rochester. But the proposed endowment campaign at
Rochester was not for technical but for liberal education, of a
sort he had earlier regarded with indifference. Yet, whether
because of personal esteem for Rush Rhees or because he was
beginning to value general culture more than he had, he
promptly made known his intention to support the new
Rochester undertaking. Rush Rhees wrote him at that time:

I have your letter in which you confirm your proposal given to me in
our conversation earlier in the week, to duplicate any amount up to a
total of $500,000 which the Trustees of the University can raise during
the present calendar year, for the purpose of increasing the endowment
fund of the University.

In acknowledging this most princely offer I am glad to say that our
Executive Committee have unanimously and enthusiastically undertaken
the task of raising the $500,000, which together with your promised gift
will increase our resources by $1,000,000, and plans are now being
crystallized to carry that undertaking through to the earliest possible
conclusion.

That you have deemed the present occasion to be of sufficient significance to offer towards the support of the work which I am doing
here by far the largest single gift we have ever received, and by that
offer at the same time to stimulate other gifts totaling a like amount,
fills me with pride I cannot well control, in having won a friendship so
eloquently expressed. Your friendship awakens in me also the profoundest
determination to do everything in our power to make it certain that the
passing years will convince you that your generous investment in our
work here at the University has been worth while.

Great enterprises have a beginning, a middle, and an end.
It is not always easy to discover the middle. The year 1912
was a turning point not only in the life of Rush Rhees, de-
ciding him to spend the rest of his days in Rochester, but also
in the life of George Eastman. For it was then that he enlarged
the scope of his philanthropy from utility to liberal culture.
From that time on he gave not only to technical education,
from which he could see direct and practical advantages, but
to a wider educational program, for the administration of
which he must trust others. His earlier experience with some
college men in his employ had been disappointing, whereas
the work of the Massachusetts Institute of Technology he
could judge for himself by the high caliber of the men it sent

him. The time had now come when, just as he trusted experts
in science, he began to trust some experts in general education,
in particular his friend Rush Rhees.

In this critical year, 1912, when he began a new and wider
program of philanthropy, George Eastman was fifty-eight years
old. He grew more in the remaining twenty years, intellec-
tually, aesthetically, generously, and humanely, than in all his
previous life. Having made a fortune, he gave good fortune
away. Any reader of the Ackerman biography will recall that
the ten years following that date included not only World
War I, with its tremendous business losses abroad and its
colossal war benefactions, but the prolonged strain, irritation,
and expense of the Goodwin patent suit and the attorney
general's determined efforts to dissolve the Kodak Company.
Yet it was during those same years that Mr. Eastman conceived and carried out his plan for the Rochester Dental Dispensary, followed by the establishment of similar institutions
in other cities at home and abroad. It was then that his interest
in musical education led first to experiments with an existing
musical institute and then to the foundation of the Eastman
School of Music, to be described in the next chapter. During
that decade from 1912 to 1922 those other important enterprises, the Community Chest and the Rochester Bureau of
Municipal Research, already discussed, were being not only
largely financed by Mr. Eastman but helped by his wise counsel and energetic decisions. He erected and later enlarged a
fine building for the Chamber of Commerce.

Like Rush Rhees, he was often absent from Rochester.
Unlike Rush Rhees, he had a large executive staff at home,
competent to carry on the business without him. A strange
man; a man of restless energy and imperious will; a killer of
lion, elephant, and rhinoceros; a good shot, lover of camping
and wildlife, proud of his own cooking and his guns, able to
enjoy with equal zest the rough ways of the wilderness and
the luxuries of wealth; a patron of art, who spent money like
water for music that he loved and music that he could not

understand; a businessman who tolerated—sometimes—the eccentricity and egotism of genius; a genial host, a welcome guest, who disliked publicity and would seldom make speeches, even of thanks; a handsome bachelor who respected all women, admired many, cherished a few, but loved his mother best; a citizen who wished to make Rochester the best city in the land for children to grow up in; fond of bright flowers, old masters, and old friends.

Portrait painters put on canvas his clear-cut features and keen gaze. They painted what they saw; but they could not know that beneath the mask of a man accustomed to power was a man loath to pose, ill at ease with strangers, unwilling to be stared at, reluctant to be praised. They could not paint proud humility or kind severity. They could not reconcile in his cryptic expression the defier of competitors and of government itself with the friend of any child with a toothache. They could not show in one face both the parsimony that grudged unnecessary postage and the generosity that gave millions for Negro education. They painted Mr. Eastman, not G.E. Nobody could—not even a Rembrandt or a Franz Hals. His life was a question, and he died without the answer.

Who really knew George Eastman? He liked to tell a story about a child who lived in a tenant house on the rear of his large estate, and whom he used to meet in his garden, on that neutral ground between seventy and seven which is one-half fairyland. She was asked by a neighbor, "Do you know Mr. Eastman?" "Sure, I know him. He's the man that lives in our back yard."

The history of his interest in children's teeth and tonsils and adenoids, and what he did about them, has this double value, that it shows his strong support of any program for removing the handicaps of childhood, and also formed a natural approach to his later emphasis on preventive medicine. Boys and girls in the schools, impeded by removable physical defects, were his special concern. Correction of those defects he left to experts, but he established several principles that governed many of his other activities in later years at the School of Music: All such welfare enterprises must be efficiently but economically run, no money wasted, no necessary expense spared. Children's parents should pay something, even a nominal sum, in order not to pauperize them. By careful follow-up records, long-range studies of results should be continued. Children exceptionally high or exceptionally low in the scale of health or ability should receive appropriate treatment, but raising the general average is equally important.

Such tendencies in philanthropic enterprises showed his systematic mind and his belief in mass improvement. He was not inclined to cultivate individual or personal relations with beneficiaries, or to favor special protégés. Nor was he always intimate with those to whose welfare projects he contributed. Having a social conscience without a social temperament, he often preferred to promise by mail and keep a promise with a check. But when he found men who looked upon him with sincere liking, humorous indulgence for his peculiarities, and genuine admiration for his modest munificence, all barriers were down. Rush Rhees was such a man. It was to him that Mr. Eastman wrote in 1914, replying to a letter urging him not to resign from the Pundit Club, a whimsical explanation of his unwillingness to write papers:

When anybody says that the two papers I did write were good, I feel like a man I knew in the early days when people crossed the plains with wagon trains. This man was a tenderfoot, but he had to fit himself out like the rest. One day he and another member of the party came upon a band of antelope unawares. He killed one with his six-shooter. When they got it back to camp he was hailed as the crack shot of the party. He let it go at that, but he never dared shoot off his gun on the whole trip after that. If these papers weren't accidents in the way they hit the Club, they were certainly better than I could do again.

Rush Rhees understood George Eastman because they had some traits in common. Both were naturally reserved and reticent. Both were amused, not embittered, by the transparency of many self-important men with whom they had to deal. Both saw through shams and pretense. Both were realists in their practice, idealists in their long view of human progress.

During the memorable year 1918, when the great burden of the World War lay heavily on both men, they met even more often than before, especially in connection with the War Chest, its local money-raising and its problems of allocating appropriations for foreign relief. Mr. Eastman's musical Sunday evenings at home were continued, and he had other things than war on his mind. He casually asked Rush Rhees, "Why don't you have a school of music?" The answer cost him a fortune, and will be found in the next chapter. Immediately after the war the General Education Board began planning to establish new medical schools in strategically located cities, considered Rochester for one of them, and in 1920 approached Mr. Eastman seeking his co-operation. That cost him another fortune. Medicine will be the subject of the chapter after the next.

Since the schools of music and medicine require separate treatment, and since this chapter is primarily concerned with the personal relations of two men rather than with the expansion of the university, it will be necessary here to pass over all details connected with the beginnings and early growth of those schools. But since from that time on Rush Rhees's time and thought were more and more occupied with them, so that he was forced to spend less time in his office in Anderson Hall and had less contact with undergraduates, it must be observed that his unshakable conviction as to the importance of the College of Arts and Science was never changed. In numerous addresses at educational conferences and at other universities he voiced his faith in liberal culture. One such utterance in those years of transition from a college to a university was the following from a Rutgers address:

> The finest accomplishment of college education is seen when it makes a man superior to his task, so that he may make a superior performance of his task, and then have a rich margin of intellectual life left for intellectual enjoyment and for fine public service.

Another passage in the same address is even more pertinent:

A successful man of business, himself not a college man, said to me not long ago, "If I had a son and he wouldn't go to college, it would break my heart." I at once began to indicate my approval of his judgment by referring to the service of college studies in the disciplining of common elements of intellectual life and in furnishing a broad horizon. He interrupted me, saying, "I am not thinking of that sort of thing at all. I am thinking of what he would do with himself after he had made his pile." To that man the satisfactions of life loom as the large concern of human education.

Here are two different but not contradictory estimates of what college education can do for a successful man: first, during active life it can give him intellectual and aesthetic interests for leisure hours; second, it can enrich retirement. Both views George Eastman had reached gradually during his later years. There were others besides Rush Rhees who by their indirect influence and example may have helped him to adopt them. His contacts with eminent visitors who were his house guests broadened his vision. Cultivated women among his hostesses and guests also brought grace to his home and refinement to his taste. Friends, music, and time improved him, as they improve most men who have enough of them.

By 1924 it had become evident that the College of Arts and Science could not keep pace with the new demands of an enlarging university, in either equipment or endowment, without large additions to its resources. Proposals for removal of the College for Men to a new site near the School of Medicine and Dentistry were made by George W. Todd, a businessman not hitherto connected with college affairs, and James S. Havens, an attorney and former congressman. Under Mr. Todd's energetic leadership a campaign to raise $10,000,000 was organized and carried to successful completion. There were 13,651 subscribers to the fund. Mr. Eastman contributed with his usual liberality.

He did more than that. Immediately after the Greater University of Rochester campaign, in addition to paying his subscription in full, he largely increased his previous gifts to the schools of music and medicine, and capped the climax by adding $1,500,000 to the endowment of the College for Women. This last was indeed a dramatic reversal of his "not interested" verdict some twenty-six years earlier. He did nothing by halves. When Eastman changed his mind he changed history. Letters of Rush Rhees at that momentous crisis show how astonished he was by the rapidity with which things were now coming his way. To one trustee he wrote:

I think you can imagine that I have found it difficult to keep my feet on the ground and my breath at a normal rate of respiration since this thing happened. I remarked to Mr. Eastman when he first outlined the plan to me that I assumed he must realize what it meant to an institution to have such confidence reposed in it. He smiled and replied, "I have the confidence." It is our obligation henceforth to prove that the confidence was justified.

In George Eastman's statement explaining why he was distributing his Kodak stock, there is no emotion. He writes as if he were drafting a prospectus; indeed, he was.

One of the reasons why I welcome this disposition of my Kodak stock is that it separates me from money-making for myself, and will give me the benefit of a somewhat more detached position in respect to human affairs. I look forward with interest to finding out how much the changed conditions will affect my slant on current affairs.

A friend of mine who had advance knowledge of this transaction asked me why I selected these four institutions as the beneficiaries of this distribution. The answer was easy. In the first place the progress of the world depends almost entirely upon education. Fortunately the most permanent institutions of man are educational. They usually endure even when governments fall; hence the selection of educational institutions. The reason that I selected a limited number of institutions was because I wanted to cover certain kinds of education and felt that I could get results with the institutions named quicker and more directly than if the money was spread. Under the best conditions it takes considerable time, sometimes years, to develop the wise expenditure of money in any line, no matter how well prepared one may be. I am now upwards of seventy years old and feel that I would like to see results from this money within the natural term of my remaining years.

After explaining his reasons for increased gifts to the Massachusetts Institute of Technology, Hampton, and Tuskegee, he continued:

As to Rochester, the town in which I am interested above all others, we are all set now to develop our University on the broadest lines and make it one of the outstanding universities of the country. By that I do not mean one of the largest but one of the highest rank in all of the fields which it has entered. The citizens of Rochester have never shown any inclination to "lie down" on any great civic enterprise, or to "let others do it." This, I suppose, is one of the reasons that has actuated the General Education Board and other friends of the University outside of Rochester to aid in large undertakings for the University here. But for the fine response of our citizens in the recent University campaign, I should certainly not have allotted to the University of Rochester so large a proportion of the properties which I am now distributing.

Rochester is well started on its way toward being the finest city in the world to live in and bring up families. As a place to earn and spend money, to maintain health, to obtain education and recreation, it stands unrivaled. All that I can see that it needs now among the fundamentals is a civic center and a modern system of municipal government.

A more informal expression of Mr. Eastman's later attitude toward college education is found in a letter which he wrote during the 1924 campaign to a well-to-do citizen who, when solicited, had expressed indifference toward the university and what it stood for in the community:

Fifteen or twenty years ago I used to feel pretty much the way you do about college education. There was a long time when I would not hire any young college graduate. In your day and mine a large proportion of the boys who went to college were rich men's sons who did not really have to work when they came out. Nowadays practically all the bright boys try to go to college, and the war developed the fact that it was the college graduate who made good as an officer and leader. We now instead of looking askance at college graduates send out scouts every spring to engage the cream of the college men to fill our ranks. So you see my position has completely changed. From the Kodak point of view I consider it a very highly desirable thing to have a good college here, not only to help train good men but also to make Rochester an attractive place for Kodak men to live and bring up their families.

That in his later life George Eastman came to accept the principle of educational giving without too narrow specification as to how his gifts should be used is another indication of the influence upon him, not only of Rush Rhees, but of Julius Rosenwald, Abraham Flexner, and other leaders. In a letter Rush Rhees wrote in 1929 to a correspondent who inquired on this point he said:

Mr. Eastman's recent gifts to us have not been designated for endowment, nor have they been designated for use in current expenses in any set proportion. Moreover, we do not use such funds for current expenses, rather for equipment and the like. A university is nearly always hampered by insufficiency of current income. Our policy has been to make up deficits if they occur. We have never as yet drawn on capital funds for that purpose since my connection with the University. Mr. Rosenwald's policy of authorizing the use of limited amounts of what might be regarded as capital gifts for current expenses is as interesting as it is novel. Mr. Eastman insists that his gifts to us are not specified for endowment, but he approves the policy of reserving so much as is possible for income-producing purposes.

Having gradually withdrawn from active management of the Kodak business, Mr. Eastman was able to give more time to travel and recreation, as well as to the affairs of the Eastman School of Music and its associated enterprises. He hunted big game in Africa, Alaska, and elsewhere, visited Japan, entertained many notable guests in his large mansion on East Avenue, and had a few years of that "ease with dignity" for which he had longed. Many honors were offered him, of which only a few were accepted. In 1930, when he received the medal of the American Institute of Chemists "for outstanding service to the science of chemistry and the profession of chemistry in America," Rush Rhees was again his interpreter:

When one takes into account the magnificent liberality of his contributions for the advancement of technical education to the Massachusetts Institute of Technology, and in particular his provision for the unique developments made at that institution in the training of chemical engineers, one recognizes that the significance of Mr. Eastman for the advancement of chemical science is far greater than would be indicated alone by his faith in chemists and chemistry in the development of his own enormous business. The fact that Mr. Eastman's confidence in education as a major factor in the development of the better life of our country, shown in his great gifts to music and general education in the University of Rochester and elsewhere, marks him as one of the distinctive figures in the life of America in our time.

There was one limitation in his giving which was generally understood in Rochester, but not always elsewhere. He did not give to strictly religious work. Rush Rhees explained this attitude in reply to an inquiry:

Mr. Eastman is not affiliated in any way with any church. Mr. Eastman holds Christianity in high respect, but for reasons of his own has
made it a rule never to contribute to any religious enterprise. How
liberally he interprets this policy may be inferred from the fact that he
has been by far the largest contributor to the funds of the Rochester
Y.M.C.A., but I believe that he does this because of his regard for that
association as a character-building agency.

Mr. Eastman shrank more and more from public appearances
and crowds, declining to make speeches or even to listen to
speeches. In 1930 the Society of the Genesee in New York
made strenuous efforts to have him as guest of honor at its
annual dinner, but without success. The next year he did
accept, and on February 9, 1931, at the Hotel Commodore in
the presence of a distinguished company he received the congratulations of his fellow townsmen, his New York friends, and
eminent speakers from elsewhere. A bound volume of autograph letters from his associates and friends was presented to
him, also an engrossed parchment scroll. One of the speakers
on that occasion was Rush Rhees.

That was one of George Eastman's last public appearances.
He watched with keen interest the building operations at the
new River Campus of the university, but firmly refused to have
his own name attached to the campus in any way—a refusal
respected while he lived, and even more respected after he
died by explaining its motive and ignoring it for the sake of
posterity.

The sands were running out. George Eastman was a sick
man, growing weaker all the time. His friends knew it, though
the public did not. His last year showed courage, patience,
and fortitude. During the winter it became evident that recovery was unlikely, but that life might be prolonged by
complete rest and careful nursing. He would not have it on
those terms. After a long and active life to be bedridden, helpless, an object of pity, smiled at as people smile for the sick,
whispered about behind the door in hidden commiseration—
that was not in the book for the old hunter. He was through,
and he knew it.

On March 14, 1932, a little after noon, when all that was vital in life was done, he sent people away, and wrote: "To my friends: My work is finished. Why wait?"

He did not wait.

Rush Rhees wrote to Frank L. Babbott, Mr. Eastman's life-long friend:

Harriet and I saw him last Saturday and had a very happy visit with him, remarking as we came out that he was more like himself than at any time in the last six months. We have seen him about once a week, and for the last three weeks he has seemed happier and more normal. However, his physical weakness continued. It was pitiful to see him try to get about. I am very much comforted by the way in which his real friends in Rochester have taken the manner of his going. No one could call George Eastman a coward.

When George Eastman's will was read, the only thing in it that Rush Rhees knew about in advance was the gift of his residence to the university for the use of its president, together with sufficient special endowment to cover the cost of mainte-nance. "I should like to have the experiment made for say five or ten years, and then if the expense seems unwarranted, you are at liberty to make such disposition of the house and con-tents as you think best. It is my idea that it would be a good thing for the city to have the President of the University a social leader, and that to be such a leader he ought to have the proper equipment." Of this intention President Rhees had been confidentially informed as early as 1925.

He knew nothing of the rest of Mr. Eastman's will, or of its codicil, leaving most of the remainder of his fortune to the university and raising the total of his contributions to it to a larger amount than any other of his benefactions. Much of this was for music and medicine, but there remained an unspecified fund to be used in the discretion of the trustees. Mr. Eastman could hardly have foreseen that within a short time after his death income on investments had so fallen and expenses so increased that the affluence which the public expected has not yet arrived. Contrary to a general impression is the fact that except in memory and hope, fine equipment and large tasks, Rochester is not rich. A good university never has enough.

Rush Rhees delivered tributes to George Eastman on several occasions: at a memorial service in Eastman Theatre on March 23, 1932, at an anniversary meeting of Kodak employees on March 14, 1934, and at the dedication of the Kodak Park Memorial on September 15, 1934. The main thing to remember about Rush Rhees in relation to George Eastman was that he thoroughly appreciated Eastman as a great man and loved him as a friend.

Most people outside Rochester when they think of the name Eastman think of money and photography. They should think also of music, medicine, generosity, and humanity. For these his last years were lived; by these his work still lives. His last words were not quite true. He said his work was finished. It is not finished; others must carry it on. To live up to his gifts and his high expectations, as Rush Rhees said in another connection, "We have a long way still to go."

Notwithstanding Mr. Eastman's aversion to monuments, there are two—that at Kodak Park and Rush Rhees's inscriptions on the stone pillars at the entrance to Eastman Quadrangle on the River Campus. He had refused to have his name attached to any building there; and it should be here remarked that the same was true of the Eastman Laboratories and the Eastman School of Music, his preference in each case having been overruled by the trustees. For the inscriptions at the River Campus, Rush Rhees chose words carefully. On one pillar is carved:

> Eastman Quadrangle. This quadrangle is dedicated to the memory of George Eastman, whose ideal for the service of the University of Rochester was as high as his gifts for that service were great.

On the other:

> Rochester, a city of happy homes, was George Eastman's cherished vision, and he gave lavishly to promote its health, education, and civic life. Like benefactions enriched others in America and foreign lands.

With those inscriptions on stone may be compared a shorter one, also by Rush Rhees, composed in 1906 for a bronze tablet in the Eastman Laboratories on the Prince Street Campus:

> This building given by George Eastman is
> dedicated to the study of life and energy
> for the larger knowledge of truth.

"The study of life and energy"; though meant for biology and physics, the phrase was prophetic. "The study of human life and energy" is a good name also for biography, good for this chapter, good for this whole book. Human life and energy are all that save the world from spiritual disintegration. They make science, art, history, philosophy, and literature. They keep the past and shape the future. They outlast war and are the only hope for peace.

Life and energy, even when they seem to have departed, live on. They survive in words, ideas, beauty, and truth. On bronze, stone, canvas, and paper we find durable signs showing where life and energy once were, and what they did. Transient radiation of light, sound, or thought shows where—for an instant—that same life and energy are again, or seem to be. But their real home is the spirit.

XII

BEAUTY

Beauty is the moment of transition, as if
the form were just ready to flow into
other forms.—Emerson

Yet should there hover in their restless heads
One thought, one grace, one wonder, at the least,
Which into words no virtue can digest.—Marlowe

To feel beauty is a better thing than to understand how we come to feel it.—Santayana

⟫⟩⟩⟨

ART as a desirable element in liberal education was
recognized at Rochester long ago. From 1872 to 1886
President Martin B. Anderson gave lectures on the history of
painting, sculpture, architecture, engraving, and etching. They
included some discussion of aesthetic principles, and of the
historical relation of the fine arts to civilization. These lectures
were attended not only by students but by ladies from the city,
and were illustrated by photographs and prints from the president's private collection. During the nineties no such opportunities were offered on the campus, except in the fine arts
section of the college library. The real beginning of systematic
instruction in the history of art dates from the coming of Dr.
Elizabeth H. Denio in 1902.

Dr. Denio was a graduate of Mount Holyoke, a Ph.D. of
Heidelberg, who had taught German and history of art at
Wellesley until her retirement. By the liberality of Rochester
friends of the university she was appointed to a lectureship,
and for fifteen years showed young people how to look at pictures. Being an experienced teacher, with her own large col-

178

lection of photographs and lantern slides, she made the history
of painting interesting to her students, most of whom were
women. She retired in 1917 and died in 1922, a much respected
pioneer who in early days had been an apostle of beauty amid
unpromising surroundings. As an example of an energetic
woman who after ending one career began another, bridging
the transition to greater things, she should be remembered.
So should the late George L. Herdle, a Rochester artist who
became in 1913 the first director of the Memorial Art Gallery.

As early as 1906, when preliminary plans were drawn for
future development of the campus in order to plot suitable
locations for new buildings soon to be erected, a place was
assigned for an art gallery. There was no prospect of its erection, no intention to solicit funds for it, at a time when other
needs seemed more pressing. But Rush Rhees, always a lover
of the fine arts, missing in Rochester the opportunity of frequently seeing good pictures except in the homes of his friends,
had this art gallery project always at the back of his mind.
There was already an educated public ready to appreciate and
use such an institution. Whether it could or could not be established the President did not know, but he had hopes. The land
lay waiting.

Then in 1912—that extraordinary year when so many good
things came at once that Rush Rhees decided to stay—the late
Mrs. James Sibley Watson, of Prince Street, daughter of Hiram
Sibley, offered to build on the university campus an art gallery
in memory of her son, James G. Averell. She had been interested for years in the efforts of Dr. Denio, Mr. Herdle, and
others to co-operate with President Rhees in promoting local
interest in the fine arts. Prominent Rochesterians whose frequent opportunities for seeing art exhibitions in New York,
Buffalo, and elsewhere led them to wish to share their pleasure
with less fortunate citizens stood ready to help in sustaining
such an institution.

It was not Mrs. Watson's design that this gallery should be
primarily an academic building; it was rather to be a gift to all

the people of Rochester, placed on the campus in order to give it attractive setting and permanent protection against encroachment. The gallery was to be administered by a special board of directors, on which the university would be represented; its heating, lighting, and janitor service would be provided by the university; but all other expenses were to be met from annual dues of members and larger gifts of patrons. The university trustees gratefully accepted this arrangement, not only because it would use for the benefit of all citizens a plot of ground long intended for that purpose, but also because it would make possible more adequate art instruction for students and others.

The white limestone Renaissance building, on a raised terrace surrounded by evergreen shrubbery, when completed in 1913 turned out to be beautiful in design and proportion. Enlarged in 1926 by addition of the Fountain Court and of several more rooms, a joint gift of Mr. and Mrs. James Sibley Watson, it became adequate for large loan exhibitions and for a small but growing permanent collection. In its entrance lobby stands a marble figure of "Memory," with a pedestal bearing a bas-relief portrait head of James G. Averell, executed by William Ordway Partridge, to whom Rush Rhees wrote in 1914:

Will you let me express to you in writing the sentiment I have already expressed to you by word of mouth concerning the figure of "Memory" and bas-relief of Mr. J. G. Averell, which you have made for our Memorial Art Gallery.

In tenderness of feeling, in exquisite reserve, in freedom from any funereal suggestion, and in subtle spiritual impressiveness your "Memory" is a source of constant surprise and joy to us all. It succeeds in giving to our whole building an atmosphere difficult to describe but pervasive and uplifting, contributing in a peculiar degree to the emphasis which our Gallery aims to place upon the spiritual significance of fine art as a means for the enrichment of the life of the community. That your "Memory" is effective in this direction is made apparent by the interest and reverence of the multitudes who visit the Gallery when they stand before your marble and comment upon its beauty and significance.

Those familiar with this figure, and with others more somber such as Daniel C. French's "Death and the Sculptor" and

THE MEMORIAL ART GALLERY

KILBOURN HALL, CHAMBER MUSIC HALL
AT EASTMAN SCHOOL OF MUSIC

Augustus Saint-Gaudens's Adams Memorial at Washington, will agree that the verdict was just. Remembrance of this departed youth is serene; "nothing of him that doth fade."

Until then the college had possessed no building of architectural distinction, nothing to lead strangers to admire or students to linger before beautiful objects of contemplation. Lingering in contemplation, wonder about the past, delight in a changeless present, which are part of liberal education, had been lacking. Now there came a new spirit over those green acres when a white house to shelter perfection was set up among the elms. It was "an outward and visible sign of an inward and spiritual grace." Soon the Gallery began to seem as if it had always been there. Rochesterians needed it, loved it, made it their own. Children were brought from the schools to be guided through. Working people came on Sunday afternoons, wandering about amused, amazed, awakened. For thoughtful students what they saw here—form and design, light and shadow, color and perspective, symbol and fantasy— came as a revelation to minds brought up solely on books. The dream of Mrs. Watson and Rush Rhees began to be realized. Those two are gone, but their dream remains. The awakening of youth is the brightest hope of age.

In later years, as tapestries, medieval sculpture, early Italian paintings and furniture were gradually added to the permanent collection, those rooms and corridors took on a quality of their own, a friendly familiarity with distant lands and ages. To enter those doors was like entering another world. It took time to feel at home there, to realize that the world is one, that the past belongs to us—its loveliness without its burden. Among some people on that campus the infrequency and reluctance with which they came seemed to indicate that they preferred provincialism. Perhaps it only meant they were afraid to come too near magic, lest it might hold them. The literal fear the spirit, and avoid it.

Here for a few years Ewald Eiserhardt, that gentle soul whose youthful admiration for Dürer led him from German poetry into many wide fields of art, taught undergraduates aesthetic perception, showed them philosophy behind sculpture, and diverse civilizations expressed in architecture. One dimly lighted room, devoted to the art of the Far East, seems even now haunted by his presence, because of its stillness, inner concentration, and timeless peace.

The Prince Street Campus has in this Memorial Art Gallery and the more recently erected Cutler Union, respectively Renaissance and French Gothic, two buildings of an architectural excellence unsurpassed by anything on the River Campus. These two charming buildings at Prince Street, and the interiors of Eastman Theatre and Kilbourn Hall on Gibbs Street, are the best examples of pure beauty yet achieved at the university. They were a great satisfaction to Rush Rhees. They needed no apologies or explanations to visitors. No longer was his institution devoid of that grace beyond utility, that refinement of proportion, that lifting of sight into vision, which he missed in childhood, glimpsed in youth, and at last inherited in his crowning years.

If in earlier chapters the practical and worldly side of this remarkable man has been overemphasized, in order to show how his idealism could adapt itself to limitations, remember that while he could still enjoy, he had joy. Sunset on amber windows in Cutler Union tower, the "Vision of St. Dominic" by El Greco in the Gallery, Beethoven and Brahms in Kilbourn Hall and Eastman—these too were part of what life brought him: surprise, humility, gratitude, and peace, as in St. Dominic's face when he saw the beatific vision. Rush Rhees never, like some Rochesterians, took marvels as matters of course. To the end they still refreshed him. Something was deeply hidden in him which, like a child, a poet, or an artist, never got beyond wonder. Beauty was never dulled, never lost. The first intensity remained to light the last maturity. Such men never grow old. As Sir Thomas Browne said, they live by an invisible sun within them.

Music also was necessary to Rush Rhees. From 1892, when
as a resident of Newton Centre he became a regular concert-
goer in Boston, he never missed an opportunity to hear good
music. Weekly concerts by the Boston Symphony Orchestra,
string quartets, organ recitals, great pianists and singers, ora-
torios and other choral works rendered by the Handel and
Haydn Society, musical evenings with Newton Centre friends,
were more than entertainment to him. They were an important
part of his life. Though not himself a musical performer, he
was a cultivated amateur. Boston was a musical center, with
the New England Conservatory of Music, noted composers and
critics, and many annual visits from New York orchestras and
opera companies. All this he left behind when he came to
Rochester, and missed it.

Some indication of the delight he had always found in great
music may be seen in the following extract from a letter replying to a request for his impressions of Paderewski:

I am very happy to reply to your request concerning impressions of
Mr. Paderewski. I first saw and heard him at a concert in the old Music
Hall in Boston in 1892. Before that time I had heard several of the
distinguished pianists, but I was convinced then that I was listening to
a master of that great instrument. The most notable impression was that
perfect technical mastery was completely put to the service of musical
interpretation. It was the greatness of the man's spirit even more than
his technical skill which impressed me. Never shall I forget his playing
of Beethoven's Sonata Appassionata. I have heard him many times since,
always with confirmation of my earlier impression.

One other contact with Mr. Paderewski revealed another side of his
extraordinary mind. It was during the war, and he made an address at
a large luncheon in the Chamber of Commerce on the subject of Poland,
its rights and aspirations. He talked for about three-quarters of an hour
without a note of any kind. Two things seemed to be remarkable: first,
the scope and accuracy and command of the English language. While
he had some of the accents of a foreigner, his choice of words and
understanding of fine distinctions in the meaning of words was a source
of amazement to me. But even more remarkable was the evidence of his
intellectual grasp of the political problems which he was discussing.
I then realized that one reason for his marvelous artistic supremacy is to
be found in the clear operation of an unusually keen mind. That experience I have used frequently in talking to music students concerning

the importance of cultivating their minds as earnestly as they trained their fingers and voices.

In other words, he saw in Paderewski a man commanding music, not music commanding a man. That was the sort of musician and music that he preferred. Enjoyment of music for him seems to have been both intellectual and emotional, a love for ideas, an understanding admiration. He could like music that he did not understand, and understand music that he did not like; but when both these aspects of appreciation were combined in a great composer or a great performer, then perfect art brought perfect happiness. One hour could keep the quality of eternity.

Such hours were uncommon in Rochester when he came. There had always been music of one sort or another, for there were musicians and music lovers among the older families, some of German ancestry, others with a long American tradition of culture. There was a Tuesday Musicale, a fortnightly meeting of ladies who met to hear good music and to listen to lectures about it. There was a small orchestra, which in addition to playing for dances and receptions gave occasional subscription concerts of classical music, augmented on some occasions by players from New York. The repertory of this orchestra was gradually extended as its leader, Hermann Dossenbach, received encouragement in his pioneer efforts from influential patrons. For Mr. Eastman's friends after 1906 there were also the string quartet and organ recitals on Sunday afternoons at his large house, now known as Eastman House.

All this earlier musical activity was on a tentative and informal basis, in which the purpose was to undertake no more than could be well done. Superficiality and haste have never flourished in Rochester. Its people have always had standards beyond their resources. They are hard to please.

Musical critics are likely to be condescending toward small-town ambitions. Seldom do they make constructive suggestions, such as that of Elbert Newton to Hiram W. Sibley which led to the establishment of the Sibley Music Library. The city needed not only reference books on musical history, biography, and theory, but instrumental and choral music scores for the use of students and conductors. Mr. Sibley authorized the purchase of such a collection, mostly imported from Europe, increased year by year, and shelved until 1922 in the college library building erected in 1874 by his father. This musical library was for the use of the public, who from its beginning about 1905 until its removal to the Eastman School of Music drew from it for home use volumes of Beethoven sonatas, Mozart symphonies, Wagner operas, folk songs of all nations, thereby greatly enlarging the musical intelligence of the community. Another effect of this wise benefaction of Mr. Sibley was that it increased the concertgoing public. Request programs were called for. Mr. Dossenbach was able to give more concerts to better prepared listeners.

Convention Hall, in which these Dossenbach concerts were given, as well as recitals by visiting soloists, was totally unsuitable because of its lack of comfort and its faulty acoustics; yet music lovers continued to support the concerts, not without heavy deficits that had to be made up by the patrons. Audiences varied with the weather, but expenses did not. A snowstorm could spoil a season's record. Yet on June 25, 1910, Rush Rhees wrote to Hermann Dossenbach:

I cannot adequately express to you how highly I appreciate the work which you and your orchestra have done during the years since the orchestra was organized to advance the interests of music and give pleasure to the lovers of music in Rochester.

When I came to Rochester ten years ago I was surprised by the apparent apathy of our citizens with reference to music. During the past decade that apathy has disappeared, and a lively and increasingly intelligent interest has taken its place. In working the change you and your colleagues have had a most important part, and I desire personally as a citizen to express to them and to you my heartfelt appreciation.

The work of your orchestra has been noteworthy for its steady development in confidence and accuracy of rendering, and for the intelligence and sensitiveness of your interpretations, and for the range as well as the high character of your programs. As a citizen I have had increasing pride in the fact that Rochester is able to present as its own so creditable an orchestra in concerts of the high character which you have maintained.

To you and to your associate musicians, as well as to the generous friends of musical culture who have lent you their support, all Rochesterians are largely in debt.

Rush Rhees's praise stimulated its recipients to greater exertions. It was not meant to make them complacent, and never did. That Mr. Dossenbach's efforts had about reached their limit, unless wider horizons could be opened before him, was the basis upon which a few of his patrons sent him to Europe for further study in 1911-1912. This project, supported chiefly by Mr. Sibley, Mrs. Watson, and Mr. Eastman, was one of the results of the formation of a Musical Council for the city.

On May 15, 1911, a meeting was held at the Chamber of Commerce to organize a permanent association for the better co-ordination and support of music in Rochester. Four classes of members were established: (1) one representative each from the Tuesday Musicale, the Dossenbach Orchestra, the Symphony Orchestra, the Oratorio Society, the Musicians' Union, and the like; (2) a representative from each of the daily newspapers, presumably the music critic; (3) fifteen representatives of the general public interested in music; (4) four ex-officio members, the mayor, the president of the Board of Education, the president of the Chamber of Commerce, and the president of the university.

Musical interest had grown so rapidly during the previous decade that rival organizations had threatened to hamper by competition the very cause to which all were devoted. It was not sufficient to increase the lists of subscribers to the several enterprises unless co-ordination and the prevention of unauthorized ventures could be arranged. In the very month in which the council was organized, a two-day choral May festival previously planned, at large expense, resulted in a heavy deficit. Rush Rhees uncomplainingly did his full share not only in subscribing for this unfortunate loss but in soliciting others to make it good. A new organization cannot start "in the red." But few people like to pay for a dead horse—especially if they are not sure it ever was their horse.

Such discouragements would have led some men to drop the whole thing. Not so Rush Rhees. He was in it for better or worse, for richer or poorer. During all those critical years between 1911 and 1920 his wise counsel and cheerful facing of complications did as much for the future as the thousands that others poured into musical undertakings. People think now of George Eastman as the only "angel" of Rochester music. In the end he was—the archangel. But at the beginning others carried more of the burden. At first he even declined to become a member of the Musical Council. On May 17, 1911, he wrote to President Rhees: "It is not feasible for me to give the time that would be required." He thought better of that. Mr. Eastman's first reactions were often wrong; he did not hesitate to change them.

Mr. Dossenbach's year in Germany was profitable to him in many ways, and he returned full of ambition for larger things. A second choral venture for 1912 was advised against by the President; he wrote:

My own feeling is that it is better to handle one enterprise at a time. It would be wiser to get the orchestra well started before going after the choral situation with too much aggressiveness. That will mean, of course, that you must postpone for a while your ambition for the Ninth Symphony; but sometimes the longest way around is the shortest way home.

A so-called Rochester Conservatory of Music was organized in 1911 by several local music teachers as a private venture, giving lessons in piano, violin, voice, and theory, on a fee basis. It had no connection with the university, though it would have welcomed such recognition. A successor of this school, later known as the D.K.G. Institute of Musical Art from the initials of its three proprietors, acquired in 1913 from the Board of Regents a provisional charter, which was to expire in 1918. Its building was opposite the Prince Street Campus. During the war years, when leading sponsors of music in Rochester had many other things on their minds, the orchestral concerts were nevertheless continued. The Institute enlarged its faculty and steadily improved its work. But the whole musical future was uncertain. Capital was not available to endow the orchestra or the school, and there were some who felt that the ultimate solution of the problem did not lie in that direction. Something larger was needed.

Then it was, in 1918—the last and worst year of the war—that George Eastman's question to Rush Rhees, "Why don't you have a school of music?" was asked and answered. Nothing but the best would do for either man. Mr. Eastman purchased the property and charter rights of the Institute of Musical Art and presented them to the university. Application was made at that time to the Board of Regents for amendment of the university's charter in order to permit it to add other schools and grant other degrees than those originally contemplated, and the necessary legislation was arranged in due time. The full intention of Mr. Eastman to build a theater and establish a high-grade university school of music was not announced until 1919. Land had to be obtained, preliminary plans drawn, and the general outline of the project determined, before the news could be made public.

Now that these origins have already passed into history, it is difficult for those who did not live through the protracted period of struggling experiment to realize what this culmination meant to Rush Rhees. Knowing as he did the full extent of Mr. Eastman's magnificent gifts to the Massachusetts Institute of Technology and of his donations to war funds, it did not at first seem to him possible that Rochester was about to become a musical center by princely endowment from the same source. At the time the public announcement was made, Mr. Eastman in an interview explained his motives. He said:

It is necessary for people to have an interest in life outside their occupations. Work, a very great deal of work, is drudgery. I see no possibility of getting away from this condition. Hours of employment have accordingly been shortened, and as production increases—as it must increase—they must be still further shortened. What, however, is going to be done with the leisure thus obtained? Leisure is unfruitful because it is not used productively. We do not know how to use it fruitfully. All sorts of sports, recreation, and diversions must be developed if we are to make full use of our leisure.

I do not imagine that music is going to occupy all the leisure interests of people. Do not think that I am a reformer—far from that. I am interested in music personally, and I am led thereby to want to share my pleasure with others. It is impossible to buy an appreciation of music. Yet, without appreciation, without the presence of a large body of people who understand music and who get enjoyment out of it, any attempt to develop the musical resources of any city is doomed to failure. Because in Rochester we realize this, we have undertaken a scheme for building musical capacity on a large scale from childhood.

As was his usual policy, President Rhees first acquainted himself with other university departments or schools of music, and with the best standards required for granting music degrees. He also co-operated with Mr. Eastman in working out details of his comprehensive scheme. That scheme was so far-reaching in its intention, so idealistic and practical at the same time, that even now some casual observers do not understand the relations of its several aims to one another. Those aims, or part of them, may be thus summarized:

(1) To provide professional musical education of the highest quality for proficient students of sufficient talent to enable them to make music their career.

(2) To organize a preparatory department for talented boys and girls, enabling them to have the best instruction in instrumental music at an early age when such training is of the highest importance.

(3) To co-operate with public schools in improving school orchestras and bands by lending musical instruments, especially wind instruments, to those unable to purchase them.

(4) To maintain a special course for teachers of public school music, including not only musical and pedagogical theory but instruction in piano, sight reading, conducting, and reasonable proficiency on two orchestral or band instruments.

(5) To erect, under one roof with the School of Music, a large motion-picture theater, equipped with an organ, an orchestra pit, and a stage adequate for opera as well as con-

certs; motion-picture programs accompanied by high-grade orchestral and organ music, such as already existed in New York, to serve the triple purpose of entertaining the public, educating musical taste, and earning profits to supplement the endowment of the School of Music. Since all profits would be used for educational purposes, not for private gain, there would be no commercial aspect.

(6) The large theater would be available on one evening of the week for concerts of symphonic music by the theater orchestra, and for musical recitals by visiting artists, arranged in series supported by subscribers. It would thus supersede Convention Hall.

(7) A small hall in the same building, also equipped with an organ, would provide a suitable environment for chamber music, small student orchestras and choirs, and solo recitals by advanced students.

No greater proof could be found of the executive ability of George Eastman and Rush Rhees than the fact that, although the motion-picture feature of this program had to be abandoned after a few years for reasons to be later explained, thereby greatly reducing the expected revenue, the rest of the plan not only has been carried out for nearly a quarter of a century but has been enlarged and improved.

In 1919 President Rhees, announcing plans for the new building in his report to the trustees, stated: "Acting on your instructions, I have asked that this new school shall bear his name, and he has agreed that this new department of our work shall be known as the Eastman School of Music." It required even more persuasion to get George Eastman's consent to have the theater also bear his name; he had considered some such title as "Academy of Music and Motion Pictures," but fortunately accepted, while the building was under construction, the more adequate designation "Eastman Theatre." In Rochester the single word "Eastman" now means music; an unconscious tribute to an unpretentious man, surviving by his best.

In the erection of this magnificent building George Eastman

was the dominant figure. He had more than the usual amount
of difficulty in inducing consulting architects in New York to
work harmoniously with local architects who had drawn the
ground plans in accordance with his instructions. The site
selected, on the corner of Gibbs and East Main streets, near
the business center, presented an unusual geometrical problem.
It was not a right angle, the streets intersecting at a slope
permitting a corner entrance on a wide sweeping curve.
Mr. Eastman declined to yield to the recommendation of the
consultants that this entrance lobby, one of the best features
of the building, should be altered to allow a more conventional
interior design, which would have greatly reduced the seating
capacity. He showed his characteristic independence by insisting on the original plan, and time has vindicated him. With
all this Rush Rhees had little or nothing to do, though fully
informed, but it gave him a good chance to see how to handle
architects.

The Eastman Theatre interior, admirable in proportion, rich
but not ornate, perfect in acoustics, has been pronounced by
some good judges the best concert hall in the country. Built,
as the motto on the façade proclaims, "for the enrichment of
community life"—one of Rush Rhees's many inscriptions—the
Eastman Theatre has become a palace for the people. There,
at moderate prices, symphony concerts are available throughout the season, as well as recitals by eminent violinists, pianists,
and singers, and Sunday evening popular programs at a nominal figure far below their cost. In addition, the large student
orchestras and chorus of the school often give free concerts of
high quality. To these all sorts of people in all sorts of clothes
come in crowds, listen with attention, applaud with vigor, and
go away refreshed. These purposes for which the theater was
built are still being fully realized, notwithstanding early abandonment of the motion-picture scheme which was supposed to
pay the bills. Why did that scheme fail, and how are the
bills paid?

The motion-picture project was based on two assumptions:

that enough first-rate films worthy of the stately surroundings would be available to show a new one each week or two; and that people willing to pay New York prices for the combined program of pictures, orchestra, and ballet would keep the theater well filled. Estimates of box-office receipts resting on these assumptions were found to be too optimistic. The public liked the music but did not like it enough to keep on coming in crowds week after week. Also, the quality of the films available, even after Mr. Eastman bought up several other local picture houses in order to command their booking rights, was often mediocre. For a time the Eastman Theatre was leased to one of the chains, but after losing money faster than ever, the contract was canceled, and the picture period came to an end in 1931.

The financial outlook was not encouraging. How was the symphony orchestra to be supported? Subscriptions for season tickets, even at best, will never cover the cost of such an organization, even when overhead expense is otherwise met. Orchestras are always run at a loss, and must be. Good music costs more than can be charged for it. What was the answer?

The answer was widespread popular subsidy of Rochester music by Rochester people—the Civic Music Association. This community movement, headed by leading business and professional men and public-spirited women, conducting an annual membership campaign which in no way conflicts with charitable or patriotic funds, has saved good music for Rochester. Instead of an Eastman endowment sufficient to cover all deficits and give Rochesterians something for nothing, there is a steadily maintained spirit of co-operative effort under competent management, by means of which public pleasure is increased, musical taste improved, and civic morale sustained. This cannot be done once and for all. It has to be done afresh every year, by the people for the people, like most other things worth while. Few great enterprises can be finished by millionaires and left to run themselves, least of all in education.

In developing the musical program at Eastman Theatre and

solving its early financial difficulties, Rush Rhees was not the leader, since a special board of trustees, of which he was only one, had these matters in charge. An adequate sketch of recent musical history in Rochester, which this chapter does not attempt, would name many men and women whose share in these labors and their successful issue was as great as his. But, on the other hand, the Eastman Theatre is the property of the university, its high reputation must be kept worthy of its distinguished history, and President Rhees co-operated with Mr. Eastman and with the management in administering this great trust. He was ultimately responsible. His negotiations with the city government concerning the ever-present issue of assessment and taxation showed firmness and tact. As a nonprofit institution, all surplus earnings of which, if any, must be devoted to musical education, it was legally exempt; but constant vigilance was necessary to protect that exemption. The hall can never be rented for profit, but is available for university functions and certain civic occasions. "The enrichment of community life" is its sole aim. That this aim may never be forgotten or neglected, the University of Rochester is responsible. Few other universities have an equal task and an equal opportunity.

The Eastman School of Music, a part of the University of Rochester more widely known throughout the country than any other, is largely the creation of its director, Howard Hanson. When he came to it in 1924 he found a group of more or less independent departments, with good teachers, gifted students, and unsurpassed equipment. But the first two years, both in the school and in the theater, had been somewhat experimental and complicated. Mr. Eastman had personally employed foreign artists and conductors, encountered difficult temperaments, and shown himself master. He did not stand in awe of famous artists, and wanted results. There had been comic episodes, and some not so comic. Relations between school and orchestra were not clearly defined, since teachers of orchestral instruments were also members of the orchestra.

Rank and responsibility were not fixed. Individual and class instruction did not suffer from these incomplete adjustments, inevitable in the first stages of any large enterprise, but a clear and consistent policy had not yet been reached. Mr. Eastman and President Rhees were looking for a new director for the school.

Then in 1923 their attention was drawn by the English conductor Albert Coates to a young American musician studying composition at Rome on the foundation known as the Prix de Rome. Howard Hanson, a Nebraskan of Swedish ancestry, after graduation from Northwestern University and musical study in New York, had taught theory and composition for six years, first at Northwestern, then at San Jose, California, where he was dean of the College of the Pacific. His three years at the American Academy in Rome had been fruitful in composition and in experience as an orchestral conductor. President Rhees, who had already met him in Rochester, made further inquiries at the American Academy in Rome in 1924, and decided to recommend him to the Eastman School trustees as head of the school. Howard Hanson wrote to President Rhees on January 26, 1924, after reporting his impressions of a visit to the school:

> If Rochester is to take an important place in American music, it will not be an easy task. It will take the life of some man to do it. It is not a physical task but a spiritual one. The director of your school will have to breathe fire into a great machine, and endow it with his own enthusiasm for a great cause. Rochester is not a music center, and for it to become such a center a great thought would have to be born there, which by its very bigness and idealism would direct to it all those who believed in the same things.

Howard Hanson wrote the long letter of which this is a paragraph in a New York hotel room just before going to lecture to the American Music Guild on American music. It is remarkable that after three years of European musical contacts, and wide acquaintance with musical standards and methods in Italy, France, Germany, and England, he came home to champion the cause of American music—the past, the present, but

especially the future of American musical composition, interpretation, and education.

The derivative and imitative quality of romantic American
music in the later nineteenth century, the use of native folk
tunes and rhythms by composers in the next stage, the vogue of
descriptive tone poems and program music, gradual introduction of modern dissonance—all these interested him, but none
commanded his exclusive attention. He had no fads, no scorn,
and not too much adoration. As much at home in the modal
music of the Middle Ages as with Palestrina, Bach, and the
great classical masters, as ready to interpret the West as the
East, admitting no subservience and no prejudice, he looked
backward beyond discarded fashion into permanence and forward beyond transient eccentricity toward the unknown. As
composer, conductor, friend of ambitious youth and open-
minded age, he was well prepared to lead a new movement of
national importance in what had been a rather provincial industrial city. To do that takes more than money; he had more.

In the development of the Eastman School of Music since
1924 three aspects only can be considered here, out of many
others more appropriate in some other context. This biography of Rush Rhees is properly concerned with these aspects,
because, though largely original with Howard Hanson, they
were encouraged and supported by George Eastman while
he lived and by President Rhees throughout his administration. These three aspects were the American Composers' Concerts, the rigid selection of students for superior musical aptitude, and the combination of musical education with liberal
or general education.

The American Composers' Concerts, begun in 1925 and continued ever since, are financed by a special appropriation in
the annual budget of the school. From manuscripts of recent
American compositions, submitted each year, several are
chosen to be performed in Rochester. All the considerable
costs of copying scores and orchestral parts, rehearsals, and
traveling expenses of successful competitors and invited critics,

are borne by the school. It thus becomes host and patron for a day, without other endorsement, to potential talent some of which might otherwise remain unknown. More than one young composer has first heard a composition of his own performed at Rochester, conducted by Howard Hanson, in the presence of faculty and students of the school and the general public, and reviewed in the press.

In view of the impecunious state of most young musicians, this privilege is of inestimable value. Though begun before the recent system of musical prize competitions for broadcasting orchestras, it still serves a different and equally important function. There is no prize but the hearing, no praise but applause and whatever critics may choose to say; yet here not one but many have the chance to bring their newest work before an audience. This is more than a young author can do. His story, poem, or book is read by some unknown person in an editor's or publisher's office, and may never get beyond that barrier to people who might understand and enjoy it.

At American Composers' Concerts there is a great deal of eccentric music, caviar to the general, cocktail for the few. There is also sometimes music of a strange new beauty, never heard before, perhaps never heard again, but present in the air and in the imagination for fifteen minutes once in a lifetime. This too is art.

It is also a gift from the dead. At a cost of several hundred dollars of Mr. Eastman's wealth, made long ago from photography, it has been possible to translate a composer's manuscript into sound waves from an orchestra, so that many can hear with their ears what he alone heard in his head. Perhaps once in half a dozen times it is worth hearing; and that one time is priceless. What art has to do with money is a big subject, never yet exhausted; but here is a concrete case where capital serves creation. Only time will tell whether genius grows best by encouragement or by starvation.

Selection of candidates for admission to the Eastman School of Music, or to any other good music school, differs fundamentally from admission to a college. It has to be based not merely on intelligence, industry, and application as indicated by academic records, but on musical aptitude sufficient to justify a favorable prediction for the student's future career. In the case of voice candidates, the possibilities of the voice itself have to be decided by audition before good judges; for others, previous musical preparation and proficiency must be appropriately weighed; but for all alike there are in addition purely objective tests for discrimination of tone and rhythm, for musical recognition and musical memory, sufficient to rule out those whose ambitions exceed their capacity.

High standards both for admission and for retention in the school must ensure that neither performers nor teachers of music shall be graduated from the Eastman School of Music without being really good musicians. This might seem axiomatic, but it is not; for many highly intelligent young people possess enough musical taste and ability to justify their giving time to the cultivation of music as an avocation, but not as a profession. The Eastman School of Music cannot receive as candidates for its degree Bachelor of Music young men or women of first-rate academic ability but deficient musical aptitude who wish merely to increase their musical appreciation.

More than most schools of music, Eastman under the leadership of Howard Hanson and Rush Rhees laid emphasis from the beginning on general culture. The two men agreed absolutely that without adequate knowledge of literature, history, and other fine arts besides their own, musicians however talented will always be at a disadvantage. They must know foreign languages, even as tools in their studies; but they must also know how to speak and write their own language better than many older musicians ever learned to do. Whether they are to teach music, as many of them ultimately do, or to be professional singers or players, they should have a higher education, equivalent in some respects to that of a college graduate. Neither in mathematics nor in science can much be expected, because of the large amount of time required, which many hours of daily practice make impossible. But by a few required nonmusical courses in the first half of their course, and some free time for nonmusical electives in the second half, it has been possible to make out of singers, pianists, organists, and violinists men and women of good general information and culture. They have to work harder than any other class of students except chemists, engineers, and medical students to attain this desirable combination of skill with refinement, but the best of them succeed. When they have time to breathe, they may even enjoy it. Musicians have to be enthusiasts; they would never get anywhere if they weren't.

Rochester is one of the few universities where a college student of sufficient musical ability can major in music for a Bachelor of Arts degree. This arrangement, made possible by a special curriculum worked out co-operatively by the Eastman School of Music and the College of Arts and Science, meets the needs and desires of those musically gifted students who wish a larger proportion of academic studies than is possible in the Bachelor of Music program. It is not a refuge for inferior musicians or dilettantes; if they attempt it, they soon drop out. Really good graduates from this course, if they can afford the time and money, may continue for another year or two at the School of Music and earn another degree. These opportunities bring to Rochester some excellent students from distant parts of the country. Scholarship aid, though never sufficient to meet the needs, encourages many young people, who have just heard the word "Eastman" as a name both for music and for hope, to find both beside the Genesee.

In this chapter on beauty—the discovery and advancement of beauty by Rush Rhees as man and president—the sections dealing with the history and methods of the Eastman School of Music may not seem relevant. In their details these matters belong to administration, and he dealt with them as university business. Intellectual and practical rather than aesthetic considerations were generally uppermost. He was concerned with carrying out George Eastman's great design for improvement of public taste by good music and by musical education. For expert advice in both fields he had to rely on others. It was primarily a question of the best use of money and time for the cultivation of a fine art. But what could keep it fine?

Any art by which men have to make a living is partly a business. Musicians who play in symphony orchestras may supplement their earnings by playing in dance orchestras, where something else than fine art prevails. Painters who do posters and illustrations as a trade, architects designing a factory or a hospital, radio script writers, Hollywood poets, box-office dramatists, erotic novelists, even interior decorators for the vulgar rich may, or may not, sell their souls. If there is no market for their best, they can give it away. If they cannot give it away, they can at least keep it for their children—who will probably not want it. There is no such thing as mass production of beauty at a profit; but a great deal of ugliness passes for beauty when it pays or becomes a fashion.

Anything is fine that shows or promotes refinement of skill by imagination, or of matter by mind. Nothing is fine that coarsens or cheapens the few things that make life worth living. Beauty is perfection beyond reach that keeps men reaching. Perception of beauty in common things, admiration for it in uncommon persons, creation of it, more feeling for it, less talk about it—these are part of the good life and the liberal education which Rush Rhees worked for and partly achieved.

In one of his last public addresses, that delivered at Albany in 1933 at the 150th anniversary of the University of the State of New York, speaking on "Liberal Education, Then and Now," he said:

So much as is needful for intelligent understanding of painting, sculpture, architecture, or music will clearly contribute to such a power of clear understanding and right thinking as the college aims to develop. The essential in all such aesthetic studies is an intelligent appreciation of the contribution made to life by art. It is not fanciful to find therein some recovery of the values recognized by the old medieval curriculum, which coupled music with arithmetic, geometry, and astronomy in the *quadrivium* in which culminated the liberal training of medieval students. And side by side with this new interest in aesthetic studies is an even more interesting movement for the recapture of religion as a subject for serious, intelligent attention by liberally educated men. Liberal education should concern itself with the whole man, and therefore, *a fortiori*, with the highest life of the spirit of man.

All fine arts—painting, sculpture, architecture, music, poetry, drama, dancing, and the rest—began with religion. They praised the gods; the world was a temple. They will never again approach perfection until modern men train their highest powers to serve the highest good.

XIII

MEDICINE

I swear by Apollo the Physician, and Aesculapius, and Health and Hygeia, and all the gods and goddesses, that according to my ability and judgment I will keep this oath and stipulation: I will follow that system of regimen which, according to my ability and judgment, I consider for the benefit of my patients, and abstain from whatever is deleterious and mischievous. Into whatever house I enter I will go into it for the benefit of the sick, and will abstain from every voluntary act of mischief and corruption. Whatever, in connection with my professional practice or not in connection with it, I see or hear in the lives of men which ought not to be spoken of abroad, I will not divulge, as reckoning that all such should be kept secret. While I continue to keep this oath unviolated, may it be granted me to enjoy life and the practice of the art, respected by all men in all times; but should I trespass and violate this oath, may the reverse be my lot.—The Hippocratic Oath, as taken by new Doctors of Medicine on Commencement Day at the University of Rochester

RUSH RHEES never asked for a medical school. The proposal came from the General Education Board early in 1920, in circumstances so unusual as to seem like chance. It was anything but that, being the deliberately calculated result of a survey of American medical schools made by Dr. Abraham Flexner years before. Because Albany, Syracuse, and Buffalo all had medical schools but Rochester none, and because it is harder for reformers to make over an old school than to found a good new one, geography partly decided this momentous question. But if there had not been a good college in Rochester, to which the General Education Board had already made large grants for college endowment, the offer would never have been made. In June, 1920, President Rhees made the following announcement:

201

About four months ago it was brought to my attention that competent judges of the needs of medical education in the United States were of the opinion that our city offers a very desirable location for a medical school of the highest order. This idea caused me great surprise. It was not the first time that the possibility of a medical school connected with the University had been suggested to me. But my reply had always been: medical education is the costliest form of professional training, and the University of Rochester is not interested in undertaking such work without resources sufficient to make that work unquestionably of the first class. I had no idea that Rochester could command such resources. Furthermore I had the opinion that the trouble with medical education in this country was not that it had too few medical schools but too many.

It was not strange that he was surprised. The General Education Board had hitherto confined its activities chiefly to college endowments and improvement of Negro education in the South. Two other Rockefeller agencies, the Rockefeller Foundation and the Rockefeller Institute for Medical Research, had been among the organizations through which by large gifts medicine and public health in the United States and throughout the world had been advanced. But Dr. Abraham Flexner, after years of investigation of medical schools for the Carnegie Foundation and of colleges and southern schools for the General Education Board, had now just succeeded, late in 1919, in securing from the Rockefellers a large special appropriation for improving medical schools. Grants had already been made to enable the Johns Hopkins, Washington University (St. Louis), and Yale medical schools to adopt the full-time system for clinical departments, and thereby to stimulate medical research. He had not made much headway in his attempts to persuade the great medical centers in New York City to take so radical a step. There, as in Chicago, the separation of preclinical and clinical teaching in different parts of the city seemed an impassable barrier to the new method. Columbia and Cornell might perhaps be brought to see the light if a new medical school could be established elsewhere in the state, built right, from the ground up.

It was the same strategy that Dr. Flexner later followed to stimulate medical education in western state universities by a

large grant to the University of Iowa, and in the South to
Vanderbilt University at Nashville—an object lesson, plus
rivalry. In the end, as he tells the story in his delightful auto-
biography *I Remember* (Simon and Schuster, 1940), it certainly worked. The transformed Johns Hopkins, Yale, and
Washington University medical schools were to be Exhibits A,
B, and C; Rochester was to be Exhibit D, provided Rochester
would co-operate. The General Education Board did not finance
educational projects unaided; it nearly always required large
local subscriptions as a guarantee of local support.

Rush Rhees was already well known to Dr. Wallace Buttrick
and Mr. Frederick T. Gates, of the General Education Board,
not only because he had corresponded and conferred with them
in regard to previous grants to his college, but because they
were both former Baptist ministers, graduated from Rochester
Theological Seminary—though long before he came to the city.
They had high respect for the educational wisdom and financial
soundness of his administration during the preceding twenty
years. They had also recently learned of George Eastman's
great gifts to Rochester for a music school, and to the Massachusetts Institute of Technology. Could he perhaps become
interested in a medical school? It seemed not impossible, for
his Dental Dispensary indicated concern for public health.
The first step was to approach President Rhees. On a visit to
New York early in 1920 he readily promised Dr. Buttrick to
arrange an interview with Mr. Eastman by Dr. Flexner. The
latter tells most amusingly the story of several talks with the
Kodak magnate at his home, and how his original offer of
$2,500,000 was gradually built up to $4,000,000, plus the Dental
Dispensary, valued at $1,000,000, the General Education Board
to give an equal sum.

That was a momentous decision for Rush Rhees. It gave
him no relief from heavy administrative burdens, but increased
them. It would involve extensive building operations, preceded
by perplexing problems of location. It would, as he foresaw,
take most of his time for several years, simultaneously with

building and organizing the music school discussed in the previous chapter. Was there real need for another medical school in western New York? Was the need great enough, and the opportunity promising enough, for all the time and thought it would involve?

He was not unprepared to face such questions; he was seldom unprepared for anything. Medical education had been one of many subjects, outside college teaching, which he had been led to investigate through his relations to the State Department of Education and the Association of Colleges and Universities of the State of New York. As early as 1904 he was inquiring into the seven-year plan for combined college and medical education, by which medical schools accepted certain college courses in science and colleges certain first-year medical courses, so that a student having spent three years in college on a planned curriculum might receive his college degree at the end of one successful year in the medical school. The study of this proposal, subsequently adopted at Rochester and elsewhere, had required some examination of standards in medical education. He already knew enough, early in his administration, to decline local overtures for a Rochester medical school carrying with them no promise of adequate support.

His experience in establishing the Department of Vital Economics on the Ross Foundation had involved some acquaintance with recent physiological research and with medical men. Many of his friends, in Rochester and elsewhere, were physicians, as were several trustees. He was well acquainted with leading Rochester doctors, in connection with his Community Chest duties in making up annual appropriations for hospitals, and even earlier by reason of a tentative proposal of the Rochester Academy of Medicine to erect a building for its members' use on the college campus, a scheme never carried out. Several of his relatives were physicians; and he had got his name from his great-uncle Dr. Benjamin Rush Rhees, a medical pioneer in Philadelphia a hundred years before. In these and other ways he had gained no small acquaintance with some of the problems of elevating the medical profession, as one of the chief means of social progress.

Most of all, through reading annual reports of the Rockefeller Foundation and various monographs written for the Carnegie Foundation by Dr. Abraham Flexner on medical education in the United States and Europe, he was well aware of the new emphasis on medical research as an indispensable basis for the art of healing. These Flexner studies, based on intimate acquaintance with the great work of Dr. William H. Welch and his colleagues at the Johns Hopkins Medical School, were severely critical of most American medical schools. In the first place, those schools were in part staffed by busy practicing physicians who could do little research themselves, because hospital duties, lectures, and private practice as consultants left them no time for it; in the second place, many famous medical schools gave preclinical subjects in one place and clinical in another place near a hospital, sometimes miles away, so that necessary correlation was complicated by distance.

Dr. Abraham Flexner's penetrating and often caustic comments on American colleges and so-called universities had also been carefully noted by President Rhees in his conservative development of his own college during the previous decade. In fact, Dr. Flexner's influence on higher education during his long service, first with the Carnegie Foundation and then with the General Education Board, until his later retirement to organize the Institute for Advanced Study at Princeton, has been as great in raising the level of all graduate study as in the strictly medical field. This was the man to whom, second only to Dr. William H. Welch, the great Johns Hopkins dean, President Rhees had to look for wise counsel and constructive suggestions during the earliest stages of the medical development at Rochester. Mr. Eastman also had for him a high respect, as the most persuasive salesman he had ever met.

Six questions had to be considered before the new medical school could even begin as a hole in the ground: (1) Who should be its head? (2) On what principle should this dean

206 RHEES OF ROCHESTER

when appointed select his faculty? (3) Since the $9,000,000 promised at the start (in addition to the Dental Dispensary) would be necessary for endowment and for medical school buildings, how could the hospital be separately financed? (4) Where should the school and hospital be located? (5) On what basis should dentistry be related to the school, the Eastman Dental Dispensary near the Prince Street Campus being already in use as a dental clinic? (6) Since a medical school requires a larger amount of clinical material than a hospital for paying patients can provide, could the city be induced to build a municipal hospital as part of the university medical group? Many other questions soon arose, but all of these six, except possibly the last, had to be settled at the beginning.

The first question was the most important. The head of the school must be a leader in medical research, capable not only of solving his own problems but of picking first-rate men at an early age and giving them ample opportunity and stimulus for long productive careers. He must be able to get along with all sorts of people, without compromise and without offense. He would come into a city with four old and well-established hospitals and several smaller ones, receiving aid from the Community Chest, and some of them also receiving city payment for indigent patients, with all of which the new university medical center would be in competition, if it hoped to keep its beds filled. His time, hitherto given largely to original research, would be partly taken up with administration, without which neither his own research nor that of his colleagues could succeed. He would pay that price in time and energy for the opportunity to head the first high-grade medical school begun from the ground up in many years; the first new school of importance, in fact, since the Johns Hopkins in 1885. Many other good schools had been improved, but no other of the highest quality had been begun. It was a great chance and a great burden. Who should have it? Presumably no one who wanted it; for a man good enough for that kind of job is likely to prefer to stay where he is.

Dr. Welch, himself a pathologist, recommended that Rochester should put a good pathologist at the head, and suggested his former assistant, Dr. George H. Whipple, then director of the Hooper Foundation at the University of California. Dr. Simon Flexner, of the Rockefeller Institute, agreed in this choice. The first efforts of President Rhees to interest Dr. Whipple by mail were unsuccessful, but he did not give up. He made a special trip to San Francisco to persuade him. Being in the midst of a large research project involving several expert assistants and extensive animal experimentation, Dr. Whipple would not even consider the proposal unless adequate equipment for continuing that study could be provided when the medical building was planned. The answer was that he could help to plan it for himself, and for others like him. His special field was the chemistry, physiology, and pathology of the blood and liver, as bearing on anemia, including pernicious anemia, a hitherto incurable disease. Even then he was working on the use of liver in combating blood deficiencies, a field in which he later shared with two others the Nobel prize in medicine for 1934. Other honors came in due time.

Dr. Whipple's acceptance of the deanship was President Rhees's first success in this great enterprise. On his California trip, on which Mrs. Rhees accompanied him, he visited the Mayo Clinic at Rochester, Minnesota, and other western medical centers. With much satisfaction he reported to Dr. Flexner and Mr. Eastman that the transcontinental journey had accomplished its purpose. Letters and telegrams would not have done it; even the large prospective endowment alone would not have done it.

An important part of the future of Rochester was settled at San Francisco on a winter day when a doctor changed his mind. This chapter and this book are made up of critical decisions. What goes on in a man's head that makes him say "Yes" or "No," and stick to it all his life?

For department heads in the yet nonexistent medical school it was the recommendation of Dr. Welch and Dr. Abraham

Flexner, also of Dr. Simon Flexner, that young men, preferably under forty, should be chosen, on the basis of competent
research and good personality, not necessarily on the ground
of being already widely known. By the time a scientific man
has made a national reputation by discoveries or books, he is
often middle aged or elderly. The best part of his life may be
still ahead if he is capable of further growth, but his energies
are not what they were and his future will be shorter than his
past. Those "grand old men" who made Baltimore a Mecca for
learning pushed their brilliant juniors to the front. If a junior
cannot stand the honor of a top appointment, and gets a swelled
head, out he goes. Scientific competition is keen: friendly
among the best, tolerant among the good, bitter among the
disappointed, productive in all. The fittest and luckiest survive.

President Rhees and Dean Whipple, between the beginning
of the medical project in 1920 and the opening of the school
in 1925, chose as professors of medicine, anatomy, surgery,
bacteriology, obstetrics, and so on, a group of young men all
experienced in research, all sympathetic with the Johns Hopkins
idea of constant advance in knowledge as the basis of medical
progress. In answer to a query as to their youthful appearance,
one of the advisers said: "If a man is not good at thirty, he is
never going to be good."

For the hospital, George Eastman was personally responsible
for securing from the nonresident daughters of the late Henry
A. Strong, his former Kodak associate, a pledge of $1,000,000.
The hospital was to be a memorial to their father and mother.
These ladies, Mrs. Gertrude Strong Achilles and Mrs. Helen
Strong Carter, wished the building to express in some way the
warm and philanthropic side of their parents' interest in victims of illness and misfortune. In planning the Strong Memorial
Hospital it was Rush Rhees's sympathetic understanding of
the humane spirit of this gift that led to the interior design of
the main waiting room, with its large fireplace, pleasant lighting, comfortable seats, paintings on the walls, and a memorial

inscription underneath the clock, setting forth for all comers the good wishes of the donors after their own time was over:

> HENRY ALVAH STRONG
> HELEN GRIFFIN STRONG
> May the kindliness and human
> sympathy which characterized
> their lives continue forever
> through the ministry of this
> hospital

In such ways as this, Rush Rhees was better able than George Eastman, George Whipple, or anyone else to interpret science in the language of kindness. Good words can neither heal the body nor save the soul; but they can share trouble, bring consolation, and lighten the inevitable. Even the courteous voice of a clerk at the hospital information desk or of a telephone operator at the switchboard can carry cheer to the depressed and courage to the disheartened. To live daily among crises, whether as doctor, nurse, or clerk, makes the right sort of people kinder and the wrong sort crosser. Strong Memorial Hospital has made friends simply by not being a machine. Every hospital was originally a place for hospitality. This one still is.

By means of separate financial provision for the hospital, it became possible to erect the medical school buildings largely from the income, over several years' time, of invested capital already turned over to the university. In this way, by strict economy in construction, it was planned to retain as a permanent endowment the larger part of the $9,000,000 fund. Ultimately not only were overdrafts replaced, but Mr. Eastman made further gifts, which he supposed would yield sufficient income to cover all future deficits on hospital operation. Financial problems of later hospital development, though they caused much perplexity to President Rhees, do not have much space in this chapter, nor in this book. It is meant to be a human story with no adding machine; just a man pushing ahead, a great idea at work.

Where should the new school be? With a dean, a prospective faculty, a promised hospital, and millions drawing interest, there was still no place to put them. Many Rochesterians are not aware that careful studies and surveys were made of the possibility of placing the medical school and hospital on or near the old Prince Street Campus. There was still a little free space on the original campus, the university had acquired some land on adjacent streets and could have bought more. Some were strongly in favor of keeping the whole institution together— or rather, near together, for the Eastman School of Music site, already selected, was half a mile away. It soon became evident that although the immediately necessary medical buildings might be crowded into that general neighborhood, in spite of its central location it had three defects: (1) it was too near the main line of the New York Central, with attendant noise and smoke; (2) too close to college buildings and residences for ambulance and outpatient service, supply trucking, animal houses, and other inevitable accompaniments of a hospital and school based on laboratory research; and (3) even if these objections could be met, no room would be left for future growth of the College of Arts and Science.

The college had already during the war been obliged to acquire as a football field a block of ground a mile east of the campus, since then abandoned. The question of removing the college itself, or a part of it, in order to allow for college expansion was not at first considered and will not be considered here, though it soon became involved with the medical school location. It forms the subject of the next chapter.

For reasons above stated and others, it soon became evident that the medical school would have to find other quarters than Prince Street. Some advised a site far outside the city, near the lake, where there would be good air and plenty of room. Others said, on the contrary, why not build it on the congested north side beyond the tracks, among indigent people who would be its most numerous clinical patients and outpatients? All sorts of places were suggested, some by people with land to sell, others by disinterested parties considering solely the general good.

The final selection of a tract of land on the southern edge of the city, not far from the river and northeast of a large city park, was based on ample size with moderate cost; isolation from other buildings; proximity to the Lehigh Valley branch line, which, although convenient for hauling building supplies and coal, had not enough heavy traffic to be objectionable; and sufficient land for a municipal hospital. The site called for relocation of some streets and improvements in transportation, but these, it was believed, could readily be arranged. On the south was ample land for a nurses' dormitory and for future expansion. Distance from the center of the city was the principal objection, but no nearer location with equal advantages could be found. On the whole, the selection of this tract for the medical school and hospital has proved to be a wise one.

Dentistry had to be connected in some way with the enterprise, because of Mr. Eastman's interest in that subject and his inclusion of the Dental Dispensary in his gift to the university. The close relation of this branch of medical science to focal infections, oral surgery, and general diagnosis had led some progressive medical reformers to the view that dentists should have exactly the same preclinical training as physicians for the first two years of their course. This view required that they should meet the same high standards of admission as premedical students—a college degree, or its substantial equivalent, and thorough preparation in advanced chemistry, physics, and biology. Furthermore, the principle of original research should extend to the dental field, and dental graduate students should undertake laboratory studies in pathological and hygienic problems affecting the teeth.

This high conception of the dental art, agreed upon as theoretically desirable, together with excellent facilities for apprenticeship in dental practice among school children at the Dental Dispensary, led the administration to adopt for the new institution the title "The University of Rochester School of Medicine and Dentistry." After some years' trial, so few qualified candidates for admission to the dental course appeared that ordinary training for the dental profession was discontinued. Postgraduate dental research and education at the school were retained. This later modification of policy does not properly belong in this sketch of beginnings, but is necessary in order to explain why the School of Medicine and Dentistry now graduates no dentists. Mr. Eastman's intentions in the whole matter were clearly set forth in his letter of June 25, 1920, to the trustees, quoted by Ackerman (*George Eastman*, pp. 392-394).

A new Rochester Municipal Hospital had been under discussion for years, because the limited facilities in existing hospitals for adequate nursing and free medical care for indigent patients were becoming overtaxed; because provision for contagious diseases was obsolete; and because the city Health Department had high ideals for raising the general level of public health among the poorer citizens. Now that a teaching hospital, staffed by medical and surgical experts in a completely modern plant, with emergency and outpatient departments, was about to be established, the opportunity for giving to the city's less prosperous families, unable to pay full medical fees, the advantage of such facilities seemed obvious. Nevertheless, it took careful negotiation between President Rhees, Mr. Eastman, Dean Whipple, the university's attorneys, and the city government to adjust legal and financial problems, and reach an agreement which led to ultimate completion by the city of the Rochester Municipal Hospital, adjacent to Strong Memorial Hospital and the School of Medicine and Dentistry.

This large hospital group, with its nurses' dormitory, staff house for interns, heating plant, and other accessory buildings, now bears comparison in internal convenience, though not in external appearance, with many of the best medical centers in the country. The Municipal Hospital, like all the rest of the group, was built for use, not for show. In this respect it presents to reasonable observers a pleasing contrast to ornate and costly public buildings elsewhere.

These initial problems of the medical enterprise having

been considered and decided, President Rhees turned over to
the dean and heads of departments the detailed planning of
their laboratories for research and rooms for instruction. For the
hospital plans he employed a consultant from the Johns Hopkins
Hospital, who worked with the newly appointed hospital doctors. Two fundamental principles were adopted: First, by an
ingenious ground plan, connecting the several floors of the
medical and surgical parts of the hospital on the south with
laboratory and clinical facilities of the school on the north, long
corridors and plenty of elevators gave access to everything
under one roof, yet with ample light and air. Thereby the work
of doctors, interns, students, and nurses was greatly simplified,
and much time was saved. Second, no large wards were permitted. The word "ward," as having unpleasant connotations,
was avoided. The word "division," meaning a room for several
beds, capable of being separated by curtains, was substituted.
It was hoped that these divisions, in which charges were con-
siderably lower because of the economy in construction and
service, would attract most of the paying patients, and require
only a few private rooms. It did not work out that way, and
many more private rooms have since been added; but the semi-
private arrangement of the divisions has been a pleasant contrast to the barracklike interiors of some older hospitals.

As already hinted, fine architectural appearance in a strictly
utilitarian structure meant nothing to George Eastman. He disliked it. When he was planning a building like the Eastman
Theatre he employed the best consultants, artists, and decorators to make it beautiful. But for a laboratory, lecture hall,
hospital, or factory, all that was needed was plenty of room,
light, and air. Walls, windows, roofs, cubic space, well proportioned and well connected; anything more was waste. External features such as stone cornices and other stone trim,
intended by the architects to relieve the bareness of brick,
were cut out. In this policy Rush Rhees agreed, knowing that
every extra dollar put into stone meant that much less for
income; and knowing also that from a distance the general

effect of large masses of plain brickwork, if well proportioned, can be pleasing to the eye. The factory type of construction used in the medical school part of the building, with brick interior walls and concrete floors and ceilings, for economy in both construction and maintenance, was intended "to demonstrate how economically a thoroughly effective equipment for scientific laboratories can be provided." The skyline of the medical group as a whole is not bad; and in recent years landscape planting, with vines on the walls, is beginning to mitigate an architectural style which Mr. Eastman himself once called "early penitentiary." At first rather forbidding, it may become imposing.

The completed School of Medicine and Dentistry was opened in October, 1925, with impressive ceremonies attended by distinguished medical visitors from other cities and from Europe. George Eastman was just back from an African hunting expedition. Between that time and the end of Rush Rhees's administration, ten years later, the President gave a great deal of time to medical affairs. Both there and at the School of Music he was often present at conferences on matters of general policy. Questions of considerable delicacy arose from time to time, in which his long experience in handling differences of opinion without arousing resentment was indispensable. A few examples of the sort of thing he had to deal with, in co-operation with the medical faculty, may show that his presidential relation to the new school was by no means merely nominal.

Only members of the staff could bring their private patients to the hospital. This meant, of course, that a large number of Rochester doctors were listed in the catalogue as part-time instructors or lecturers, giving a limited amount of time to instructing medical students assigned to clinics where they might be working. This list of part-time doctors, coming to the school at more or less regular intervals to see patients, and if necessary to assist in clinical teaching, was large enough to include some who also had similar access to other hospitals, so as to avoid even the appearance of exclusiveness or competition. Yet inevitably from time to time for one reason or another some physician not on the staff at Strong felt dissatisfied.

Good feeling among the hospitals of the city, built up by Rush Rhees and others in connection with the Community Chest, and fraternity among physicians hitherto maintained by the Academy of Medicine and the Monroe County Medical Society, was of highest importance. Any unfounded suspicion that the University of Rochester, with its large Eastman and Rockefeller endowment, was likely to hinder rather than help the cause of medicine in Rochester was something that could not be ignored. Any real discrimination or competition must be corrected, and no ground must be left for professional jealousy or hard feeling. These things exist, and everybody knows they exist, but it has sometimes been the fashion to ignore them on grounds of professional ethics. When they are hushed up but persist beneath the surface, they still do harm. Medicine is not only a profession but a business, and competition is just as keen as anywhere else. To expect that all medical men should unselfishly co-operate in every new program for improving public health without even considering its effect on their own practice is a utopian dream; and Rochester is not yet utopia.

In matters like this alleged conflict of interests between the new hospital and older medical groups, Rush Rhees showed his shrewdness. He assisted in co-operating with city welfare authorities to see that other hospitals got their fair share of city-paid patients as in the past, even when this meant that many beds in the Municipal Hospital remained vacant, while overhead remained the same. More frequent talks by university doctors at Academy meetings, more invitations to medical lectures at the school by visiting specialists, more reciprocity, more amenities, fewer rumors and less gossip, are a good thing among doctors—as the equivalent would be among ministers, lawyers, professors, or any other well-meaning but contentious class. Frankness, with a good story and a good laugh, is a potent prescription that costs nothing.

Wherever prejudice and jealousy are found, truth is hampered and progress delayed. No business and no profession is altogether free from them, no college, no school. Rush Rhees in his presidential capacity throughout the whole university, and in his relations with all other institutions, all arts and sciences, all parties and all religions, tried to make peace and keep peace without betraying his trust. But the trust came first.

Although physicians of the School of Medicine and Dentistry probably do more free work at the Strong and Municipal hospitals than the staffs of most other hospitals, the Strong has never received a cent from the Community Chest. Annual deficits of other hospitals are met by Chest appropriations. The Strong deficits, which are heavy, come out of the income of general funds of the university left by Mr. Eastman's will. They are simply a part of the tremendous cost of medical instruction. Without clinical material among patients who pay less than cost, medical students could not study the variety of cases they must study before they can become good doctors. Public critics should understand these matters better than they do; for it is easy for outsiders to say, either that the university is so rich that it can afford to go on indefinitely running behind in current operations by drawing on reserves or, on the contrary, that the management must be careless not to live within its means.

This one brief digression into the field of finance, otherwise barred, seems necessary because in his public relations Rush Rhees sometimes had to face misapprehension and answer unjust attacks; yet he never lost his head, his temper, or his friends.

In quite a different aspect of public relations he sometimes had to speak for the medical profession better than it could speak for itself, as being more disinterested. Such a situation often arose in regard to animal experimentation. Miscalled "vivisection" by fanatics, who thereby imply that dogs are "cut up alive" for the amusement of anatomists and pathologists, the use of animals, under proper conditions of anesthesia and humane treatment, for study of disease and new methods of treating disease, is indispensable to medical progress. Nearly

every year bills are introduced into state legislatures to pro-
hibit all such experiments. Any medical man knows that there
is not a single important recent discovery, whether in surgery,
medicine, or pharmacology, that has not required animal
experimentation to test its validity and its safety. He also knows
that anesthetics and narcotics to prevent or relieve pain, careful feeding and proper attention, have to be employed to ensure
the success of any experiment, even if humane feeling did not
demand it. But many doctors feel so strongly the stupidity and
irrational sentimentalism of some antivivisection propaganda
that they cannot always keep their public utterances on a level
likely to persuade persons sincerely misled. Here is one of many
letters which Rush Rhees wrote on the subject:

Wherever we touch on steps of progress relating to medical science
and treatment, if we examine the method of gaining the necessary
knowledge, we come immediately to the fact that animals were used to
gain the necessary information. In the laboratories of this University
many experiments are performed on animals, the dog among others, and
I am convinced that every effort is made to minimize discomfort and to
protect animals against unnecessary suffering. The procedure is exactly
the same as in the hospital of the University, where anesthesia is given
during operations, and drugs like morphine are used after such operations
to minimize discomfort of post-operative nature.

Not only has man benefited by animal experimentation, but also the
dog has been benefited. Distemper, which formerly raged unchecked in
large colonies of dogs, now can be controlled with 100 per cent success
by a new distemper vaccine developed by English bacteriologists, now
of great service to the dog, protecting these animals against long continued sickness, disability, and death.

The University authorities, including the Trustees, feel the necessity
of continuing the use of animals for experimental purposes, as we assume
that medical science must progress and gain new knowledge of diseases
as yet beyond human control. To promote legislation to cripple or ob-
struct this type of research would be nothing less than disaster.

Medical research at the School of Medicine and Dentistry
under the direction of Dean Whipple and his associates went
steadily forward from the beginning. Year by year new facts
about disease and the treatment of it were worked out co-operatively by members of the staff and by graduate students. To the
general public the technical reports of these discoveries as pub-

lished in medical journals were of course unknown, but the President kept track of them and took solid satisfaction in them. Scholarly research about the past, in fields like history and literature, he also valued and appreciated, for he had done some of it himself in earlier and less crowded years. But scientific research about the causes of disease, especially of obscure and apparently incurable disease, had now a greater fascination for him as an interested observer. Moreover, if new light on a disease enabled scientists to suggest a way to prevent it or to reduce its severity, that seemed to him more exciting than new methods of accelerating travel or cheapening luxury. Preventive medicine was one of his chief concerns, and has always been prominent in Rochester.

Before the School of Medicine was begun or even thought of, he had written in his annual report for 1916, apropos of the Lewis P. Ross bequest for research and public information about the physiology of nutrition:

It is certain that this gift lays upon us a large task, but it also opens before us a great opportunity to be of service to mankind. Mr. Ross clearly intended that his estate should help people to understand, better than most now do, how to order their physical lives for their own greater health and happiness.

He had already, when the Ross Foundation was first established, quoted the phrase from Mr. Ross's will, "to the end that human life may be prolonged with increased health and happiness," and had announced "that the aim of the Department of Vital Economics will be primarily to make available for the general community the best information concerning matters of hygiene and nutrition for the greater health and happiness of mankind." Though that department, since the opening of the School of Medicine and Dentistry, has been devoted chiefly to research and teaching, the President continued to feel that sound and nontechnical medical counsel on wholesome living and avoidance of illness was a part of the university's duty to the public.

Medical and other scientific research rapidly increased the

number of Ph.D. candidates. Graduate work in the college up
to that time had not gone beyond the M.A. and M.S., but now
it was not only possible but necessary to reward advanced study
with the higher degree. A standing committee of the college had
been in charge of graduate work, but as the amount of such
work increased a more formal method of administering it was
required. There were other problems besides graduate degrees
that affected the College of Arts and Science, the School of
Medicine and Dentistry, and the Eastman School of Music. A
University Council was organized to decide such questions. In
its meetings deans and professors from the several schools of
the university met—as they also did in the University Library
Committee—for informal conference and formal decisions. This
council, as an administrative device, had in the President's
judgment not only the practical value of preventing conflicting
usage within the university, but also the highly desirable function of promoting mutual understanding among scholars, whose
daily work lay far apart but whose ultimate aims were, or should
be, all the same—human enlightenment and amelioration. It
broadens any teacher's outlook to be called on to understand
problems distant from his own.

During the last fifteen years of his administration, when much
of the President's time was spent on university business as distinguished from college business, he never lost sight of the central position of the College of Arts and Science. Supplementary
grants from the General Education Board for graduate work in
science at the college, in order to strengthen the medical school
on its preclinical side, made possible large extension of advanced study. To keep the growing institution from going off
balance was his constant aim.

One of his strongest convictions in regard to medical education was that a broad, liberal college course, preferably of four
rather than three years, was highly desirable for young men
intending to study medicine. He deplored the decline in the
proportion of cultivated and well-read physicians as compared
with former times. All attempts to confine the premedical course

chiefly to science he definitely opposed. In his opinion, literature and social sciences should be, as in the past, a part of the
background of scientific men, without which they become
specialists out of contact with some of the most important
movements of their age.

Yet with all his zeal for general education, the success of
the School of Medicine and Dentistry was to him a cause of
peculiar satisfaction. To have transformed the College of Arts
and Science was a contribution to human intelligence; to have
assisted in founding a School of Music, giving scope for youthful talent and pleasure to the multitude, was a rare opportunity; but to preside, as first among peers, at the birth of a
great school of healing, where life itself is the mystery, the
goal, and the reward—this was his unexpected duty, his high
honor, his late labor. On the new university seal he had added
to the book of Athena and the lyre of Apollo the caduceus of
Hermes; and *Meliora* was still his motto for all three.

Is it not a strange paradox of human life that sometimes
when it is waning it seems to grow? As health declines, the
health of others matters more. When happiness is impaired by
the disappointments and bereavements of age, the happiness
of others becomes the chief—perhaps the only—care. So
begins that transfer from self to not-self which marks the
pilgrim's progress toward something wider than his world and
longer than his life.

A man's first twenty-five years are all ambition and preparation; his next forty are mostly hard work, with little time to
look beyond his daily task and his personal responsibility; but
his last ten, if he has been fortunate enough to begin some
great work which he can never finish, and has found young
men to carry it on better than he could, may be best of all.
In the time that is left he can remember great moments and
forget himself. Medicine, quite as much as religion, may have
meant that to Rush Rhees. Both were part of his hopes for a
better world.

At a Rochester Commencement in Eastman Theatre, when the dean of the School of Medicine and Dentistry says, "Candidates for the degree of Doctor of Medicine will please rise," persons of imagination, who know the past too well to fear the future, may become conscious of invisible witnesses. Those need no seats; they breathe no air; they are not in space, or even in time. They are only names to conjure with, but they are here.

Great physicians, from Hippocrates, Galen, and St. Luke to Osler, Cabot, and Welch; great scientists, like Pasteur and Lister; fortunate discoverers, like Long, Morton, and Simpson; philanthropists, like Grenfell and Trudeau and Schweitzer; beloved Rochester physicians, like Edward M. Moore, Charles A. Dewey, and Edward W. Mulligan; great givers, who when their own health and happiness were failing, tried to ensure health and happiness for others—as if money could buy them; rich old men, like Lewis P. Ross, Henry A. Strong, John D. Rockefeller, and George Eastman; wise old men who "saw life steadily and saw it whole," like Martin B. Anderson, David Jayne Hill, and Rush Rhees—all these are waiting to hear one promise renewed, to see one more Commencement, to watch young men march out.

What do these venerable ghosts expect young doctors to do with all this new learning? "To prolong human life with increased health and happiness." It is not so stipulated in the code, but it is implied in the hopes of all who watch them. What does it mean?

To see life and happiness begin and grow and end; the best never lost, the worst never told; never to withhold skill or effort that might heal the body or save the mind; to protect the helpless, lift the weak, quiet fear, and lessen pain; yet knowing that all these will soon be gone, and everything else but honor; keeping faith with the dead, the living, and the unborn.

Can it be done? Is it worth doing? Are the odds too great, the rewards too small? Only the unseen witnesses know, and being sworn to secrecy they will not tell.

Graduates listen to the dean, reciting the quaint but solemn sentences of the Hippocratic Oath. They may feel slightly silly, or slightly scared. Is this a superstition, a sacrament, or a little of both? A sudden change comes out of the pagan past with that little prayer of Hippocrates for joy in life, in the practice of the art, and in the respect of men; and then that self-imposed curse for the faithless at the end of the ritual.

With that high challenge before them, to increase human health and happiness, some men who have no gods, not even Apollo, may inwardly reply, with no profanity, not even a sound to break the stillness:

"I doubt if I can always live up to that, but by God I'll try."

XIV

EXPANSION

Years of the modern! Years of the unperform'd!
Your horizon rises.—Walt Whitman

EIGHT irreversible decisions determined the history of Rush Rhees's administration: (1) admission of women in 1900, with the origin of which he had nothing to do; (2) beginning of applied science in 1905, when the conditional Carnegie offer of $100,000 was accepted; (3) Rush Rhees's decision in 1912 to stay at Rochester; (4) acceptance in 1912 of the offer of the Memorial Art Gallery, completed in 1913, the location of which dedicated the Prince Street Campus—at least its southern half—forever to educational use; (5) decision in 1918 to establish a School of Music, erection of which on Gibbs Street in 1921-1922 began the decentralization of the university; (6) decision in 1920 to establish a School of Medicine, and in 1921 to locate it several miles from the old campus; (7) decision in 1921 that the College for Men should be removed to the Oak Hill tract now known as the River Campus; (8) decision in 1921 that the College for Women should remain at Prince Street.

None of these decisions can ever be changed. It is useless to inquire whether they were all inevitable. The eighth was finally settled in 1934 when Cutler Union was built. Only the seventh has ever been seriously questioned. Since that too is irrevocable, it would be unprofitable to do more than to set forth the steps that led up to it. Since the River Campus decision was the last great act of President Rhees's career, its grounds should be here recorded, so that it may never be misunderstood.

Normal growth of the College for Men and the College for Women, separated on paper in 1912, would ultimately require more buildings both for women and for men, for which more land would be needed than was then available. Sibley Hall would not have been permanently adequate for the growing University Library; it could be enlarged, but not indefinitely. While more land south of University Avenue might have been acquired at high prices, no whole blocks were available. While expansion toward the north was then possible, it was later closed by erection of the Masonic Temple. Even though land enough somewhere in the vicinity might have been purchased for new buildings, outdoor athletics for men would still have had to be centered at the football field on Culver Road, a mile east of the Alumni Gymnasium, involving for part of the year a mass transportation problem—though not so great as that caused by the River Campus decision. Large funds necessary for an extensive college building program could be more readily raised for an entirely new site, especially if alumni support favoring a separate College for Men could be enlisted. Finally, President Rhees had accepted the opinion of his Johns Hopkins advisers that it was highly desirable for the medical school and the college to be near together, not only in order to facilitate more efficient use of laboratories and libraries, but especially to promote personal contacts.

Though the importance of the last of these considerations was not fully realized at the time, the others, even without it, would have been controlling. It is doubtful whether ten millions, or half of that, could ever have been raised for new buildings scattered through the Prince Street neighborhood. The prospect at Oak Hill for more spacious athletic grounds, a larger gymnasium, a stadium, a group of new fraternity houses, and a students' union, made an advertising appeal which Mr. Todd's committee pushed for all it was worth. The idea of a "Greater University," greater in size as well as in quality, brought results because it reached all classes in the community. There is a great book in a glass case at Rush

Rhees Library containing the engrossed names of many thousands of people who gave out of their abundance or their poverty to something that touched their imagination. The River Campus did that, and will always do that, not merely for what it is, but for what it may become.

While the location of the School of Medicine near the river south of Elmwood Avenue, for reasons of adequate space, isolation, and low cost of land, was logically separable from the decision to remove the College for Men to the neighboring Oak Hill site across the tracks, the two soon became inseparable. In particular, the relocation of railroad tracks and roads, the building of main sewers and heating tunnels, and the size of the heating plant, were engineering factors that required prompt decision of the whole question. Negotiations with the railroad company and with the city government would take time. Likewise the agreement with the Oak Hill Country Club for purchase of its land was conditioned on its finding another site and building a new clubhouse and golfcourse, which also took time. During this period of uncertainty, when the public had only partial information, many had doubts as to the wisdom of so radical a departure. But the President's farsighted decision has been confirmed by experience. More and more in the future, especially in connection with graduate research in science, and in some premedical undergraduate courses, such as physiology and bacteriology, contacts will increase. Better acquaintance of college teachers and medical teachers, by adequate provision for a faculty club on the River Campus, also is desirable. In all possible ways the underlying unity of the institution, university rather than diversity, needs more emphasis. Learning is too centrifugal.

Between November, 1921, when the decision as to site was publicly announced and November, 1924, when the money-raising campaign was successfully carried through, much preparatory work had been accomplished. On May 21, 1927, President Rhees, just back from a long journey through Egypt, Palestine, Greece, and Italy, went to Oak Hill to start a new culture. All he did for learning that day was to take a spade and dig a little hole in the sod of a bank overlooking the Genesee. Trustees, faculty, and alumni stood by smiling and watched him work. Then a big steam shovel swung around and began scraping down a hill that had been there ever since the glacier left. The earth was changed. The River Campus was begun.

By extensive grading operations the whole top of the hill was removed, and its rather commanding height was reduced to a level terrace for the main quadrangle, with land falling away north and south to a lower grade for dormitories, athletic buildings and fields, and fraternity houses. Several architectural studies were made showing alternative arrangements of the quadrangle buildings before the adoption of the present plan.

When it was decided to put a round tower on the library, to make it the central point of perspective from the west or southwest, and then to omit the whole eastern half of the building, it was apparently not realized how many people will always approach from the east. The view of that monumental building is good only from the west; from all other directions it is conspicuously unsymmetrical. The original plans provided for a dignified eastern façade and an interior court, with the tower at the center of the building, as it should be. In reply to a suggestion in 1932 that this obviously incomplete building should be finished as soon as possible for aesthetic reasons, as well as for needed office space, the President wrote:

Personally I have not felt that an unfinished building is in itself an objection, advertising as it does the plans for the future. However, I do realize that unless that aspect of the matter is understood the position of the tower on our building is perplexingly eccentric.

Classical Revival was chosen for the architectural style of the quadrangle. Some Colonial features appear in the fraternity houses, which though not built by the university were subject to the approval of its architects. Brick with stone trim on the inner façades of buildings in the Eastman Quadrangle, stone colonnades between them, Doric and Ionic columns in the

RUSH RHEES LIBRARY TOWER FROM THE RIVER

EASTMAN QUADRANGLE, RIVER CAMPUS

porticoes, stone carving on the pediments and around the door-
ways, and admirable landscape planting, give a harmonious
and stately appearance from within. The plainness of the outer
walls allows for future extensions.

The unique round tower of Rush Rhees Library dominates
the whole, rising above a circular colonnade to a stone lantern,
186 feet above the ground. This tower contains the bookstack,
with sufficient empty space for many years of expansion. The
interior of the library is beautifully decorated, especially the
Welles-Brown Room for leisure reading and the circulation and
reference rooms on the second floor. Carving in stone and
wood, and pleasing use of color and gold, give warmth and
richness. The Treasure Room is a delight to bibliophiles.

The stone lantern on the tower contains a fine chime of
seventeen bells, presented by the family of the late Albert W.
Hopeman in his memory, music from which is heard several
times a week for a considerable distance throughout the neighborhood. This Hopeman Chime, at the summit of the highest
building, revives an old Flemish folk art to crown the other
arts and sciences below. As in other chimes and carillons of
the Old World and the New, the larger bells may sound a little
harsh when heard too near—too much cling for the clang, with
the deep hum-tone, an octave below, hovering long in the air.
But distance softens them, evening charms them, and memory
will always link them with youth and time and the river. Those
bells have rung for the dead, the living, and the immortals;
for joy, for prayer, for peace. What they will ring for a century
from now, who knows?

The trustees had much difficulty in persuading Rush Rhees
to allow them to name this splendid building in his honor.
When the time came to carve a name over the entrance some
pressure had to be brought to bear by his friends. They knew
that in the course of nature it could not be many years before
he would be no longer at the head of the institution into
which he had put so much of his life and thought, and all of
his loyalty. They overruled him. This should be known. To a

correspondent at a distance to whom he sent announcements concerning the new campus he wrote:

> You will find references to the Rush Rhees Library. Please note and duly emphasize the fact that that name was given the principal building on our new campus without my consent and over my protest. Not that I am insensible of the honor which has so been conferred upon me, but that it makes me wince a little to see the President of the University of Rochester apparently in the role of providing a choice monument to himself. The designation of that building marks the only difference of opinion between me and my Board of Trustees for over thirty years.

Rush Rhees Library is well named. As for Rochesterians Eastman means music and Strong means healing, Rhees means books. Because he was more than a bookman he deserved this honor. Because for him books were vital, this is not a tomb for dead authors but a home for living ideas—including his own. He wrote only one book on paper, because he lacked time. Here is his other book, on stone, which defies time.

Rochesterians as well as visitors often wonder why it was decided that the College for Women should be permanently located at Prince Street. These were some of the reasons:

The Memorial Art Gallery must always have vacant land around it to avoid impairment of its architectural effect. It must also be heated from the central heating plant. The northern part of the campus could not be sold, even though older buildings were sacrificed, because the land would revert to the heirs of the original owner if it ceased to be used for education. Though Catharine Strong Hall and Anthony Memorial, and the land on which they stand, were under no such legal restrictions, there was a moral obligation to the donors and their heirs.

Removal of women students from Prince Street to the River Campus would have made difficult or impossible that close relation with the Eastman School of Music and the Memorial Art Gallery which had been one of the chief assets of the College for Women. Moreover, evening University Extension classes in Catharine Strong Hall and Anderson Hall could not be transferred to a new location far from the center of the city.

The most important reason of all was that in 1912 the President, the trustees, and the faculty had formally adopted the policy known as "co-ordination," which specifically called for permanent separation of men and women in prescribed courses. Co-ordination was not a restrictive or negative policy, but a positive affirmation that the College for Women would be better off if allowed to develop its own traditions and customs, without imitating, adopting, or rivaling those of the men. As pointed out in Chapter VIII, co-ordination was at first largely theoretical. Even after completion of Catharine Strong Hall and Anthony Memorial it continued to be partly such. There was still neither room nor money to have a real College for Women, as that term is commonly understood. But in 1930 there was room enough, and in 1932 there was money enough.

Yet a complete, self-contained College for Women is not yet in sight. A drift toward mixed classes on both campuses, involving extensive daily intercampus transportation, began almost at the start and was not checked. The result is that the four-mile drive through city traffic, which in bad weather is a handicap to education and good temper, is now regarded as if it were an inevitable consequence of the River Campus decision. It was not.

However this problem resulting from the wide separation of the two colleges may eventually be settled, it should not obscure the magnitude or the wisdom of the major achievement. When one remembers that in October, 1930, a year after the beginning of a long financial depression, the university was able to dedicate a ten-million-dollar campus, built all at once on a single plan, the timing, the audacity, and the foresight of that plan seem marvelous. Unparalleled generosity, energy, co-operation, and good fortune of many men working together for a great cause brought about a magnificent culmination.

At the dedication, though many congratulations centered on material advancement, a higher note was sounded in the address of Principal **L. P. Jacks,** of Manchester College, Oxford, when he said:

As Aristotle pointed out long ago, the good life is a very difficult affair, and will always remain so. It needs a great soul to play the part of a good man in the modern world. A great drama has been written for the acting of that part, a noble theatre has been built for its presentation, the stage has been set for the performance to begin, the tickets have been sold, and the audience is all ready to assemble; but what is the good of all that until great actors come forward to play the parts?

The acting of new parts is not easy. I have often thought that the greatest delusion of our time is the belief that the good life can be made easy. Widespread is the notion that psychology will presently come forward with some formula which has only to be pronounced to set the performance going; or that philosophers will work out some theory of the universe which makes the good life automatic; or that a social system will be set on foot to supply happiness to everybody, as electricity is brought to our homes. I see no signs that any such thing is coming to pass. The drama of the good life cannot be acted by pressing a scientific button. It cannot be done on those easy terms; neither on the social scale nor on the individual. You need great actors.

Expansion of a university is not measured by acres, registration, or endowment. The addition of money or of men does not improve the quality of its life. That cannot be achieved solely by intelligent effort or reorganization. Neither is it accomplished by moving from one place to another, or calling old things by new names.

Expansion that amounts to anything is growth from within. It is like the life force that bursts the shell of a seed, penetrates the ground with roots to gain more life from the earth, sends up stem and branches and leaves to win more life from sunshine and air, to withstand winds and cold, to know when spring is coming and leaves should open, to know when fall is coming and leaves should go; but flourishing chiefly to make new seeds for other plants, other times, other lives.

The University of Rochester grew slowly for seventy years, fast for fifteen. This sudden acceleration was not mushroom growth. Though due to nonrecurrent external causes, it would not have come without gradual increase of public confidence during quiet years. That the fruits of earlier labor, not only of the President but of generous benefactors, happened to be harvested at a time when national prosperity was temporarily declining was not only fortuitous but fortunate. It would have been unfortunate if it had brought lessening of effort. Material expansion is now represented by many buildings and investments, which are means, not ends. What the future will make of them depends not on things but on men. The university should never despise its small beginnings, and never seem too proud of its recent unearned inheritance.

Only what men have worked for and understood and loved is really theirs. In that way Rush Rhees and his college belonged to each other. Rochester helped to make him what he was; he helped to make it what it is. They grew up together, changing to what neither would have dreamed of when they met. In him and in his university the best was latent from the first. Time brought it out. Time will bring out more.

XV

CLIMAX

I count not myself to have apprehended; but this
one thing I do, forgetting those things which are
behind, and reaching forth unto those things which
are before, I press toward the mark.—St. Paul

Riches and honor are only an appendix to the book
of life. We can live without them.—Morgan John
Rhees, 1794

RUSH RHEES resigned in 1930 at seventy, but was urged
to keep on. The trustees would not even consider his
retirement in that culminating year, when the new College for
Men on the River Campus was completed and dedicated.
During that first academic year under the new conditions,
when many problems were still to be adjusted, long experience
and knowledge of the past gave him superior power of adjustment. But he was not satisfied to do merely that. There was
needed a comprehensive plan for future development of the
College of Arts and Science, to give it intellectual enlargement
and efficiency worthy of its new environment. This applied to
both campuses, for at Prince Street, Anderson Hall had been
completely remodeled inside, only the brown sandstone walls
and mansard roof remaining of the original structure; Sibley
Hall had been improved; and Carnegie, abandoned by the
Department of Engineering, had been refitted for other departments. There was room and incentive for better teaching on
the old site as well as the new.

Much of the President's time for several years was given to
educational studies. Committee sessions and faculty meetings

were devoted to the fundamental questions of what college education should accomplish and what it does accomplish. There were statistical inquiries based on the results of various testing programs, designed to compare the actual knowledge of students at successive levels, and their improvement from entrance to graduation. These figures could also be compared with those reported from other colleges, sometimes with pride, sometimes without. In all this there was a definite attempt to get away from mere theorizing about higher education—deductive reasoning from assumed definitions—and to learn objectively what is the actual material on which the college has to work.

Improvement should begin with the freshman year. Students entering college at the age of seventeen or eighteen should receive in the very first term a new intellectual stimulus, an adult approach to self-directed study, an invitation to the world of scholarship. It was Rush Rhees's opinion that teachers are inclined to underestimate the potential intellectual capacity, not of superior students but of the average. In this and in some other respects it might be better to assume that a freshman is a man before he really is, in order that he may soon become one. That the best teachers in a department should take their turn at freshman teaching he regarded as no waste of superior talents. No teacher is too good for good beginners. Few are good enough.

There had been revisions of the curriculum in 1913, 1920, and 1927, but another was needed. The President's most emphatic warning was always against the tendency to multiply courses. He was aware that no college can teach all the things that somebody wants to know, and saw no reason why it should. Foreseeing ultimate development of more advanced graduate work, he recommended that little specialization be undertaken in undergraduate class instruction; that should come later. The individual student might indeed be encouraged to specialize by his own efforts under proper supervision, but the curriculum should not be indefinitely expanded. Straining for breadth might encourage superficiality. It seemed to him that every college graduate should know at least two subjects well, well enough to use them later without relearning and correction of early mistakes.

How thoroughly he went into the history of college education is illustrated by the range of his reading in 1933 for his Convocation address at Albany in October. He chose as his subject "Liberal Education—Then and Now," a comparison of the college curriculum in the later eighteenth century with the successive changes of a hundred and fifty years. He read histories of all the oldest eastern colleges, biographies of pioneer college presidents, and much eighteenth century material. In that notable address he showed that comprehensive grasp of educational theories and facts which had marked his whole career. He well knew that in every period some claims made by reformers for the superiority of their *a priori* principles have been only partly supported by *a posteriori* evidence. This was true of the old inflexible classical curriculum; of its extreme opposite, the unrestricted elective system; and of all successive later stages of progressive higher education, including our own.

That each stage is better in all respects than that which it supplants is often taken for granted. Perhaps it is safer to say that for each advance something is sacrificed which need not have been wholly sacrificed. For example, the prevalent utter ignorance of Greek and Roman culture which superseded not thorough knowledge of that culture, but some influence of it, some respect for it, Rush Rhees regarded as a distinct loss, which might have been avoided. Better methods of language teaching, designed less for grammatical drill than for facility in rapid and extensive reading of the classics, even assisted by translations, might have saved Latin, even Greek. They may come back.

Again, he heartily approved wide intellectual curiosity about many things, though he did not regret the passing of the unrestricted elective system which was supposed to encourage it. Any intelligent person could learn some things without "taking a course" in them. He had done that himself. It is part of what libraries and encyclopedias and bibliographies are good for. A lively mind finds its own answers for some of its own questions.

Throughout the Albany address of October 12, 1933, which embodied his mature opinions about the aims of college education as "clear understanding and right thinking," there is the note of underlying continuity beneath apparent random experiment. He summed up his conclusions as follows:

Ever since the middle of the eighteenth century the American college curriculum has been "unfinished business" in our educational endeavors. Sometimes there has seemed to be scant directing intelligence in such endeavors, as we have adopted now this, now that new scheme for curriculum organization, and added now this, now that to the growing list of college studies. But in it all there has been a devoted pursuit of the ideal of richer service to American youth. And now with increasing clearness we see an emerging consciousness that the aim of liberal education is the emancipation of the mind of youth from the shackles of ignorance; of prejudice, which is something other than ignorance; of superficial judgment; and of narrowness of outlook on life. We are seeking constantly a modern equivalent of the great tradition, of the older learning, for the richer service of the men of today and tomorrow. And in this we are true disciples of the men who in 1784 sought by the establishment of this University of the State of New York to insure to the youth of their time and of coming time a full possession of their intellectual heritage.

Educational problems were of no less interest to Rush Rhees at seventy than at forty. His own work was nearly over, but his concern was now with the next generation. Much may be ultimately learned about a teacher's real caliber by noting whether he does or does not drop interest in his profession when it ceases to be his daily occupation. Rush Rhees never did. He was both scholar and teacher all his life; always a teacher because always a learner.

A second engrossing interest of these last five years of his administration was the University Library. Scientific experts had designed their own laboratories and selected their own apparatus for the new campus. For the so-called humanities the library is the laboratory, deserving as much liberality in appropriations and as much care in spending them as the machines and instruments of scientific research. For the first time, and only for the first few years, large appropriations for books were available. In the course of time, before financial stringency required radical cutting of library expenses, the relatively limited college library brought over from Prince Street in 1930 had been greatly augmented in quality as well as in size.

A valuable collection of autograph letters presented by Mr. Charles A. Brown, of the Board of Trustees, a gradually increasing number of rare books acquired by gift or purchase, historical material about Rochester and the Genesee Valley, archives and papers of early Rochesterians, including Lewis H. Morgan, found safe storage in the fireproof quarters of the new building. That it has already become a resort for scholars working on original material is a proof of the wisdom of this policy.

This was a fitting occupation for a scholar's closing years. To collect, to conserve, to exhibit, and to interpret rare books and documents was a privilege which the University of Rochester in its leaner years had coveted in vain for its scholars. Now it began to be possible, and was valued by the President as well as by the librarians, the faculty, and the generous friends of the university. Treasures well guarded and well used have a way of growing by gift and bequest. The Rush Rhees Library has had such gifts, and hopes for more, to honor the name over its doorway, and other names not less illustrious.

These important concerns, improvement of college education and enlargement of library collections, were accompanied by heavy administrative duties at the School of Music and the School of Medicine and Dentistry, already surveyed in preceding chapters. Throughout these later years the complexity of the President's problems necessarily increased. To turn rapidly from one thing to another, with detachment and concentration for each, yet relating all to the ultimate purpose, is to command the order of the day. To withdraw from irrelevant details, delegating much to others, turning always more often toward the center, the true goal, the end which all means serve—this is the mastery of maturity. A wise chief, leaving mistakes behind, discarding the impossible but not the ideal, trusts the future to youth to whom it belongs, and awaits release.

In calling the last five years of Rush Rhees's administration the climax, one should not forget high points earlier and not less dramatic. Each peak in the curve of his life was not the completion of buildings or funds, but a human decision. It was a promise made and given to the world. It was somebody's saying "Yes"; a nod of the head, an elevation in the mind; a signature on paper, which long preceded digging earth, pouring concrete, setting up steel, laying brick, and making speeches of dedication. Celebration of something finished has no such exultation as gratitude and hope for that which is surely begun. Education calls its high festival Commencement; held in the morning, ending at noon.

Likewise the peak of expansion, the climax in the later life of Rush Rhees, was not merely three October days in 1930 when the new campus was dedicated. It was that, plus much that had gone before—absorbing interest in architectural planning on a scale he had never before attempted, almost a Jeffersonian design; looking forward for generations, trying to place buildings where they could always stay and always serve, yet leave plenty of room for more. The climax of that year was not all in October. It was a month's holiday at Cannes with the McCutchens (Uncle Charley's last winter, for he made no more journeys except the long one); a week in Spain, with the art treasures of Madrid and Toledo; then England for the spring; a weekend at Grasmere, with memories of Wordsworth, and of the world that "is too much with us." The past came back, the future came swiftly on. Summers are short at seventy. That was the year, with its life and death and "aspect of eternity," of which his mind must have been full when he sat in his presidential chair at the Henry A. Strong Auditorium among his guests, and listened to their words of wisdom. Thirty years seemed like a day, for the future was so long, so short, so wonderful.

One who was not there that day had already said his word. This was Dr. John H. Finley, of the New York *Times*, with whom Rush Rhees had ties not only of friendship but of spiritual affinity. After many years as a college president, at Knox College and the College of the City of New York, he had become commissioner of education of the state, and then since 1921 had been associate editor of the *Times*. His editorial of October 9, entitled "Rochester's New Glory," after describing the greatly enlarged facilities of the university, closed with the following paragraph, exalting, as he always did, men above things:

Rochester has again shown what a city whose prevailing ambitions are qualitative rather than quantitative can do in the higher ranges of community life. She has had, to be sure, her Eastman, her Strongs, her Sibleys, her Cutlers, her Wards, her Bausches and Lombs, among others who have given largely. And she has had her Todd, and above all her Rush Rhees. But the people generally have joined those of the alumni in an effort whose consummation will be celebrated during the next three days. Town and gown are one in their rejoicing.

Whenever John Finley came to Rochester, and whenever he and Rush Rhees met elsewhere, there was that perfect kind of meeting in which men of opposite temperament and similar character greet each other across the gap. Dr. Finley was exuberant, demonstrative, frankly affectionate toward those he liked. Rush Rhees was restrained, unable except on rare occasions to let himself go. They understood each other. A quiet man is lucky to have one hearty friend. Rush Rhees had many such besides Dr. Finley—Shailer Mathews, George Vincent, some of his Amherst classmates, some of his own trustees, some of the older alumni. Such men in a crisis or a climax all stand together.

On his seventy-first birthday, February 8, 1931, Rush Rhees received the congratulations of his friends and of the public with modest self-depreciation, giving all credit for what had been achieved to the workers and givers who had "made the dream a reality," to use his own phrase. But on the next day in New York, at the dinner of the Society of the Genesee where the guest of honor was George Eastman, there was beneath his own and others' speeches a kind of finality. Mr. Eastman was not a well man. He would never be really better, but he would keep up for another year. During 1931 he was persuaded, rather against his will, to have his portrait painted again. There was already a good likeness at the Chamber of Commerce, but others were commissioned by the university for the Eastman School of Music and the Rush Rhees Library. In dedicating this latter portrait, on December 2, 1931, the President said:

Although we have not been permitted to use his name here, he has consented to allow us to have his portrait here. His picture was painted recently by Mr. Charles Hopkinson of Boston, the artist who painted also the portrait in the Chamber of Commerce. There he has represented the great business leader; here, the man of idealistic vision, confident of greater good to be realized in the coming years, ready by great gifts to contribute towards the realization of that greater future, and rejoicing constantly in his ability to see in his own lifetime his gifts at work for that high end. We and those who follow after we are gone will have in this portrait a perpetual reminder of our greatest benefactor, and our challenge to render service worthy of the great confidence reposed in us.

On the same wall with the portrait of Mr. Eastman hangs one of President Rhees, painted by the same artist, by order of the trustees. Both portraits show strength. Neither shows enough benevolence. Paint cannot capture that, which, gleaming just an instant in the eyes and around the mouth, lasts forever in recollection. Life is off the record.

George Eastman's death on March 14, 1932, was a tragic peak in the drama of Rush Rhees. That death could not have been long postponed, and none was wise enough or good enough to judge the manner of it. Silence was best. Yet though speech is inadequate, decorum and respect for the opinion of mankind often require some public utterance. Rush Rhees wrote for the trustees a resolution of which the conclusion was as follows:

Our largest benefactor in gifts, he was still more our boldest leader in the adoption of the highest ambitions. And he rejoiced to see his gifts at work, aiding us in the pursuit of such ambitions. And now he tells his friends that his work is done. For him, as respects active participation, this is sadly true. For us who carry on what he has inspired, his work is only just begun. Only the future years will be able to measure the greatness of that continuing work. With us is left the task of grateful determination to make that measure adequate. "Farewell and hail" are the greetings we must give to him who has passed now into the silence. But for us he will never be silent, but rather eloquent with ever renewed challenge to seek for the University to which he gave his faith and confidence ever those "better things" which reach constantly after the best.

At the memorial service in Eastman Theater on March 23, 1932, where Rush Rhees gave the principal address, it is significant to record that there was no funeral march or note of lamentation. The program included the Good Friday music from *Parsifal*, the Cavatina from Beethoven's Thirteenth Quartet in B-flat major, a Tragic Symphony for organ and strings by Locatelli, and an Elegy for orchestra and chorus by Howard Hanson. Tranquillity and noble remembrance rose above sorrow.

That was the quality of the memorable year 1932. After a few weeks in England the Rheeses spent the summer as usual at Islesford in Maine. It ended with a great spectacle, never forgotten by any who witnessed it, the total eclipse of the sun on August 31, seen in the narrow zone of totality in an unclouded sky. Thousands of people who journeyed to Maine or New Hampshire solely for that event were prevented by local clouds from seeing what they came for. Rush Rhees had inquired in advance from the professor of astronomy at Rochester what were the special features to be noted, and was told that they were the corona, beads of light seen on the edge of the sun, shadow bands moving rapidly over the ground just before and after totality, and stars and planets near the sun. In replying to his adviser, he wrote:

The Rhees family drove on August 31 to the line of totality of the eclipse, not far from Lewiston, Maine. Unlike the experience of the investigators who had set up their apparatus in the White Mountain region, we had an absolutely clear sky and a marvelous sight of the whole performance. The corona was worth the entire price of admission. The only one of the planets that I noticed at the period of totality I took to be Jupiter.

So closed the second and so began the third of those last five college years. A great death, a great darkness, and a great glory. None lasted long.

When Mr. Eastman's will revealed that in addition to leaving his residence to the university for a president's house, with an endowment for maintenance, he had given to it most of his residuary estate, minus certain special bequests, the magnitude of his final generosity seemed at first incredible. Some Rochester people had got so used to seeing in the newspapers new Eastman gifts of millions to the university that they could not realize in this last act of his life the true climax of his whole career.

It was also in one sense the major climax of Rush Rhees's administration. The special sense in which it was a university climax was not the delusive prospect of unexpected luxury and ease, but rather a great burden of responsibility. It took several months for the executors to appraise the estate, discharge immediate obligations, and report the market value, which greatly increased the productive assets of the university. This might seem to be cause for unqualified rejoicing, as if it would lift from the financial officers of the institution all anxiety about future deficits and retrenchment. Yet it must not be forgotten that all this late prosperity of the university after 1929 came at a time of serious economic disturbance, widespread unemployment, political uneasiness, and international unrest. Between the election in November and the inauguration in March, 1933, this country passed through a severe financial crisis. The guardians of a great fortune, even in gilt-edged stocks and bonds, could take no chances. Instead of more money to spend, there was less. Economies were called for, costly improvements had to be postponed, expected increases in the teaching force were canceled. To protect the ultimate reserves, to avoid the danger of drawing on liquid assets for immediate uses that might impair the whole future of the funds, was the difficult duty of the administration.

Rush Rhees did not have to settle these questions himself, for the treasurer and the Finance Committee were charged with that duty. But as himself a trustee, and also as a director of a Rochester bank and of the Eastman Kodak Company, he was not immune from emergency business decisions. They weighed heavily on him, and strengthened his desire for early retirement. The presidency was now becoming a task so difficult, so many-sided, so perplexing, that, quite apart from its educational program, it called for a younger and stronger man. His resignation had been in the hands of the trustees since 1930, but he began to suggest that it be taken off the table. A fixed opinion that educators should retire at seventy, unless for some special reason they might be asked to continue briefly on yearly appointment, led him to apply the same principle to his own case.

In June, 1932, the Rheeses moved their possessions from their old house at 440 University Avenue into storage, and in September took up their residence at 900 East Avenue, now named Eastman House by the trustees. It was a wrench to leave the old home where they had lived through so much happiness, and through not a little sickness and trouble too; rooms full of associations with children now grown up and gone, rooms where time had clothed antiquity with charm and age with hospitality. They went knowing that it was not for long. They had disposed of old belongings, burned old letters, cleared out cupboards and attics, and said good-bye to the past. That was not easy, even though the house was not to be torn down but used as a women's co-operative dormitory. By vote of the trustees it became Harriet Seelye House, and shelters each year some hard-working, bright young women, who

EASTMAN HOUSE, PRESIDENT RHEES'S RESIDENCE, 1932-1935

PRESIDENT RHEES RECEIVES THE STUDENTS' FAREWELL GIFT

do their own cooking as well as their own thinking. The girls know in a vague way that here was once a center of grace and culture, now a center of economy, study, and ambition. In time all five may grow together. Something lingers at 440 besides the cheerful young transients, with their reading and talk, eating and sleeping; something old and fine, something wise and kind. Someday they may become aware of it; perhaps long after they have left it, as is the way of youth. It is hardly too much to say that the University of Rochester was born in that house. Quite as much as Anderson Hall it holds the past. Presidents Anderson and Hill lived there before the Rheeses came. It is nearly as old as the university. Famous men have been its guests. Patrician ladies of the old school have poured tea and coffee there. Many young seniors at June receptions have danced around the west room, before they danced away. If the walls of Harriet Seelye House could speak, they might tell more than our generation can understand. It takes time to season a house, a family, or a college. Give it a hundred years.

Entering Eastman House was for the Rheeses not a triumph but a tribute. For twenty-six years Mr. Eastman had filled it with treasures, trophies, music, and friends. Those years were full of great events, and the house was full of the years. It was not a manse, but a mansion; not a place to stay, but a gallery for exhibition. One felt obliged to share it generously with people who used to come. There should be music, for the organ, which in the past had sounded daily, must not be always closed. There should be flowers, for the gardeners were busy growing them, and they would not last. There should be work for the large household staff. The lofty conservatory in the center of the house, where the organ was, with palms, orchids, and vines, and a great elephant's head on the wall, called for guests. When it was empty it asked why.

In other rooms one could not be lonely, for there were the old masters. Rembrandt and Van Dyck, Franz Hals and Tintoretto, Reynolds and Raeburn, brilliant heads and figures, soldiers and gallants, seigniors in splendid robes, ladies in lace and satin. Highborn faces under shaded lights glowed with the pride of power and position, the charm of youth, or the commanding gaze of age. These were all of the old regime. Their place was secure. Their searching eyes asked, "What are you doing here?" But after proper introductions they could be gracious; in time they made all welcome who recognized their rank, their right, their serene permanence. Aristocrats on the walls make Eastman House a palace. Time cannot change their beauty. While they remain, the proud new world can see what the old world was. In their presence it is hard to feel superior.

It must be hard to live up to art every day. The Rheeses undertook it, and held the trust nearly three years. They left things just as they were. Change would be for their successors to decide. With ample guest rooms and efficient service, they could now entertain visitors to the university with more dignity and state, though not with more cordiality of welcome, than in the old house, which had always been crowded at Commencement. Here, too, they could have the annual luncheon for the Board of Trustees in June, after the business of the year had been transacted and the President had made his annual report.

In times of illness the spaciousness and luxury of Eastman House, with its admirable service, its elevator, its quiet and protection from interruptions, were all appreciated. The gardens were a delight. The President's automobile and chauffeur were always ready for a pleasure drive or a long journey. Nothing was like the old simple times when dollars were counted and monthly bills brought unexpected problems. All was smooth and safe and easy—all but living. An emperor said, "It is possible to live well even in a palace"—difficult, but possible. So they found it. Those last three years in office were not the happiest, but nearest to what might have been envied by those whose life is dependent on material things.

In the late spring of 1933 Rush Rhees found it possible to arrange for two academic events which gave him much pleasure. One was to preach a baccalaureate sermon at the

University of Toronto and receive its honorary LL.D., to add to others given many years before by Amherst and McMaster. His relations with Toronto had been close throughout his administration, and this final honor was most welcome. The other date was at Amherst, where his class was to hold its fiftieth anniversary in June. The Rochester faculty and trustees altered the date of the Rochester Commencement in order to permit him to preside at his class reunion. That was a joyful occasion, and according to reports he relaxed among the other gray heads and was one of the boys. Classmates who survived him have written in reply to inquiries that he had become much less reserved in his later years, more friendly and genial. "He let us see the richness of his sympathy and his understanding of the problems and difficulties his classmates had had to meet, and his deep appreciation of what the lives even of those who had been less fortunate and favored had meant to the world."

On June 10, 1933, he presented to the Rochester trustees the following renewal of his resignation:

Three years ago, having recently passed my seventieth birthday, I submitted to you my resignation as President of the University, to be effective at your pleasure and convenience. You declined to accept the resignation at that time, and I consented to continue as President for a limited period.

Convinced that it is best both for the University and for my own personal interests, I now renew my resignation, with the earnest request that it be accepted, to become effective as soon as you can select a man to take up the work which I desire to lay down.

One is reminded of Dr. Johnson, who, when reproached for not carrying on a task on which he thought he had done enough, replied: "No, Sir, I am not obliged to do any more. No man is obliged to do as much as he can do. A man is to have part of his life to himself."

The Board of Trustees regretfully accepted his resignation, but asked for plenty of time in which to find his successor. This proved to be more than the year he had hoped would be sufficient. In October at the University Convocation in Albany he made the address on "Liberal Education—Then and Now," already referred to. It marked for him the end of an era in state education; he had been active in it for thirty years, and his energetic utterances and efficient committee work put Rochester on the educational map long before material prosperity began to advertise it abroad.

The year 1934 wore on without a new president. In June, 1933, he had written to his friend Louis Wiley, of the New York *Times*:

Your letter with reference to my resignation is very generous and it is warmly appreciated. I hope that during the years of relative leisure I may be able to be of some use in the world.

In June, 1934, he wrote to his friend and classmate President E. S. Parsons of Marietta College:

I have been requested to carry on for another year. Frankly, however, I shall be very glad when administrative duties, including the writing of baccalaureates, annual reports, and other similar compositions, will be passed on to somebody else.

One pleasant interlude of the year was the belated presentation of a Polish decoration for his services in connection with the Community Chest during and after World War I. It reminded the Rheeses of a Serbian decoration he had received in 1923. That one was hung around his neck in public by a foreign lady, who stepped so close to reach that he said to her after the ceremony, "I thought you were going to kiss me." She answered, "When we get home I will," and she did.

In those days the Rheeses often spent Christmas in Boston, with Jack's family and with other relatives. It was well that so many family reunions, in Boston, Maine, and England came while they could be enjoyed to the full. There could be no more quite so free from anxiety. In January, 1935, Rush Rhees had his first attack of angina, warning of coronary weakness which meant long rest and care. He had been working too hard, trying to clear up all details of executive business before leaving office. By advice of his physician, instead of staying at home he was allowed to take a cruise to the West Indies with Mrs. Rhees and his aunt and cousin, the McCutchens. After a few days he was able to get up on deck, and the complete rest and sea air did much to restore his strength. Returning to Rochester, he remained under the doctor's orders for the rest of the spring, and was able to do a part of his official business by strictly conserving his strength. Care gave him nearly four years more.

The trustees had elected to the presidency Alan Valentine, Master of Pierson College at Yale, educated at Swarthmore and Oxford, and for a time connected with the Oxford University Press, a young scholar of energy, wide acquaintance, and keen appreciation of the responsibilities and opportunities of the university. To him and to his gifted wife, Lucia Garrison Norton, a descendant of William Lloyd Garrison, the duties and amenities of Eastman House would henceforth be entrusted.

For the future comfort and security of Rush and Harriet Rhees the trustees had purchased a commodious and attractive residence a few blocks out East Avenue, equipped with an elevator for infirmities unfit for stairs. It had a library for study, rooms large enough for the club meetings which remained an occasional part of each season's hospitality—everything for quiet living, in the only city they could now call home. But they had planned to spend the first free year after retirement in Europe, and still hoped to be able to do so.

As the end of the college year approached, the President was no longer expected to do much in the way of routine arrangements for Commencement. A substitute was appointed for the baccalaureate sermon, which had long been a strain. He wrote his last annual report to the trustees, which ended thus:

I cannot close this report without sentiments of profound thankfulness for the fullness and cordiality of co-operation which have been given your executive from the first to the last of his thirty-five years of service. They have been happy years; full of interest, rewarded by loyal friendships won in your Board, in your faculties, and among our students. . . . The opportunity which opens before our University is thrilling and challenging. Each year that may come will add to my sense of high privilege in having been associated with you and my faculty comrades in the development already attained. Each year will add to my gratitude for affectionate regard so constantly and abundantly shown, affection which I reciprocate in fullest measure.

There was the last faculty meeting, on June 13. The notes for his talk to the faculty before taking up the business of the day are preserved on a single page in his little black book. They are as follows:

Greeting—happy to meet once more; sorry to play the truant still.
Appreciation:
  Assembled intelligence. Note 1896-1900 and steady development of
    college.
  Spirit of co-operation. Priceless heritage and responsibility.
  Loyal friendliness. A treasure for all coming years.
  Habitual patience and tolerance. N.B. "The General Confession."
Our rare good fortunes:
  The growth of thirty-five years;
  The constancy of insistence on quality;
  The vista of the future.
Our new leader:
  Trust him;
  Work with him;
  Love him;
  And never quote Rhees to him.

The faculty told him what they thought of him, in words of warm appreciation for his unfailing courtesy, fairness, modesty, and patience, as well as of congratulation for the unparalleled progress during his long term of office. There were not many teachers present who had been in the faculty when he came, but those few felt as if they had seen a lifetime pass in review.

The last meeting of the Board of Trustees was not held at Eastman House as twice before, owing to the strain on the President, who had to save his strength for Commencement. It was in the beautiful new Cutler Union on the old campus, recently completed. At the close of his address to the trustees he said:

I have not come to you with a valedictory. There isn't going to be any. I met the faculty on Thursday afternoon, and being a little fearful of the excitement of lachrymary glands, it occurred to me that I might

ALAN VALENTINE AND RUSH RHEES

very properly apply to my own situation the experiences of an eminent person who was lying in what was supposed to be his last illness, and surrounded by a number of solicitous friends. He noticed that one of them was surreptitiously putting his hand under the covers and feeling of his feet, and also limbs up to his knees, evidently desiring to get the first indications of the approach of the chill of death, and he opened his eyes, and he winked at them, and he said, "I ain't dead yet."

It is difficult for me to over-emphasize the privilege of association with the members of this Board from the first time of my contact with you until this hour. I appreciate your constant interest. I appreciate your judgment, which I was going to characterize as sound but for the fact that I have sometimes felt that you were a little lacking in readiness to criticize the proposals of your executive; but that intensifies the appreciation that I have of the relations which we have had together. Your unstinted support of your executive has made the years happy.

But above all I value the rich prize of your friendship of which I have been conscious during all these years—friendship lavish in its generosity of feeling, a prize which will continue with me during all my conscious life—here or hereafter. You need hardly be told that I appreciate, and I cannot tell you how deeply I appreciate the very liberal provision which you have made for my comfort and Mrs. Rhees's comfort in the years that remain to us for residence in Rochester. For Rochester will continue to be our home, although this coming year we propose to indulge ourselves in a desire we have cherished for a good many years of spending some time on the other side of the sea; but we hope for continued fellowship under the guidance of your new leader.

It will be the grief of my life if under your new leader you give any indication that you are turning to your old friend for suggestions with reference to the administration of the University of Rochester.

The vista of the future is alluring. I can think of no institution in this country which has such possibilities or has such a measure of freedom from the necessity which besets most endowed institutions. My particular plea to you, unnecessary I know, is to trust your new leader as you have trusted me, to trust him as I am confident he is worthy of your trust; to work with him and love him, and by all that is holy, never quote Rhees to him.

Now gentlemen, if I may be excused, I will revert to the conditions of bondage in which I have lived in these last months, and go away back and sit down—but possibly I may confidentially say, go home and lie down.

In reply to the word of one of the trustees, "We are not going to say good-bye," he said as he left the room, "Not good-bye then, but good morning."

There remained Commencement, on June 17, 1935, when he had to award degrees and to give the address to the graduating class. The subject of it was the duties which accompany the "rights and privileges" to which they had just been admitted. Social, economic, and civic responsibilities must be accepted. Ethical standards of the community and of the chosen profession must be more highly regarded than personal advantage. "So, my young friends, we send you out with joy. Your way will not always be smooth, but your spirits can be unbowed as you quit yourselves like men." A Pauline farewell.

During all these last public appearances he showed, notwithstanding some physical weakness, his power of will that commanded calmness when most men would have faltered, his power of looking back without too much emotion, and of looking forward without apprehension. All his long life he had concealed feelings when they were too strong and mastered obligations when they seemed too great. Now, though his heart was weak, his mind was firm, his words precise, his will supreme. At the end as at the beginning of his public life he seemed to rule not by feeling but by reason. Really he ruled and lived by faith—his faith in his reason, his faith in himself, his faith in others, and his faith in God. He was justified by faith; for what he believed, he was.

XVI

PERSONALITY

What another would have done as well as you, do not do it. What another would have said as well as you, do not say it. What another would have written as well, do not write it. Stick to what exists nowhere but in you. Fit yourself to fill a place that no one else can.—André Gide

Höchstes Glück der Erdenkinder
Liegt in der Persönlichkeit.—Goethe

Cogito, ergo sum.—Descartes

HE COULD HAVE BEEN almost anything he wished. A teacher or a preacher who could not have done anything else is not much good at that. He was good at both; also a good businessman, a scholar, writer, and speaker, an executive and organizer, a carpenter and cabinetmaker, even a general handy man in a pinch. He was a golfer, though not a sportsman. In his youth he declined an editorial position on the *Youth's Companion,* but he became another kind of companion to youth. He might not have succeeded as an artist, but would have been a good builder. He would have been an excellent banker; a good lawyer, a better judge; a poor politician, but a good governor. He had too much truth for some professions, too few illusions for others.

On the other hand, though he handled chisel and plane with precision, he never could run a typewriter without making mistakes. He was a good loser, but other people had to retrieve what he lost. Without a guardian he might have missed engagements and left many letters unanswered. In early days, his papers, so he said, had a perverse way of getting buried under other papers, turning up just in the nick of time for belated reply. Credit must be given to his secretaries for saving him from many embarrassments, and to his wife for remembering what he forgot.

These details are mentioned for the enlightenment and consolation of alumni and friends who supposed that "Prexy" was too perfect to be human. Far from it. He had the defects of his virtues. He had no redeeming vices, unless smoking a pipe is a vice for a Baptist minister. People may wonder what a good man says when he hits his thumb with a hammer. The answer is, he doesn't hit his thumb, he always hits the nail; that is why he is good.

When he lost things, he always tried to get them back. If he left a memorandum book or a toilet case on a train or in a hotel, he would write or telegraph immediately, often with success. His laundry returned studs and cuff links left in his dress shirts, and was always thanked for this carefulness. On one occasion it took several weeks to find out the name and address of a laundress to whom he was thus indebted, because she had been away on account of illness. He wrote her:

Dear Madam:

In response to my request the laundry has informed me that you were the lady who so thoughtfully called my attention to the fact that I had left a pair of cuff-links in a shirt which I had sent to be laundered. Recognizing that what you did was a part of your routine duty, I also recognize that you secured me from loss of cuff-links whose value to me is due to associations which are of much more importance than the actual value of the articles. I therefore ask you to allow me to hand you the enclosed check as an expression of that appreciation.

He had a way of putting an important letter in a pocket letter case, in order to consider it at leisure before replying. When he changed his clothes he would forget all about it, and ask his secretary to find the paper which should have been on his desk. He never blamed anybody but himself for such lapses, and his apologies, though humorous, were abject. Engagements entered on his desk pad, unless he copied them into his little red pocket diary, might easily be forgotten.

Fortunately his absent-mindedness never had serious results. It was a source of endless diversion to his office associates.

Considering the fact that he was an extremely observant person in some ways, the following incident will show why it was sometimes impossible to take him seriously. During the family's summer absence in Maine, the superintendent of maintenance in Rochester reported to the treasurer that something must be done about repairing the cupola on top of the President's house on Prince Street. It was one of those quaint old glassed-in structures, with windows on all sides, meant perhaps for viewing the landscape or the stars; rather a conspicuous Victorian survival, neither beautiful nor bad, but of no earthly use. Since the wood was much decayed and there were likely to be leaks, the treasurer asked the superintendent why he didn't just take it off the house, mend the roof, and say nothing about it. The superintendent did not care to take the responsibility without consulting the President, but the treasurer did not like to bother the chief during his vacation, and promised to stand back of the superintendent if there was any trouble. Off came the cupola.

During the first week after the President's return, as he sat in his office right across the street, and walked back and forth many times a day, the treasurer expected inquiries. There were none. The next week nothing happened. It began to look as if the President was seriously offended and took this way of showing it. After a month or so, the treasurer got tired of waiting for the showdown. They were walking along Prince Street, and he said:

"Dr. Rhees, do you notice anything different about your house?" The President took a look.

"No, what's wrong with it?"

"Take another look. Look at the roof." A light dawned, a grin spread. He was slow to notice, but quick to react. Instantly he replied:

"The king has lost his crown and didn't know it."

There were other occasions when he did notice things and

ignored them. There was the time when some student hid an alarm clock inside the chapel pulpit in Anderson Hall, the repeating kind for refractory early risers, set to go off during the prayer, and pause, and then ring again and again until it was turned off. It worked all right, but the President went right on praying and never cracked a smile. What he prayed for is not known. Another time there was tissue paper woven among the piano strings so that when the pianist began to play the hymn it sounded like a banjo. The presidential face could not have been more impassive if he had held four aces.

He did remarkable things with that frozen expression. Whispering or reading in chapel he would not tolerate, but never spoke of it. He would simply stop speaking and stare fixedly at the offender. Silence and that stare set up converging lines of force all over the room, centering on one spot, so that the spot turned red. One such boy wrote him:

Last Thursday morning I caused an interruption in the chapel exercises by so far forgetting myself as to give my attention to the person sitting next to me rather than to you. I humbly beg your pardon for the offence, and assure you that the silent reprimand which you administered was so humiliating as to be constantly on my mind and so to prevent any recurrence of such an interruption on my part. Trusting that you see my position, and credit me with thoughtlessness rather than with malicious intent, I am,

Very sincerely yours.

The reply was characteristic of the President's courtesy and underlying kindness of heart toward all such youthful breaches of good manners. He knew that good manners were going out of fashion, and could not be directly taught at college age, but hoped for the best when delayed adolescents finally grew up. He wrote:

I sincerely appreciate your letter received this morning, and desire in the first place to say that the episode to which you refer had entirely passed from my mind, but that I was perfectly sure that your attention to the matter which you were reading in chapel was due to an inadvertence. Please rest assured that I shall remember nothing of the episode except the pleasure which I find in your own manly letter. That will remain as an additional element in the regard in which I have ever held you, both for your own sake and on your father's account. With sincere friendliness,

Very sincerely yours.

Much may be learned about a busy man by the way in which he answers letters from children, and from young people who attribute to him omniscience. There was a time when Rochester school children were encouraged to write to prominent citizens requesting a favorite quotation or precept, to be copied into their composition books for some class project. A seventh-grade pupil wrote to President Rhees:

Our class is making a scrapbook which has to contain a quotation for every day of the year. It is to be named "A Thought a Day." We have selected the names of some few outstanding men and women to ask for help in our project. Will you be so generous as to give us some thought or quotation that has helped you in your success? We will greatly appreciate your kindness, and will esteem it a great favor.

He answered:

The thought which has been helpful to me is that expressed in Ecclesiastes 9:10, "Whatsoever thy hand findeth to do, do it with thy might." In your class scrapbook, "A Thought a Day," you may use this quotation as being my selection.

To another schoolgirl who inquired "What book that you read before you were sixteen years old made the greatest impression on you?" he replied:

It is quite difficult to canvass my memory of literary interest prior to my sixteenth year in reply to your inquiry. I should say that, after the Bible, Bunyan's *Pilgrim's Progress* would probably be the book I should name.

He wrote many letters to distressed fathers and mothers whose sons had been placed on probation or required to withdraw. When they brought charges of unfair treatment, he gave them the facts; but when they admitted the facts and merely wanted him to know how grieved and surprised they were at the collapse of all their hopes, he was kind. In such cases he seldom or never changed his mind, but tried to show them that the boy's best interests lay in making a fresh start somewhere else, generally to earn his own living. College was not a nursery or a psychiatric clinic. The boy had already had his second chance; there was no third.

When a student or former student died, he often wrote letters of sympathy. When he was thanked by the mother of a student killed in World War I for his remarks at the funeral, he replied:

I am particularly glad of your word concerning the importance of respecting the sanctuary of sorrow of those who are under the shadow of grief. I have felt that keenly in the past, a feeling which has been intensified by experiences of not a few funerals.

He found many new ways of applying the Golden Rule. When a Chinese exchange student, arriving after the beginning of the term and unaccustomed to the country, was due early Saturday morning, and might not know where to go or how to get there, Rush Rhees met the train at six o'clock, but the boy did not appear. Later came a telegram explaining that he had missed the train but would come the next day. Sunday morning at six the President was at the station again, brought his guest home, kept him over the weekend, and on Monday found him temporary lodging at the Y.M.C.A. The thing one notices most is that he went himself; he did not delegate hospitality. He never became too important or too busy to do a small kindness, and never talked about it.

For several persons with exceptionally poor eyesight, who could get no relief from ordinary glasses, he arranged to have special lenses and frames fitted by an expert. The grateful wearers of these costly optical instruments would never have known where to go or how to pay for them. Money was not mentioned. Not merely by generosity but by intelligent understanding he had helped them to see the world as it is. They never asked him; he saw for himself that they could not see.

It never occurs to some college officials that a newly arrived student may be not only lonely and poor but actually hungry. It did occur to Rush Rhees. When he saw that hungry look he wasted no words in sympathetic consolation but fed the freshman and helped him to get started. An alumnus of early days wrote:

Dr. Rhees literally fulfilled the ancient injunction. I was hungry and he took me to his home for a square meal, after which he gave me the money to pay a month's board. I was ill clad, and he gave me the money to buy clothes. He found me steady employment during most of my college years. He never pauperized me. It was all on a "strictly business" basis. I borrowed the money and was obligated to return it. My orders were to find boys who were in trouble of any sort, to report them to him, and to keep quiet about it.

No man handicapped by natural reserve and shyness ever made more genuine and habitual attempts to show the friendliness he really felt. When the faculty was small, more or less like one big family, there would be a faculty party on the campus in the autumn or spring. The Rheeses would join heartily in the games, charades, or even "going to Jerusalem," with young instructors and their wives. Early in the summer there might be a faculty picnic in one of the parks. The President knew the faculty children, remembered their names, and would inquire for them in later years. Even if he was not equally interested in all the boys and girls whose fathers taught in his college, he knew that their parents were; it was a point of contact outside the profession, which he somehow craved.

Once he was mistaken for a grandfather by the tiny daughter of a school principal in another town, to whose home he went for dinner before being taken to the school for a Commencement address. Here was a short, stout, gray-haired gentleman with a little gray mustache, blue eyes, and a smile. He must be grandpa; she ran to him with a happy greeting. For a moment he did not know quite how to meet it, but then she was welcomed as any little girl should be if she wants to be.

In dealing with people outside the academic group he learned how to be all things to all men. He seldom talked back or argued with quarrelsome or obnoxious opponents. He once wrote: "I am a great believer in the policy of letting silence cure opposition." Once by expert advice he departed widely from this rule. It was in the early days of the Community Chest, when as chairman of the budget committee he had to meet all delegations from local organizations which wished to protest against alleged inadequacy of appropriations voted by the committee. A group of foreign-born representatives from a local charity came to the office and raised a storm. His quiet and pleasant explanations were unavailing. They departed muttering, with excited gestures of both upturned hands. Rush Rhees consulted a prominent citizen accustomed to dealing with that sort of interview.

"They stormed and shouted and pounded the table," said Rush Rhees. "I gave them all the figures, but they pounded all the more."

"Did you pound the table?"

"No, of course not. Why should I pound the table?"

"You must pound the table, doctor. They expect it. When they shout, you shout too. When they pound, you should pound harder. Just try it."

When the delegation returned at the appointed time, the chairman closed the door of the conference room, but a little company of eavesdroppers listened outside. Presently voices rose, the table was thumped. The listeners winked at each other as Rush Rhees's voice rose above the tumult and drowned out all the rest. He pounded the table; he put on a good act; he laid down the law; he may even have waved upturned hands, though no one watched at the keyhole. The uproar soon subsided to a cheerful murmur. When the door opened, everybody was smiling and shaking hands like old friends.

Patience and humility are virtues at the right time and the right place, but should not be overdone. Perhaps in early youth Rush Rhees had been too timid to assert himself, and had, as the jargon goes, overcompensated. At any rate, he replied as follows to a former theological student who was thinking of leaving the pastorate to become a teacher and had asked advice:

I believe that you are thoroughly competent to undertake advanced work and to master a subject as a teacher. I believe also that you can teach, or do anything else that you wish to turn to, provided you have gained or can gain a certain element of self-assertion, which will displace the hesitancy and shyness which characterized your work as a student. I think you never would be likely to err in the direction of conceit. I therefore do not hesitate to mention this qualification of self-assertion as one which you will need to cultivate if you are to be a successful teacher.

To one of his own subordinates, who secretly regarded the President's written and spoken style as excellent but sometimes rather elaborate and formal, he said in friendly counsel, "Cultivate the lighter touch." If what he meant was "Cultivate a lighter touch than either yours or mine," it was certainly good advice; both needed it.

In 1903 a minister who had known him at Newton, and had heard him in a public address since his going to Rochester, wrote commending what he called Rush Rhees's "aggressiveness" in his defense of the small college and its bid for students. He meant well, but the patronizing tone in which Rochester was mentioned did not altogether please, as the reply indicated:

I thank you for your reply to my letter. I shall be glad of any practical result that comes from my "aggressiveness." You need not to be told that a college of Rochester's size does not seek to compete with Harvard in respect of wealth of opportunity and fullness of equipment. In respect of efficiency of education, and the invaluable influence of personal contact between mature instructors and young men, Rochester and other small colleges are venturesome enough not to shrink from close comparison with the larger institutions. This I say simply in justification of the "aggressiveness" which you admire. The large colleges have what we cannot offer. They very often lack that which is our chief strength; hence our readiness to enter the lists with them.

He met many people who had too much self-assertion with too little back of it worth asserting. Some of them later realized this. An alumnus some years out of college wrote:

I have since come to know that the best of worth-while progressive accomplishments come about by growth and development and not by fiat. Time has convicted me of my ignorance and crowned your wisdom. This is my confession—contrite and sincere. I have come to know you better since I left Anderson Hall than you ever let me know you there, and to appreciate your worth.

The President replied:

You and I did not always agree with reference to University policy, but I think we always respected each other's independence and honesty. At least I know that I did yours.

When his advice was asked, as it often was, by men considering a change of occupation or of a place of work, he rarely gave any positive opinion except this—that he strongly disapproved of dropping an unfinished task in order to find something easier. Ministers, after a year or two in a difficult pastorate, would get an offer at a higher salary elsewhere, and wished him to confirm their "divine call" to accept it. He never did. Occasionally one of his own professors would fail him suddenly in midsummer, with complete irresponsibility as to the outcome. Concerning one such incident he wrote to a non-resident trustee:

With reference to difficulties concerning which you speak, I wonder whether you are familiar with a bit of doggerel which Mrs. Rhees's father used frequently to quote, which runs something like this:

> Some of our ills we have cured;
> The rest we have somehow survived;
> But what terrible woes we've endured
> From those that never arrived.

The philosophy contained in these lines has long been a comfort to me. As a consequence I try to avoid those which are never going to arrive, and to take with a reasonable amount of humor those which in their passing give proof that difficulties may be survived.

Much of Rush Rhees's best philosophy was undoubtedly conveyed in conversations of which there was no record. He had no Boswell, and was not given to Johnsonian talk. But many must have felt like a university president who wrote him in 1913:

I have in my mind an interrupted conversation with you at some hotel—I know not where—which left a deep impression on me. Why is it that we cannot meet the people with whom we really want to talk, and each day must meet those to whom we have nothing to say, and who have nothing to convey to us? Geography is an impertinence and an interruption to life.

Ten years earlier another correspondent wrote:

I wonder if you realize the depth of my appreciation of your talk with me in Rochester. This increased when I learned afterward how very busy you were at the time, and how many things you had to decline to undertake because of the pressure you were in. The block of time you gave me out of that afternoon had a higher value than I knew, and I question whether I deserved it. Yet you set before me very clearly an aim in self-discipline and as well stimulated me to effort in it. Therefore I cannot regret your giving me the time even at such cost. Please know that I prize the interview.

Rush Rhees wrote to another friend:

I would give a good deal for an opportunity to sit down and have an old-fashioned chat with you. The years roll on and our work grows daily more complex, limiting the freedom of human fellowship that would delight us all.

He helped many men to rise in the world. It was his belief that sometimes the best way to help a young man was to encourage him to burn his bridges and start a new career, always provided he was capable of it. He did not think any man worth his salt was tied down for life merely because he had picked the wrong profession, or married young, or settled down in a soft job at good pay. Ambition for Rhees of Rochester meant "going around" to find something worth doing, and doing it.

There was an able man in the college office working at clerical tasks which had no future. He would have been a convenient man to keep. Instead of praising him and using him, Rush Rhees practically kicked him upstairs. He did this, not by writing a letter of recommendation full of smooth phrases that could have been made with a rubber stamp, but by traveling seventy-five miles for a personal interview with a prospective employer for his assistant. This took a day of his time, and cost him a lot of trouble in finding a successor. He did that for several young secretaries in later years—kept them just to the point where they were too good to stay, and then helped them along. He never used men as if they were tools. He was more ambitious for others than for himself. He would do a lot of "running around" to keep a good man from getting stuck in a rut. Dead ends for youth he deplored, all the more if well paid.

Mention has already been made of Rush Rhees's friendships with men of somewhat more genial and expansive temperament than his own. The way in which he responded to their familiar letters shows how hard he tried to play up to them. On one occasion, when he had accepted an invitation from Shailer Mathews to preach at Chicago although it conflicted with other engagements, Dean Mathews began his letter of thanks: "You are as good a Christian as I, and that is saying a good deal." Several years later Mathews wrote: "I look back on my visits and talks with you as typical of the good times we are going to have in Heaven, where theology does not consume, and administrative duties do not break through and steal our time and friendship."

Friendship and religion were not far apart for Rush Rhees. Both were forms of comradeship, for which he felt a hunger as keen as his sense of partial unfitness for it. Of others and of their religion he sometimes said what his friends could have said of him, as for example this tribute to Augustus H. Strong:

His religious thought and feeling were the breath of his life, the atmosphere in which his whole being moved. They never obtruded on his friends' attention, because they were so manifest that there was no escaping them, and they were therefore wholly natural, proving how fully one can be in the world and not of it.

Of George D. Olds, formerly professor at Rochester, later president of Amherst, he wrote: "His faith and his life were one." And of President James M. Taylor, of Vassar:

He was not unaware that his academic vision and purpose were regarded by some of his contemporaries as very conservative. With a quizzical smile he would acknowledge it, and then with fearless confidence and clear understanding reaffirm the faith that was in him. Firm as a rock he stood for culture, for character, for rational Christian thought and aspiration. And his own utterly winsome self made these things alluring to others who had to do with him. How such lives shine in our naughty world.

Whenever in the course of the years some special occasion led his college associates to try to express collectively their admiration and respect for his leadership and his sterling character, his natural shyness prevented him from enjoying the receipt of praise as much as he did the giving of it. More than once when he returned from Europe in the spring there would be a faculty dinner, with speeches humorous but sincere, and occasional verse to give an academic flavor. He liked such frivolities, but could not say how much.

On his sixtieth birthday there was an afternoon call from the faculty at his home, with presentation of two antique arm-chairs. Mrs. Rhees was in on the secret, and knew that the party was as much in her honor as his. As power behind the throne, dispenser of faith, hope, and charity, gracious hostess in the New England tradition with the hearty Rochester man-ner, she shared his triumphs, as she had his trials of patience. He once wrote: "So far as any success has come to my adminis-tration, the wife of the president has contributed a major share of it." In 1925 the faculty presented them with a silver teakettle and the trustees with an urn, with congratulations for the quar-ter century of service.

Of their home life when the children were young it is not necessary to say more than that it was a happy Christian home, where Sunday morning prayers and church attendance were expected, but where there was no puritanical or repressive atmosphere. The children were brought up to know the Bible and to respect religion, but there was no excessive piety to alienate them, no compulsion to cause later reactions. Rush Rhees once remarked in a public address:

I am convinced that very many of us are unaware of that which is sometimes resulting from the religious teaching of our children when we pass on to them in Sunday School traditional formulas that we do not take the trouble to analyze for ourselves, or to inquire whether those formulas will stand the critical test of the life which these youth are going to have to live for themselves. I tremble sometimes when I think of the responsibility we have for the difficulties we have created for our children.

For a minister who had given years to religious education, that is a frank confession. Most professional leaders in that field are so sure of their *a priori* reasoning that they are inclined to shy away from *a posteriori* investigation of results. The subject is still unsolved. Religious education in childhood is more difficult and more important than all the sermons ever preached.

Rush Rhees's humor was always delightful to his family. Among the standing family jokes there was one about "brewis," a much overrated dessert for hard-working housewives to offer when other resources fail. When he was married, Rush said he would be glad to eat anything for dessert except brewis and coffee jelly. They had been favorites at his boardinghouse, and he never wanted to see either of them again. He never did see brewis at his own table, but whenever there was talk about getting more variety in the family menu, he would ask, "Can't we have brewis?" If a guest asked what brewis was, he would say it was stale Boston brown bread crumbs with enough water poured over them to make a soggy mess, served up lukewarm as a pudding. The children took up the joke, and clamored for brewis when they could not think of anything else to say.

When the children grew up, they had every encouragement to choose their own interests and follow their own bent. During the usual period of finding themselves, their parents were understanding and ready to wait. It was a great satisfaction to them when Jack decided to go into medicine. Henrietta's interest in science led her into bacteriology, in which she found a career. Bob's desire to study philosophy was assisted in every possible way by his father. All three children married happily. Henrietta's home wedding to Dr. John D. Stewart in 1937, when her father performed his last marriage ceremony, was a new beginning for Rhees, Seelye, and Stewart traditions, on their long way to the future. Rush Rhees was a perfect host, and enjoyed large family reunions. There were many such in early days at Rochester and Northampton, as well as during the summers in Maine.

When Rush and Harriet were married, the Seelye family had already for years been spending their summers at Southwest Harbor, and they themselves passed their first two vacations there. After that they went each summer to Little Cranberry Island, at first in rented cottages, and after 1913 in their own cottage, built by local labor from their own plans. Mrs. Rhees's father and mother, her two brothers Ralph and Walter, her sister Mrs. Scudder, and all their families also were members of the little Seelye colony at Islesford. For eight or ten weeks every summer the Rochester Rheeses were there, but Rush was generally obliged to return to the college two or three times in July and August, and conducted his own business correspondence at the island, so that it was by no means all vacation.

His two principal recreations at Islesford were cabinetmaking and cruising around the islands in his motorboat. He spent much time in his shop, where his grandfather's tool chest was still doing service, though equipped with many new tools. He was a skilled and careful workman, who took pride in the many pieces of furniture which gradually enriched the cottage. In 1924 he wrote to George Eastman:

I am far removed from business; unless you would call some very amateurish attempts at cabinet-making business. My chief occupation is studying how to fit together by mortises and dovetails some pieces of quartered oak that I am trying to make into a sideboard for Harriet. It is no end of fun, and calls for some pretty active thinking, which constitutes a large part of the fun. I began the thing last year, and do not expect to finish it until next summer—which constitutes another factor in the fun. You will infer that I am not working at it very strenuously. I do nothing strenuously here—except loafing.

He smoked many pipes and deliberated many hours at his work-bench, but the sideboard, like all his other projects, was finally completed. He did not drop things because they took a long time, nor lose interest when they became difficult. Hard wood and hard work challenged his skill and rewarded it. Besides the buffet, which had three drawers and four cupboards, he made a fireside bench, a writing table with a drawer, a settle, a nest of three tea tables, a "lazy Susan" for the table, and innumerable shelves and other conveniences for the house. All his furniture was made with mortises, tenons, and dovetail joints, not with screws, and was beautifully finished. Rochester people who never saw the work of his hands did not really know him. He fitted wood as well as words.

He depended on local carpenters, mechanics, painters, and gardeners on the island, not only in the summer, but for fall and spring work. His relations with the islanders were not like those of many "summer people" with their helpers. He never condescended, flattered, overpaid, or tried to beat them down. It was all man to man—even if the man was a boy. They respected him and liked to work for him. Being a taxpayer, he took such part as he could in town affairs and the local school. He valued highly the unconscious compliment he once received when an islander, complaining that "city folks" did not understand Maine ways and the way of the sea, added, "Of course that don't mean you; you're different." After thirty years or so in New England one is still a newcomer; but at least he was no longer a novice. Perhaps that acceptance was partly due to his lack of effusiveness, which suited the Maine climate.

Rush Rhees, born in Chicago, brought up in Williamsburgh and Plainfield, never saw New England until he went to Amherst at nineteen. Yet people in Rochester generally thought of him as a New Englander, for his twenty-one years at Amherst, Hartford, Portsmouth, and Newton Centre had left their mark. But he did not have a New England inheritance. His calm intellectualism was as readily understood and accepted by Bostonians and Harvard professors who spent their summers on the Maine coast as by Maine men themselves. He was a welcome preacher each year at the union church in Northeast Harbor. Summer visitors and distinguished scholars heard him there in complete agreement with his ethics, whatever they thought of his theology. He was just as much their sort as he was the Islesford sort. In any society he moved as one created equal and endowed with "certain unalienable rights."

One of those rights was freedom of thought. Another was freedom of feeling about his thoughts, the right to sentiment. In view of all that has been said in earlier chapters as to his preference of reason to emotion in settling questions of social and civil life, it is well here to say that in his attitude to religion, art, and all the deeper and more personal aspects of life and destiny he was not without sentiment. The word is out of fashion. Yet a man who has no sentiment about his home, his wife, his children, his friends, or his country is a man not to be trusted, but the prevailing code is not to show it. Sentiment is not emotional thinking but thoughtful feeling, in which reason rules.

Rush Rhees was never "sentimental," but all his sermons and most of his addresses closed with thoughtful feeling. He was never "academic," if that means impractical theorizing. But as head of an "Academy" in the high Athenian sense—a grove where men learned to think, a society of scholars searching for truth—he was always academic. He was nothing too much.

Considering the fact that love, honor, loyalty, patriotism, and religion are all sentiments in one aspect, and could not survive without emotional force to transform thought into action, it is not amiss, so near the close of a long life devoted to those high values, to inquire whether reason alone could have done what Rush Rhees did.

In thirty-five years a small and struggling college was transformed into what the University of Rochester was when he left it. Intelligence and good fortune were the main factors in that transformation. But why in 1912 did its president decide to stay with it, when common sense might have led him to choose what seemed a better opportunity? Why did Mrs. James Sibley Watson build the Memorial Art Gallery? Why did she do so much in both art and music to bring Rochester children face to face with beauty? Why did George Eastman, having by keen foresight and business judgment planned a great musical center for the enrichment of leisure, name its exquisite small hall for chamber music after his mother? What was Eastman's love of music but thoughtful feeling for something he did not quite understand, but enjoyed and wished others to enjoy? What is all amateur musical appreciation but more or less intelligent emotion? What is Cutler Union but James G. Cutler's sentiment for Gothic, and for women's rights to be taken seriously? He wanted a tower, with something below it worthy to be crowned. After he died it came.

Science has no room for sentiment. There was none whatever in the founding of the School of Medicine and Dentistry. Yet what but sentiment paid for Strong Memorial Hospital? What but sentiment has helped to humanize it? What but thoughtful feeling justifies such medical traditions as the Hippocratic Oath? All rituals, anniversaries, and commemorations are sentiment. Alumni associations are based on sentiment. Reason alone could never hold men together except for evident personal or social advantage. Everything that has most intimately to do with human life, from naming the baby to burying the dead, is graced or dignified by sentiment, often most deeply felt by those who say the least. Life is biology and value. Only its value, caused by one man's thoughtful feeling and ultimately measured by the thoughtful feeling of other men, is long remembered. The rest disappears.

Rush Rhees was an intellectual, with intellectual love of God and man. He knew that unrestrained emotion is a curse in life, art, literature, and society. He also believed, as his life and words bore witness, that right emotion under strong control, not mere reason alone, will be the only salvation of the coming age. Reason could not prevent the collapse of a world order believed to be secure. It was tried and failed. If it is tried again, without the support of character, it will fail again. Only strong love like Lincoln's for peace, and strong hatred like Jefferson's for tyranny and cruelty can do with the aid of reason what reason alone cannot do. Such love and such hatred Rush Rhees had. They will be remembered longer than his opinions. It was not wisdom but the love of wisdom that was the guide of his life.

The last phase of his personality to be shown is seen under the aspect of eternity. On May 31, 1918, he spoke at the funeral of Mrs. Aristine Pixley Munn, who gave to the univer-

sity the land on which the first buildings of the College for
Women were erected in 1913. She was over a hundred years
old when she died. So quiet and gentle a life might have been
forgotten, even by some who in later years enjoyed her gift,
if Rush Rhees, interpreter of the silent, had not spoken for her.
His centennial tribute to an old lady of a past era contained
the essence of his own best thinking about life, his thanks-
giving for many years of grace. From his original pencil manuscript, rescued from the files of his business correspondence,
these were his words:

Was there ever a more perfect setting for a service such as brings us
together this afternoon? The quiet of the approaching evening, the soft
air of coming summer, the fields stirring with new life, everywhere the
promise of new life, of coming harvest, of the reward of man's labor by
the God of abundant life. For it is not with grief and sorrow—except for
our own lonely hearts—that we are gathered in this home which for so
many years has been the dwelling place of a triumphant life.

The Master said to his disciples: "I am come that they may have life,
and that they may have it abundantly." Such life has filled this home
with glory. The abundance of life is realized when death has ceased to
seem a crisis to be dreaded, and becomes simply an episode in the course
of life eternal. The rare spirit who has now passed beyond our sight
knew that abundance of life. Death did not interest her particularly. She
neither feared it nor longed for it. More than once she spoke of it as
simply a passing into another room in God's great mansion of the soul.
Her thought was filled with the life God gave her to live here. The life
to come was simply like the dawning of a new day, or the coming of
summer. "Great peace have they that love thy law," sang the Psalmist.
That peace filled this home, always busy with present tasks, always
seeking in them to do the will of God.

Such a view of life is not passive and resigned. There was no room
for that sort of patience in it. Life was exciting in its daily interest,
quietly thrilling in its ever new opportunities for growth in knowledge
and understanding. I have never met a more eager mind than hers who
now has passed on to the next room in God's house of life. Everything
in nature and in the doings of man possessed a thrilling interest for her.
Each new day was a new adventure. And when death was thought of,
it seemed to be with interest only in the new possibilities it might offer
for new knowledge of the meaning of God's gifts to His children. The
peace of this home was an active virtue; it came to one who for a
hundred years habitually was a worker together with God.

It was not a life that knew no tribulation. No great life escapes that.
The long, long years of widowhood in this home are a quiet witness to the

discipline that refined this spirit. But what a refinement they produced! The patience they developed was glorified by rare humor and a great lightness of heart that only the deep springs of life can sustain. The peace of this home was begotten of those fruits of the spirit blended with a singular sanity, with singular wisdom, and with eager interest in all that life gave and promised.

The last days were shadowed over with grief—not the result of weakening of mind and body, not the mark of any faltering confidence and faith—but a heavy burden of grief for a world at strife, racked with cruel and unutterably wicked war after two thousand years of opportunity to learn the ways of the Prince of Peace. That grief is a crowning testimony to a life habitually lived in the presence of God.

The wise man said, "The hoary head is a crown of glory, when it is found in the way of righteousness." That crown of glory we have seen here, that way of righteousness we have observed as this saint of God has trod therein. And here this glorious summer afternoon, at the close of this stage in the great adventure on which God sent her spirit one hundred years and more ago, we with reverence, with gratitude, and exultation of spirit, gather with those who knew her best and loved her most, to bring our tribute of honor, and to seek from this sacred presence a new sense of the glory and the triumphant possibilities of the life which God gives to His children.

XVII

RETIREMENT

The port, well worth the cruise, is near,
And every wave is charmed.—Emerson

WHEN the strain of office was removed and Rush Rhees
was back at Islesford for the summer, he seemed much
better. Plans were resumed for the year abroad to which he
and Harriet had long looked forward. They had expected to
spend most of it in Italy, and their passage was engaged for
October. But by that time the prospect of an Italian war in
Abyssinia was so threatening that they could see it was not
the year for living under Fascist rule. Therefore they canceled
their reservation, and spent the autumn in Boston.

This unexpected sojourn at the old Hotel Vendome for six
weeks in October and early November, 1935, was one of those
bright intervals of quiet happiness that sometimes come after
or before a crisis. Here they could see almost every day their
older son, Dr. Morgan John Rhees (Jack), who was then on
the staff of the Massachusetts General Hospital, and his wife
Helen and their little girl. Jack had never been strong. During
his Choate School days, and again during his college course
at Rochester, rheumatic fever and its consequences had made
it hard for him to carry out his ambition to become a doctor.
Yet by hard work and persistence he had succeeded. Having
turned his attention to hospital administration, he became
superintendent of the Baker Memorial, and later of the Pratt
Diagnostic Hospital. For a few years he rose steadily in the
esteem of all who knew him, not without occasional illness
which would have discouraged a less determined man. He

had but a few more years, and in 1941 followed his father to
Mount Hope. That which is hidden even from foreboding adds
poignance to happiness that has not long to last.

In Boston, in the October days of their first unburdened
year, Rush and Harriet with their children near them, with
friends of older times dropping in, with little daily walks along
Commonwealth Avenue, learned how to enjoy complete
leisure. There was no need to hurry, no use to worry, nothing
more to do that they did not want to do. "In the afternoon
they came unto a land in which it seemèd always afternoon."

Now and then a Rochester alumnus or alumna, hearing that
the Rheeses were staying at the Vendome, came somewhat
timidly to call, not wishing to intrude on retirement. They
were so cordially welcomed, questioned about their work, and
thanked for coming that they wondered why anyone had ever
thought the President hard to know. But it was not so much
that he had really changed; it was they who had ceased to be
afraid of him, because now he was just a dear old friend. Sometimes age and October show us that before winter comes.

On November 15, 1935, for the audience assembled in
Rochester at a university luncheon after the inauguration of
President Valentine, by request of the committee of arrangements, Rush Rhees sent radio greetings from Boston, closing
with these words:

There is the task of keeping clear in the minds of students and of the
public the supreme importance of quality in learning as distinct from
quantity of varied information. There is the danger that the pursuit of
high quality, by means of too early and narrow specialization, may blind
our eyes to the great service which men of cultivated minds may still
render to their communities, even though they may not follow academic
careers after the years of formal education are over. And there is the
menace from the proposals of educational theorists which may make
students the subjects of experimental procedure rather than the comrades
of older scholars in the pursuit of learning.

Because I believe Alan Valentine is the man to guide Rochester
towards fulfillment of its best destiny and its richest service, I rejoice in
your recognition of his leadership and join you in bidding him hail and
God speed.

Instead of Italy for the winter the Rheeses' destination
turned out to be Hawaii. About the middle of November they
sailed with Henrietta from New York for San Francisco via
the Panama Canal. There were many stops along the way at
Central American and South American ports, and Henrietta
often went ashore with acquaintances, but Rush and Harriet
stayed aboard, except where landing was easy. After a week
in San Francisco they sailed for Honolulu, where they arrived
on Christmas Eve. For more than three months they stayed
at a pleasant homelike hotel, enjoying outdoor sunshine and
the agreeable people they met. There were many drives and
short excursions. Rush occupied himself with reading up the
history of the islands from the earliest times. He went in some
detail into the character and influence of the early settlers,
both the missionary group and the traders. It interested him
to attempt to trace the effect on social psychology of interracial
contacts, of climate, and of unusual political relations with the
American government. He wrote a paper about it for his clubs,
the Pundit and Fortnightly, which he read after he got home,
much to the pleasure of his hearers.

On the way home from San Francisco in April the Rheeses
stopped over in Arizona to see the Grand Canyon. Returning
to Rochester in the spring, they found waiting for them the
comfortable home on East Avenue which the trustees had
provided. With their own furniture again in its place, with
pleasant views, good neighbors, and the prospect of another
summer in Maine, this first adjustment to the third and final
Rochester residence was easier than it might have been earlier.

It was Rush Rhees's fixed policy to sever completely his
academic relations and not to attend university ceremonies
after his retirement, believing that when a man quits he
should quit. But he did speak once or twice at chapel services
when invited, believing that to be a part of the life of the
university in which he could give encouragement without
advice, and faith without apology.

Apart from summers in Maine and winters in Jamaica there

were not many more journeys. In earlier years the Rheeses had been great travelers. Their many European visits, their Mediterranean tour of 1927, their several sojourns in Italy and on the Riviera, had given them during the busy preceding years needed rest and refreshment. About every two years after 1924 they had gone to England, partly to be with their younger son, Rush Rhees, Jr., who after completing his university education at Edinburgh and Cambridge, became a teacher of philosophy at Manchester, later at Swansea in South Wales. He had married a Scottish girl in Italy, and became eventually a British citizen. His parents often saw him in England, and he sometimes visited them in Maine. Especially did they enjoy the spring of 1934 at Cambridge, with daffodils by the river, tulips in college gardens, and King's College Chapel against the evening sky. That was the last year that Rush had been really well. Now that his wandering years were gone, memories of them enriched retirement. He had seen the world. It was a good world then.

There was to have been one more voyage. Passage to Barbados had been engaged for February 25, 1939. But the pilgrim's progress was almost over. Someone asked him, a few days before the end, when he was leaving Rochester. He named the 25th of February, and added, "I wish we were there now."

Now I saw in my dream, that by this time the pilgrims were got over the Enchanted Ground, and entering into the country of Beulah, whose air was very sweet and pleasant. In this country the sun shineth night and day; wherefore this was beyond the Valley of the Shadow of Death, and also out of the reach of Giant Despair, neither could they from this place so much as see Doubting Castle. Here they were within sight of the city they were going to, also here met them some of the inhabitants thereof; for in this land the Shining Ones commonly walked, because it was upon the borders of heaven.

XVIII

DEPARTURE

The great business of life is to be, to do,
to do without, and to depart.—John Morley

So wie der Mensch gelebt hat, so stirbt er auch, und was er im
Leben gewesen ist, wird er auch im Tode sein. Der Tod wird es
offenbar machen.—Wilhelm Schamoni, *Das wahre Gesicht der
Heiligen.*

He who has found Him, seeks no more; the riddle is solved; desire
gone, he is at peace. Having approached from everywhere that
which is everywhere, he passes into the Whole. As rivers lose
name and shape in the sea, wise men lose name and shape in
God, glittering beyond all distance.—*Mundaka-Upanishad,* from
The Ten Principal Upanishads, translated by Shree Purohit Swami
and W. B. Yeats. The Macmillan Company, 1937.

CHRISTMAS, 1938, was a happy holiday for Rush Rhees.
He and Harriet went to Boston as usual in order to be
with Jack and Helen, Henrietta and John, and the two grandchildren. Rush seemed contented, at peace with the world.
Everything was going well. Jack was rising in his profession.
Henrietta and her husband were happy in their new home.
Bob and Jean were well settled in England. Rush himself was
not quite so tired. There was the prospect of one more mid-
winter trip to the West Indies, where they could sit in the sun
and watch the sea. Life had been good to them. "God rest you
merry, gentlemen, let nothing you dismay." Once more the
carols.

Then on the 27th came a telegram from Rochester that
called him back. His old friend and neighbor, William B. Hale,
of Prince Street, jovial comrade for thirty-eight years, a leading

member of the Board of Trustees, had died suddenly, and the family wished Rush Rhees to conduct the funeral. He could not refuse. They returned to Rochester, and on Friday the 30th Mr. Hale was buried. At funerals Rush generally read the service, with the usual Scripture passages, and offered prayers suitable for the occasion, but without any address or eulogy. This time, departing from his custom, he gave a short address. A single page in the little black loose-leaf book which he always used for notes of his addresses contains the following outline:

> Funeral of Wm. B. Hale, 12.30.38
>
> Paul to Timothy
> "We brought nothing into this world, and it is certain that we can carry nothing out."
> Words true only of material possessions.
> In fact, each man carries with him into the presence of God the character that he has shown through his earthly life.
> After nearly forty years of friendship with William Hale, I find in him a character marked by
> Integrity in all his dealings;
> Fidelity in all his duties;
> And, crowning all, a ruling kindness of heart for all he knew:
> His associates,
> His employees,
> His intimates.
> The Most High asks of men that they do justly, love mercy, and walk humbly with Him. Into that Presence W.B.H. has carried his character.

That is all. The opposite page is blank. All the rest of the book is white paper. That tribute to his friend, about carrying character into a "Presence," was the end of a Christian ministry which began with his first sermon fifty years before.

The Hale funeral was not easy for him. That marvelous control over his deepest feelings which always kept his voice firm and his face calm did not fail him, but the strain was there. On Sunday he caught cold, and could not throw it off. After resting on Monday, he felt strong enough on Tuesday evening to go to the Pundit Club dinner, where he seemed to be in good spirits. On Wednesday he stayed in bed, but was up for dinner.

Late Wednesday night the coronary pain came on suddenly. Though the doctor came promptly and applied the usual treatment, it was useless. In the presence of his wife and his faithful physician, at half past one in the morning of Thursday, January 5, 1939, the tired heart stopped. Spared the last decline, when he was called he received from the mercy that surrounds us leave to go.

In the daily rhythm of human life comes an ebb between three and four in the morning when it is neither late nor early. Time waits. "Day unto day uttereth speech, and night unto night showeth knowledge." In that poise of hesitation, when traffic is hushed, vitality low, spirit alert, those who are awake think of those who are asleep. That is an hour when children enter the world and old men leave it. Souls are passing, into life and away, over them all a great compassion. Beginning and end seem no farther apart than Gloria from Amen. They are "as yesterday when it is past, and as a watch in the night."

On the bright winter day after Epiphany, January 7, 1939, friends of Rush Rhees met in front of Henry A. Strong Auditorium, with a wide view of river and sky. They looked west and up, then went in. Quiet music and quiet words reminded them of a quiet man. There were not many people there, for no effort had been made to fill the house with mourners. He would not have liked that. Only those came who could not stay away. Perhaps some came for respect who went away with love. For half an hour the hall was filled with the peace of the dead, the gratitude of the living, and the grace of God. They all seemed one—a holy spirit. That afternoon was not like any other—unless perhaps a little like that strange last day of August, 1932, down in Maine. Then people had come hundreds of miles just to stand still one minute and a half, watching the sun's corona; splendor encircling darkness, "the power and the glory forever"; never seen before or since, yet always there; totality. Now after seven years another pause, another silent waiting; not long, but long enough. Life cannot stand it long. Time stopped, the world passed by. Then "the shadows lengthened, the evening came, the busy world was hushed, the fever of life was over, and his work was done." So Rush Rhees gave his last benediction, as he had given his first fifty years before. His life was not divided; complex, but all one in the end.

There is a quiet place in Rochester where none is forgotten, all is forgiven, and even the lost are found. It is called Mount Hope. A glacier made it, a city named it, a century has hallowed it. Some people never go there unless they have to, but they miss great society. Noble names can be seen, and visitors can wait undisturbed for the unseen. More than the past is there, more light in the tops of the trees than shadows below them, more color than elsewhere in May and October, more beauty than should be spoken. The sacred grove with the golden boughs is for birds and silence. One should not talk; a place still enough for contemplation is hard to find. Here it is.

In the older part of Mount Hope near the eastern gates a large lot was purchased in 1852 by the University of Rochester, of which the southeastern corner was sold to Rush Rhees about 1935. From its elevation above the road one looks down upon a deep hollow to the north, with a shadowy pool where a fountain flows. In one corner of the university lot is the grave of Martin Brewer Anderson, first president, with those of his wife and his father. Near them is a tiny headstone for the infant daughter of a former professor, inscribed "He shall gather the lambs with his arm and carry them in his bosom." She was not long in this world. In another corner lie two students who died in the 1850's, when the college too was

young. They were brought here because they had nowhere
else to go.

On that sunny bank lies Rush Rhees. His son Jack, the last
Morgan John, who followed him in 1941, rests beside him. The
granite monument is easily found; more easily than the graves
of his ancestors.

His father and mother, his sisters, his grandparents Rhees
and McCutchen, all lie in Greenwood, Brooklyn. His Welsh
great-grandfather, Morgan John Rhees of Beulah and Somerset, friend of Benjamin Rush and Thomas Jefferson; his great-
grandmother Ann Loxley, friend of children; her father, Major
Benjamin Loxley, friend of Franklin; the first Dr. Benjamin
Rush Rhees, friend of the friendless—these are all in Mount
Moriah, Philadelphia. They were all friends of God. "Lord,
Thou hast been our dwelling place in all generations."

The Rheeses lie apart, but the mind can unite them. Through
five generations, from the eighteenth century to the twentieth,
from Wales to the Genesee country, a long curve is now
complete. It rose from the Revolution and the sea, passes over
a grave, and ends in a chime of bells. A longer curve, the
meridian of Mount Hope, the mind can instantly project north-
ward around the globe, over the arctic and the oceans, back
from Peru straight home. Space and time have shrunk. Sun-
light on a leaf will hold them. They hide behind the forehead.
Where those two great circles cross, migration and meridian,
hovers the idea RHEES OF ROCHESTER.

Though there is no sound here but falling water from the
fountain, the mind can hear three songs. First the hymn St.
Anne, opening all great occasions—"Our shelter from the
stormy blast and our eternal home." Then Beethoven's tune for
Schiller's "Hymn to Joy" in the Ninth Symphony. Last, a
college lyric about the Genesee, the stand-up song that ends
all assemblies: "As flows the river, gathering force." River and
force flow through this valley, always going away, north to
Ontario, St. Lawrence, and the sea. Soon that water will be

Genesee no longer. It will lose a name. Yet when a river, a man, or a song becomes an idea, there is no telling where it will end. The Genesee is not only a stream but a thought. Running water and human life survive as designs. They are forms of unstable equilibrium generating power and beauty.

Our problem is, in T. S. Eliot's phrase, "to apprehend the point of intersection of the timeless with time." The timeless is not the endless. It is spiritual reality, perceived beneath appearance or conceived alone. "Eternity cannot be manifested through duration," said Spinoza. "The mind is eternal in so far as it conceives things under the form of eternity." Eternal moments—flashes from the great light; why ask more? Those who have glimpsed, however briefly, the secret life of the universe cannot be too much concerned about their own survival. Something greater has won them—spiritual quality without extension in space or time.

The granite markers at the corners of this plot of earth bear four letters, U OF R. They are bounds for the boundless. Where two worlds meet, seen and unseen, they guard the sleeping whom none can rouse, and living thoughts which none can destroy. Earth is our oldest Alma Mater, and grants the last degrees, but academies record them. Here are the diplomas. Within these few square rods, early or late, in summer or in winter, the invisible university, which is a spirit, has brought together with its last benediction old and young, distinguished and obscure, victors and unfulfilled, to rest on the hill forever.

The silence of Mount Hope is unbroken. Our meditation alters nothing and explains nothing. With or without imagination, things are what they are. Yet sometimes we see through them, not by metaphysical speculation or by fancy, but by faith. Peace is here beyond our understanding, and understanding beyond our peace. All is well.

XIX

TRIBUTES

Whatever is in any way beautiful has its source of
beauty in itself, and is complete in itself; praise
forms no part of it. So it is none the worse nor the
better for being praised.
——Marcus Aurelius Antoninus

The soul is in the body as light is in the air; the
air escapes; does not the light remain?——Plotinus

RESPECT comes to all that live right. Honor comes soon
or late to those who work for others more than for themselves. Love comes early by instinct but late by understanding,
and not all have it that should.

Rush Rhees was respected by all, honored by many, and
loved by those who knew him best. He was respected from the
first, honored even before success, and most loved when he had
laid aside the power of office. Only the power of his character
then remained, with a charm and gentleness which he no
longer needed to hide. He had more than three years to be just
himself, and no one was afraid of him any more. Many wished
they had known him better when it was almost too late to
know him at all.

His name on library stone and his spirit in essence will
gradually become the same. Friends will read and remember.
Strangers will see and be fortified. Students will learn and be
surprised. The young are always surprised to find that men
whom they cannot patronize, surpass, nor equal lived just
before their time.

Since it is futile to envy the dead either their opportunities
or their excellence, some late discoverers of Rush Rhees may

learn even in youth humility and patience, the last of the virtues. These cannot be got from books in Rush Rhees Library, where they are recorded, but only from the book of life, where they grow. His story makes one volume in that long book. His praise would fill another, but not here. The best tribute, if it were not misunderstood, would be silence. That is the secret speech of the dead, the night, and the gods.

To build of words "a monument more lasting than bronze" was a vain endeavor of Horace and Shakespeare. An ode of the one or a sonnet of the other reminds us more of the poet than of his friend. This is true even of the best commemorations. *Adonais* is all Shelley, not Keats; Hallam has faded from *In Memoriam*; Edward King in *Lycidas* is but a shadow. The dead man is buried beneath fine words, not raised again. Evocation is rare. He who would call back the departed must himself stay hidden, even if the spirit appears, or it will vanish.

The best gratitude may be anonymous—merely to say, thank God for a good man. That makes a good morning for the grateful and the remembered. He lives again, for he is now a thought, back in this world. Thanks for the absent are a kind of greeting. *Vita enim mortuorum in memoria vivorum est posita.* But their life is more than memory, it is action.

Admiration for the living and reverence for the dead are noble impulses; better than most love, for they seek nothing, not even response. The wish to express them is a good wish, though it cannot wholly succeed. They exalt human dignity, even in barbarous times like ours. Therefore, since tributes of affection belong to biography, because they belonged to the life which life-writing tries to keep alive, here they are.

Many men honored him in public and in private while he was still in the midst of his work, others near the close, and after his departure. As early as 1913, his friend John Finley wrote:

I seize a moment in this holiday to discover to you my abiding and admiring regard. I congratulate you upon your autumnal harvest. May every autumn bring you new friends of your splendid labors.

A Rochester alumnus, Sereno E. Payne, of the House of Representatives, wrote to him in 1914:

I feel an especial pride in the work you have done for the University since you have become its President. It is seldom that a university finds a president like yourself who stands among the foremost educators of the country, and at the same time has the practical ability to gather funds so necessary to the endowment of such an institution. I appreciate what you have done for the institution more than I can express, and hope that your further success may be even more brilliant than that of the past.

Mr. Payne was then seventy-one years of age, and died suddenly later in the year. Rush Rhees wrote of him:

Such a passing as he has experienced cannot be regarded as a calamity for him. It was a beautiful way for life's last summons to come.

Both men when they were old felt that strong impulse to say good words about others in the short time that remained. It was so also with former President David Jayne Hill, who on his own seventy-seventh birthday in 1927 wrote to his successor:

Among the happiest years of my life I look back upon those spent in Rochester in the service of the University. I have taken a pride in the growth of the University far beyond the measure of my part in it, largely perhaps because what I found difficult but worth while has been found to be possible.

Rush Rhees replied:

I am very much touched by your comments upon the developments of the University in recent years, and desire to tell you how constantly I am conscious of the fact that what has been accomplished in this last quarter century has been in a measure the fulfillment of the dreams you had in your own mind, and based upon the foundation which you laid in your very wise endeavor to link the institution most intimately with the city. We have been favored beyond our fondest dreams in the matter of resources for our work, and I am happy to see from your letter that you do take a just pride in the institution to which you gave at a critical period necessary and very important training.

Shailer Mathews in 1926 avoided his usual bantering tone when he wrote:

I have been thinking again and again of the tremendous things you have been able to do, and I heartily congratulate you for them all. It is a wonderful thing to be remembered by such a creative piece of work as you have done.

During the same period, when the period of expansion had begun but had not yet reached its material expression on the River Campus, George D. Olds wrote:

You undertook the captaincy when the prospects were dark, and in a trice the ship was battling steadily and victoriously to windward. In these days when the winds are no longer dead ahead but fair, you are keeping the rudder true. The fond prayer of every Rochester graduate should be that health and years may be granted you so that your hands may be long on the wheel.

And in 1929 he added:

Every honor that has come to you has meant one more responsibility, and the way in which you have met every responsibility has led to one more honor—a rare unbroken chain.

With unusual insight into the underlying motives of Rush Rhees's career, Louis Wiley of the New York *Times* wrote in 1935:

Your work has been one of love, the progress of your students close to your heart. What you have accomplished with your ability, backed by your enthusiasm, will surely be reflected in the development of the cultural arts and the influence of the well equipped men you have sent forth into the world. I hope that in your *otium cum dignitate* to be enjoyed for many years you will continue to give the world the benefits of your wisdom and learning.

Among the most energetic and most beloved of all the alumni of the university was the late Samuel M. Havens, of Chicago, a member of the Board of Trustees, who rendered invaluable service to the college in sending to it each year new students of exceptionally high grade from the Chicago area. In 1935 he wrote to the President:

Many times of late I have wondered whether you would like to be forty again and start all over in the University at its present high standing.

The answer was prompt:

Your affectionate and exaggerated appreciation of my part in the development of the last thirty-five years is received. With all due humility I cannot say that I would like to begin over again at forty to carry on here.

Perhaps the kind of tribute that he liked best was that which came now and then from men who had met him briefly many years before, and wrote after half a lifetime to tell him what they owed to some chance word or forgotten act of kindness. Such thanks bind life together. In 1935 he had such a letter:

Memory goes back half a century to a certain summer in Vermont when you, fresh from the Seminary, were the village preacher for a season. During those weeks we often walked and talked together discussing subjects of vital concern to a young man at the threshold of life. As our acquaintance was brief and your life has been so abundantly filled with large interests, you could not be expected to remember a chance contact such as ours; but my memory of you has outlived the years.

At the time of his retirement many of his associates and former students wrote personal letters of appreciation and gratitude. One friend wrote:

It has been a joy for me to see your administration in action. It is a rare privilege for one to come in contact with a great man. Character, industry, judgment, tact, and leadership of the highest order have been needed by the University during your era. You have given them to her, tempered by sympathy and kindliness toward all. A marvelous record which has brought to you the greatest love and admiration from your schools, from the city, and from the great educational world.

Another tribute of that period was an editorial in the New York *Herald Tribune*, entitled "Rush Rhees's University" which contained the following contrast of 1900 with 1930:

Three old brownstone buildings constituted the material equipment of the University of Rochester when Rush Rhees became its president. The college had a faculty of born teachers, and its two hundred students were strong in the traditions set by Presidents Martin Anderson and David Jayne Hill. Rochester was proud of it; the country at large did not know that it existed. This month the College for Men is separating itself from the College for Women, which Susan B. Anthony and other loyal friends of women almost forced upon the old male institution, and is moving out to a new eighty-seven acre campus, where eighteen new buildings already stand upon what were the fairways of the old Oak

Hill Country Club. Rush Rhees's vision and enthusiasm and organizing capacity, with the abounding generosity of George Eastman and other Rochesterians, has turned a quiet fresh-water college into a great university.

During the last few months of his term of office, because of impaired health, he was not able to appear frequently among the students and alumni, but when he did their words of admiration and affection seemed to touch him deeply. Older alumni and citizens with whom he had been long associated knew well what they were about to lose. Undergraduates, who had seen less of him except at chapel, perceived that there had been a great man among them. He did not, even for them, seem to belong altogether to the past; rather to something not measured by years, something old as the hills, new as the morning—the life of the mind.

There was a letter written just after his death which expressed this timelessness:

One close to a great mountain can see details of its structure and its intimate beauties, but to appreciate its majesty and its comparative size, one needs some distance. So in thinking of Rush, I wonder whether we who were not so close may not appreciate his greatness, not only in itself, but also in comparison with others. Yesterday a friend said to me that Rochester has just lost its greatest citizen. He was right. What Rush did for Rochester has had immediate effect, with a lasting influence ever extending in place and time.

A friend who had known him for half a lifetime wrote:

In the last few weeks I seem to be in an emptier world—first, a wise, kindly, deeply philosophical Catholic priest whose spirit I had learned to value, then an old newspaper companion who at eighty-eight not only reflected the glory of the evening sun but added to it, and now Rush, the most intimate and loved of all. When I think of such as these, poles apart in race, creed, and upbringing, I cannot help feeling that even in a distraught world where evil seems rampant there is hope in the divine spirit that dwells in the hearts of all sorts of men.

One of his former students whom he had befriended in other ways concluded his tribute thus:

Dr. Rhees's aid to me was chiefly intellectual, despite all that he did for my practical needs. He first demonstrated for me the relativity of truth, and by so doing he gave me one of the major supports of my intellectual life. He showed me how to apply this idea to religious thought, and so established the base for a lifetime of reading and study, out of which have come to me satisfaction, religious peace, and the strength to face death daily without personal fear. I have lost my best friend. So long as I live I shall contribute to his immortality by constant remembrance of him.

Another alumnus of early days wrote:

In only one other way did President Rhees influence me more than in his chapel talks. These to me were invariably of practical value, born of a rich fruitage of spiritual experience. To me also they had a warmth of earnestness that I have ever since valued. He was especially fine in discussing the Sermon on the Mount. The other channel of influence that was more significant to me than the chapel talks was a feeling of warm personal interest. Whenever I had occasion to ask for his advice and counsel, and I did make bold to do so from time to time, he never showed himself hurried, merely formal, or uninterested. He always showed me a feeling of friendly interest that I will ever cherish. That was true during my college days and in the years after as well.

The *Alumni Review* said of him, in the course of a sketch of his life:

Shy, reserved, Prexy Rhees still won the affection of his students, and they will long remember his tolerance and the occasional flashes of a keen humor.

Of printed eulogies that appeared after his death one of the most widely circulated was that of his classmate, Dr. Edward S. Parsons, in the *Amherst Graduates' Quarterly* for May, 1939, entitled "The 'Fairy Story' of Rush Rhees." It began:

In October of 1925 Rush Rhees and I happened to meet in Nashville, representing our respective institutions at the fiftieth anniversary of the founding of Vanderbilt University. At the breakfast table one morning he related in some detail "the fairy story," as he himself called it, of the development of the University of Rochester. When he became President in 1900, it was a small Baptist institution with 198 students and a very small endowment, with a group of excellent professors but with a very limited opportunity. He told me of his first visit to Mr. Eastman to solicit his help in the construction of a new building, the first and only time he ever asked Mr. Eastman for money. Mr. Eastman told him frankly, "I am not interested in education," but because the raising of the necessary money was a civic movement, he made a contribution. Later he changed his mind and said, in a statement to his business associates, "The progress of the world depends almost entirely upon education."

The article goes on to recount the story of the growth of the university, as already covered in these pages, and continues:

He was lucky. It meant everything to him to have behind him one of the most progressive and public-spirited cities in the country. He had at his right hand one of the country's most generous givers, one who was abundantly able to provide help without stint. He was very fortunate, too, in being at the head of an institution in a city and a section which the General Education Board felt to be strategically located for medical education. But though these elements in the situation were essential, yet Rhees was the great leader who could marshal them all to achieve the amazing result. Another person could have found the city of Rochester cold to his plans. Another person could have left Mr. Eastman all his life uninterested in education. Another person could have frightened the General Education Board away from Rochester.

Speaking of the fact that in 1912 Rush Rhees "was asked if he would consider leaving Rochester and becoming President of Amherst," Dr. Parsons says, "At first he was inclined to accept this suggestion," and attributes the final decision to Mr. Eastman's offer of additional endowment. "Amherst's loss was Rochester's wonderful gain."

After some analysis of Rush Rhees's temperament and a reference to his Welsh ancestry, Dr. Parsons, who knew him well, takes the same view that is embodied in this book:

This Welsh strain was no doubt responsible for Rhees's deep emotional nature. This was in such perfect control that many did not realize its strength, but it was the driving force of his accomplishment. In it, too, is to be found the explanation of his artistic sensitivity, his love and appreciation of art and music and literature. It was responsible, also, for the gift which was his in such striking measure for the apt word—his ability, on the platform or in general discussion or conversation, to express his thought in crisp, epigrammatic form. And this Welsh strain was no doubt the source of his abundant humor. This was sometimes concealed, often subtle, but it was always there, and illuminated and smoothed the way in many perplexing situations.

"The Fairy Story of Rush Rhees" closes with these words:

He had his difficulties and trials, but through them all he moved steadily forward to the goal of his great achievement. He was, what is only very rarely to be found, the union in one personality of a masterful leader and a highly cultivated Christian gentleman.

Among the many resolutions adopted by organizations of which he was a member all agreed in their recognition of qualities which distinguished him from other men; he was not like anybody else. All seem to have felt that. The University Board of Trustees included in their tribute these striking sentences:

He sought to combine the judgment of experts with his own progressive doctrines of higher education, acting never alone, but never entirely according to prevailing drifts or shifting majorities. He was a strong executive, firm but not obstinate, conciliatory but not disposed to surrender essentials. His courage in supporting unpopular causes, his fairness in difficult problems of personnel, his sense of public duty to the community, were aspects of his character perhaps most evident to those of us who worked with him in the varied administrative problems of University and city. We, who knew him well, admired him. When his plans succeeded, he shared the honors; when they miscarried, he took the blame alone.

The college faculty spoke of "his incisive mind, grasp of details, breadth of view, power of analysis, and ability to enlist co-operation."

He endeared himself to us with his kindly wit, patience, sympathy, human understanding, and sense of justice. As an administrator he imparted confidence and imbued us with his own spirit.

Directors of several business corporations on whose boards he served, including the Lincoln-Alliance Bank, the Eastman Kodak Company, and the Buffalo, Rochester and Pittsburgh Railway Company, called attention to aspects of his personality not connected with education. The Lincoln-Alliance Bank Board of Directors, of which he had been a member since 1920, said of him:

We will miss Dr. Rhees; his cheerfulness, his good humor, his tolerance. It will seem strange not to hear him speak out in meeting, asking some question, pertinent and pointed, demanding an answer invariably illuminating to all of us. He enjoyed his membership on this Board. He felt that here he was surrounded by friends interested in a common cause. He modestly disclaimed being a financier. He failed to appreciate, however, that for many years he was the most trusted and valued custodian of funds in this community. Millions were entrusted to his use, not with the thought of principal gain, but in full knowledge that these funds would be used wisely for the benefit of mankind. He was a useful financier of the first order.

Dr. Rhees was a positive man. He was careful in his deliberations, and governed always by the courage of his sincere convictions. He recognized easily the right from the wrong, and set his course quickly and with determination. An indomitable courage, a true expression of strong character, held him always to his true course.

Dr. Rhees was a learned man. He had but little interest in culture for culture's sake, but rather did he pursue the acquisition of knowledge because of the sheer pleasure it gave him in the seeking, and the satisfaction of its possession. His was a precise mind, an alert mind, a practical mind. He was not the dreamer. He valued facts.

He loved the beautiful—in literature, in art, in music, and in everyday life. He found real joy in living. At the same time he regarded it as a privilege. Probably for this reason he was eminently successful as a leader among men. He valued little the power which such leadership gave him other than the opportunity to serve his fellow man. But few worth while endeavors in the interests of community welfare were undertaken without his unselfish endorsement and aid.

Dr. Rhees was a man of great attainments. He accomplished great things because he planned wisely, held tenaciously to his ideals, and gave himself unsparingly, demanding little in return other than that he might enjoy eventually the personal satisfaction that his task, whatever it might be, was well done. He enjoyed the confidence of the entire community. It was always recognized that in any cause with which he had identified himself, his thoughts and actions were guided by sincere purpose.

With all of this, Dr. Rhees was a modest man. He was reticent, possibly austere to those who did not know him. He was always simple, kindly, a true and warm-hearted friend to those who did know him. His close associates admired him as a man, trusted his judgment, appreciated in fullest measure his fairness in the judgment of others, and were always conscious of his exaggeration of the value of their contributions and the belittlement of his own.

This short chapter of tributes, departing widely in quantity and quality from the conventional obituary note, may fittingly close with one of the best editorials printed in any newspaper at the time of his death. The following, from the New York *Times* of January 6, 1939, was by John Finley:

Here was a citizen who lived up to his own definition of liberal culture—a liberal culture "intended to free the mind from narrowness and prejudice and ignorance." And the mastery of a subject rather than familiarity with some useful technique is liberating. This he was saying at the age of seventy-five after a wonderfully liberating life. He began

with mathematics—the most liberalizing of studies, leading into infinity
—which he taught as an instructor at Amherst. Then he studied divinity,
was a New England pastor for a time, taught in a theological institution,
and at the age of forty became President of the University of Rochester.

So close was his association for thirty-five years with this institution
that it has often been referred to as "Rush Rhees's university." Its growth
in faculties, in buildings and endowment, has been phenomenal. From a
college with a few small buildings it now has three graduate schools,
notably in music and medicine, and fills two spacious campuses, one for
men and one for women. He had the proffered (or invited) help of
others, notably of Mr. Eastman, and of the people of Rochester generally.

In it all he had his special but diversified talent. His mastery consisted
in keeping himself where and when the application of that talent was
"oftenest to be practiced." He was the refounder of the institution in
which the liberal arts have a permanent and beauteous home, and the
sciences great laboratories of research, in one of the most progressive and
comely of American cities. "Equal to the church, equal to the state, so
was he equal to every other man."

In his personal note enclosing a copy of this editorial John
Finley added: "What a glorious life he lived between the two
eternities."

XX

OMEGA

I am Alpha and Omega, the beginning
and the end, the first and the last.

Time, like an ever-rolling stream,
Bears all its sons away.

And the Spirit and the bride say, Come.
And let him that heareth say, Come.

〰〰〰〰〰〰〰〰〰〰〰〰〰〰〰〰〰〰〰〰〰〰〰〰〰〰〰〰〰〰〰〰

THIS LIFE took forty weeks to begin, nearly twenty-nine thousand days and nights to enjoy or endure, one hour to end. This record of it, which took a year to write, may take ten hours to read, ten minutes to size up and dismiss. God saw that life complete in an instant as if it had been forever. Perhaps sometimes a dying man has first seen life clearly by its last flash; to see it all was to go beyond it. Which was the life, long breathing or swift seeing? Existence or essence? Duration or delight? Measured by time, what is life? Measured by life, what is time?

All that time tells cannot be told to the young. They would not listen, for they feel that time has deceived them. It has cheated them out of their youth. When they hear wind in the trees or rain at night, they think of something lost. Their disappointment is mostly bad timing; troubles of sequence or duration; happiness just missed; hours too short, years too long. When the lonely hear a train going away, or distant bells, or the end of music, these are like words not spoken, love never told. Everything came too soon or too late. They did not even know their own hour when they had it. They were prisoners of time.

Yet youth is seldom really tragic, except in war. When not joyous, as it was meant to be, it may be pathetic, or comic, or just a mistake. But if it seems pathetic to itself, it becomes comedy for cynics; if comic to itself, pathos for the wise. In either case, the malady is time gone wrong. Young men's energy is often wasted in hesitation, spoiled by haste, haunted by useless regret. No victims of moods and tenses, dismayed by calendars and the first gray hair, can understand Omega.

That secret at the end of the alphabet, great O, great circle of the sphere, comes too late for reparation, but not too late for peace. Old people have been too long familiar with the minor overtones of life to find much sadness in them, except what belongs to the world. They have got over feeling sorry for themselves. Their disappointments are not for themselves, but for those whom they loved and trusted. As for time, they are glad that the past is past, and does not have to be gone through again. Even its joys would not bear repeating. Memory can keep them. Enough is enough.

In the last act the tragic spirit sometimes relents from high drama, permitting a smile, not at the folly of others but at one's own too great expectations. Some fortunate souls keep humor to the end. They amuse others even when no longer themselves amused. They have pleasant immunities on their way out. Nobody expects much of them, or gets much. Children and dogs like them, feeling by instinct their silent good will.

But they are tired and cannot rest. That is what age is— years short, hours long. They wait for bedtime, then for morning. Their wakeful nights are full of wonder. Life, which had been a question, becomes a vigil. A deep undertone, sounding beneath all change, below the roar of traffic, murmurs of night, surf on the shore, seems like a signal, an answer almost found. The unknown is faintly heard—not seen, though the veil wears thin. No longer centered in themselves, ready to give up whatever hides the secret, they wait on the edge of some ultimate meaning. If there is any, it cannot be far away.

For that hidden meaning, that last word, the great-grandson of Morgan John Rhees waited nearly seventy-nine years. Suddenly in the night he found it—

—and took it away with him, as all his fathers had. Those that know never tell.

It is time to close this book. Rhees of Rochester is ended. There will not be another; human quality is not repeated. Yet the history of all good men is at last the same: He found his work, earned his rest, and went his way. When he had learned life he left it.

By many changing paths around Alpha and Omega, One and the Same, whom none can escape and all may adore, life goes on toward more life. Each must find his own way there.

In the *Enneads* of Plotinus there is a passage comparing life to a sacred choral dance. While we live we all revolve around the Supreme, whether we know it or not. If we look away and do not watch the leader, we are out of tune, out of step, and miss the best of the music. But when we turn to the center and see what keeps us going, we are near the beginning and the end. If we hear the song of joy, we sing while we can. When our time is over we go where we belong, and then we rest.

Rush Rhees Library tower is floodlighted on Christmas Eve. Unseen bells above the bright dome floating in darkness ring *Adeste fideles, laeti triumphantes.* Visible and invisible, light and shadow, living and dead, past and future, known and unknown, real and ideal, time and eternity, all seem for an instant ONE.

sub-specie aeternitatis

RUSH RHEES LIBRARY TOWER IS LIGHTED ON CHRISTMAS EVE

THE PUBLISHED WRITINGS OF RUSH RHEES

Bibliography by Margaret Butterfield, Rush Rhees Library

BOOK

The Life of Jesus of Nazareth; a Study. New York: Charles Scribner's Sons, 1900.
Translated into Japanese by Tatsu Tanaka. Keisheisha: Fukunaga, 1906.
Reviews of *The Life of Jesus of Nazareth: Hartford Seminary Record,* August, 1900, pp. 327-330.
  Gilbert, George H. The Life of Jesus. *American Journal of Theology,* October, 1900, vol. 4, no. 4, pp. 834-835.
  The Life of Jesus of Nazareth [Unsigned review]. *Athenaeum,* Dec. 29, 1900, no. 3818, p. 854.
  Mathews, Shailer. The Life of Jesus of Nazareth. *Biblical World,* December, 1900, vol. 16, no. 6, pp. 468-470.
  Price, Ira M. New Tools for Bible Students. *Dial,* Nov. 16, 1900, vol. 29, no. 346, pp. 357-358.

REVIEWS BY RUSH RHEES

WATSON, JOHN. The Mind of the Master. *Biblical World,* November, 1896, vol. 8, no. 5, pp. 405-407. *American Journal of Theology,* vol. 1, p. 245, 1897.
RÉVILLE, ALBERT. Jésus de Nazareth. *American Journal of Theology,* vol. 2, p. 161, 1898.
SOMERVILLE, DAVID. St. Paul's Conception of Christ. *American Journal of Theology,* vol. 2, p. 671, 1898.
BALDENSPERGER, W. Der Prolog des vierten Evangeliums. *American Journal of Theology,* vol. 3, p. 368, 1899.
RICKABY, JOSEPH. Notes on St. Paul: Corinthians, Galatians, Romans. *American Journal of Theology,* vol. 3, p. 371, 1899.
New Testament History and Theology. *Biblical World,* February, 1901, vol. 17, no. 2, pp. 145-147.
The Life and Work of the Redeemer. *American Journal of Theology,* vol. 6, p. 782, 1902.

ARTICLES

Interpretation of Matthew 12: 39, 40. *Biblical World,* June, 1895, vol. 5, no. 6, pp. 421-427.
Christ in Art. *Biblical World,* December, 1895, vol. 6, no. 6, pp. 490-502.
The Fourth Gospel, in *The Bible as Literature.* New York: T. Y. Crowell & Company, c. 1896, pp. [281]-297.
Saul's Experience as a Factor in His Theology. University of Chicago Press, 1896. *American Institute Essays in Biblical Literature, New Testament Series,* No. 7.
The Kingdom of God: a Symposium. *Biblical World,* July, 1898, vol. 12, no. 1, pp. 12-13.

The Confession of Nathanael, John 1: 45-49. *Journal of Biblical Literature*, 1898, vol. 17, pt. 1, pp. 21-30.

A "Striking Monotony" in the Synoptic Gospels. *Journal of Biblical Literature*, 1898, vol. 17, pt. 1, pp. 87-102.

Suggestions for a Sunday-school Catechism. *Biblical World*, January, 1901, vol. 17, no. 1, pp. 41 & 44.

Teaching. *Careers for the Coming Men*, pp. 21-31. Akron, Ohio: Saalfield Publishing Company, 1904.

The Supernatural Birth of Jesus . . . Is it Essential to Christianity? *American Journal of Theology*, January, 1906, vol. 10, no. 1, pp. 18-20.

The Required Religious Services of a College. *Biblical World*, vol. 28, p. 250, 1906.

The Relation of College Men and Women to the Peace Movement. *Journal of Social Science*, September, 1907, no. 45, pp. [156]-159.

The University of Rochester. William Farley Peck. *History of Rochester and Monroe County*, vol. 1, pp. 250-261. New York: Pioneer Publishing Company, 1908.

Preface. James Breck Perkins. *France in the American Revolution*, p. [v]. Boston and New York: Houghton Mifflin Company, *c*. 1911.

Did Jesus Ever Live? *Biblical World*, February, 1912, vol. 39, no. 2, pp. 80-87.

What Did Jesus Undertake to Do? *Biblical World*, March, 1912, vol. 39, no. 3, pp. 167-174.

What Did Jesus Accomplish? *Biblical World*, April, 1912, vol. 39, no. 4, pp. 243-248.

The Religion That Jesus Lived. *Biblical World*, June, 1912, vol. 39, no. 6, pp. 368-374.

The Message of Jesus to the Young Men of Today. *Biblical World*, July, 1912, vol. 40, no. 1, pp. 38-42.

Amherst's Excellent Choice. *Amherst Graduates' Quarterly*, January, 1913, vol. 2, p. 132.

The College as a Preparation for Professional Study. *The American College, a Series of Papers*, pp. 77-93.

Evangelizing Education. *Biblical World*, August, 1916, vol. 48, no. 2, pp. 67-72.

Dr. Mundy and His Alma Mater. *Ezekiel Wilson Mundy, a Book of Loving Remembrance by his Friends*, p. 30. Syracuse Public Library, 1917.

The Teacher and the National Life. *Journal of the New York State Teachers' Association*, January, 1920, vol. 6, no. 8, pp. 272-274.

Eastman School of Music. *Rochester Alumni Review*, December, 1922-January, 1923, vol. 1, no. 2, p. 38.

Tribute to Mr. Robins. *Rochester Alumni Review*, February-March, 1923, vol. 1, no. 3, p. 62.

College Objectives and Ideals. Association of American Colleges. *Bulletin*, April, 1923, vol. 9, no. 2, pp. 50-56.

The Crisis of the College. *Rochester Alumni Review*, October-November, 1923, vol. 2, no. 1, p. 14.

Morgan and the University of Rochester. Rochester Historical Society. *Publication Fund Series*, 1923, vol. 2, p. 81.

The New Endowment. *Rochester Alumni Review*, December, 1923-January, 1924, vol. 2, no. 2, pp. 37-38.

Recuperating in North Africa. *Rochester Alumni Review*, April-May, 1924, vol. 2, no. 4, p. 83.

New Members Elected to Board of Trustees. *Rochester Alumni Review*, June-July, 1924, vol. 2, no. 5, p. 110.

Present Status of Greater University Project. *Rochester Alumni Review*, February-March, 1925, vol. 3, no. 3, p. 75.

Recruiting our College Faculty. *Rochester Alumni Review*, June-July, 1925, vol. 3, no. 5, p. 146.

Faculty and Administration Attitude Toward Athletics and Other Student Activities. *Rochester Alumni Review*, December, 1925-January, 1926, vol. 4, no. 2, pp. 47-48.

David Jayne Hill's Service to Rochester. *Rochester Alumni Review*, April-May, 1932, vol. 10, no. 4, p. 95.

Rochester's Contribution to the Twentieth Century. Rochester Historical Society. *Publication Fund Series*, 1934, vol. 13, pp. [51]-64.

ADDRESSES

The Elective System and a Liberal Education. Middle States Association of Colleges and Secondary Schools. *Proceedings of the 15th Annual Convention*, 1901, pp. 36-42.

Present Tendencies in Higher Education. New York (State) University. University Convocation. *Proceedings of the 39th Convocation*, 1901, pp. 389-395.

The University of Rochester. *Addresses at the Semi-centennial Anniversary of the Founding of the University of Rochester*, 1901, pp. 107-108.

Requirements for Admission to Medical Schools, Including the Combined Baccalaureate and Medical Courses. New York (State) University. University Convocation. *Proceedings of the 40th Convocation*, 1902, pp. 274-279.

Thoroughness vs. Breadth. Address delivered before the Associated Academic Principals of the State of New York, at Syracuse, December 29, 1902. *School Review*, March, 1903, vol. 11, no. 3, pp. 200-210.

Religious Education as Affected by the Historical Study of the Bible. Religious Education Association. *Proceedings of the First Annual Convention, Chicago*, 1903, pp. 80-99. Also published in: *Biblical World*, June, 1903, vol. 21, no. 6, pp. 426-432.

The Proposed Six-Year High School Course. Discussion at 17th Educational Conference of the Academies and High Schools Affiliating or co-operating with the University of Chicago, Nov. 14, 1903. *School Review*, vol. 12, pp. 26-28.

What Should Be the Length of the College Course? Middle States Association of Colleges and Secondary Schools. *Proceedings of the 17th Annual Convention*, 1903, pp. 47-53.

The Proper Length of the College Course. An Address delivered at the Meeting of the Association of Colleges and Preparatory Schools of the Middle States and Maryland in New York City, November 27, 1903. Jamaica, N. Y. Published by the New York Association of Alumni of Rochester, 1904, 15 pp.

Response to the Address of Welcome. Middle States Association of Colleges and Secondary Schools. *Proceedings of the 19th Annual Convention*, 1905, p. 10.

Secondary English Once More. Association of Colleges and Preparatory Schools of the Middle States and Maryland. *Proceedings of the 19th Annual Convention*, 1905, pp. 71-87.

Admission to College by Certificate. Middle States Association of Colleges and Secondary Schools. *Proceedings of the 21st Annual Convention*, 1907, pp. 28-39.

Applied Science and Liberal Culture. New York (State) University. University Convocation. *Proceedings of the 47th Convocation*, 1909, pp. 86-94.

Our Heritage and Our Task. Address delivered at Rochester's Diamond Jubilee, Convention Hall, Oct. 19, 1909. Rochester Historical Society. *Publication Fund Series*, 1929, vol. 8, pp. 281-294.

The National Importance of Industrial Education. National Society for the Promotion of Industrial Education, New York Branch. *Proceedings of the Second Annual Convention held at Rochester, N. Y.*, Nov. 19, 1909, pp. 9-17.

The Baccalaureate Sermon. Delivered at the Commencement of Columbia University in June, 1910. *Columbia University Quarterly*, September, 1910, vol. 12, no. 4, pp. 421-429.

New Ideals in Education. New York State Teachers' Association. *Proceedings of the 65th Annual Meeting at Rochester*, 1910, pp. 17-23.

Comprehensive Examinations for High School Graduates and for Admission to College. Middle States Association of Colleges and Secondary Schools. *Proceedings of the 26th Annual Convention*, 1912, pp. 34-37.

What Standards Should Be Used in the Classification of Colleges? Middle States Association of Colleges and Secondary Schools. *Proceedings of the 28th Convention*, 1914, pp. 54-59.

New York State Constitutional Convention, Revised Record, Albany, 1915. 4 vols., 4510 pp. Addresses and remarks by Rush Rhees, pp. 276, 308, 406-407, 893, 968, 1366, 1413, 1436, 1563-1564, 3352, 3615, 3634-3635, 3830, 3842-3846, 3880, 3911, 4039-4040, 4128.

A College of Liberal Arts—Nevertheless. Rutgers University, New Brunswick, N. J. *The Celebration of the One Hundred and Fiftieth Anniversary of its Founding as Queen's College, 1766-1916*, pp. 243-258.

Address (at the Fifth Annual Meeting of the Association of Urban

Universities), 1919. Association of Urban Universities. *Proceedings of the Fifth Annual Meeting*, 1919, pp. 91-92.

Privilege and Obligation. Address at the Convocation of Sept. 20, 1920. Buffalo University. *Studies*, October, 1920, vol. 1, no. 3, pp. 218-226.

Address Delivered at a Meeting of the Music Teachers' National Association in Chicago, 1920. Rochester Historical Society. *Publication Fund Series*, 1924, vol. 3, pp. 24-27.

The Eastman School of Music. Association of Urban Universities. *Proceedings of the Sixth Annual Meeting*, 1920, pp. 77-80.

Tribute to President Jacob Gould Schurman. New York (State) University. University Convocation. *Proceedings of the 56th Convocation*, 1920, pp. 13-17.

Greetings from the Universities and Colleges of New York State. Hobart College, Geneva, N. Y. *The Centennial of Hobart College, 1822-1922*, pp. 35-40.

Address of Welcome to the 76th Convention, Theta Delta Chi, Rochester, June 23, 1923. *Shield*, October, 1923, vol. 40, pp. 14-16.

The Ministry of the Spirit to a Materialistic Age. Commencement Address, Hartford Seminary Foundation, May 26, 1926. Hartford Seminary Foundation. *Bulletin*, June, 1926, vol. 13, no. 1, pp. 1-7.

Iconoclasm and Religious Life, Baccalaureate Sermon, June 20, 1926. *Rochester Alumni Review*, June-July, 1926, vol. 4, no. 5, pp. 139-142.

President's Charge to the Graduating Class. *Rochester Alumni Review*, June-July, 1927, vol. 5, no. 5, p. 146.

The Gift and the Donor: James Goold Cutler. Address delivered at the Official Dedication of the Bronze Statue at Genesee Valley Park, Oct. 29, 1927. Rochester Historical Society. *Publication Fund Series*, 1928, vol. 7, pp. 95-98.

Opening Address of Dedication. *Rochester Alumni Review*, October-November, 1930, vol. 9, no. 1, pp. 8-10.

A Towering Factor in Educational Development. Address at the Fiftieth Anniversary Celebration of Tuskegee Institute, April, 1931. *Tuskegee Messenger*, May 9-23, 1931, vol. 7, no. 9-10, pp. 15, 49.

Liberal Education—Then and Now. New York (State) University. University Convocation. *Proceedings of the 69th Convocation*, 1933, pp. 14-25.

INDEX

Aborn, Everett A., 15
Ackerman, Carl W., 160, 212
Alling, Joseph T., 82
Alling, Mrs. Joseph T., 47, 48
Alpha Delta Phi, 15
American Composers' Concerts, 195-196
Amherst College, 12-18, 108-109
Amherst System, 16
Anderson, Martin B., 45, 57, 80, 178, 278
Anderson Hall, 57, 59, 110, 232
Animal experimentation, 216-217
Anthony, Susan B., 101, 102
Anthony Memorial Hall, 111
Appointments, 146, 147
Art Gallery, 57, 180-182
Association of Colleges and Preparatory Schools, 117, 118
Athletics, 150, 151
Averell, James G., 179, 180

Babbott, Frank L., 175
Baptists, 45-47
Berlin, 22, 40, 75, 89
Beulah, 6, 274
Brown, Charles R., 30
Burton, Ernest D., 30, 40
Burton, Henry F., 47, 58, 61, 102
Butler, Nicholas Murray, 7
Buttrick, Wallace, 203

Cabinet-making, 9, 265
Cambria County, Pa., 6
Carlson, Harry J., 39
Carnahan, George A., 51
Carnegie, Andrew, 57, 60, 69, 72, 73, 79
Carnegie Foundation, 205
Carnegie Hall, 72, 76, 232
Carnegie pensions, 60

Carver, George Washington, 95
Catharine Strong Hall, 111
Chapel attendance, 142
Charities, organization of, 85
Chautauqua, 40
Chicago, Rush Rhees born in, 9
Chicago, University of, 40
Citizenship, education in, 86-87
City planning, 83-85
Civic Music Association, 192
Coeducation, 105, 107
College for Women, 101-114
Columbia University, 68
Community Chest, 90-92, 216
Constitution of the United States, 145
Constitutional Convention, New York, 1915, 87-88
Cornell University, 68, 70, 145
Craigie, James H., 58-59
Curriculum, changes in, 125, 126, 233
Cutler, James G., 82, 89, 144, 268
Cutler Union, 182, 268

Declaration of Independence, 5
Denio, Elizabeth H., 178
Dental Dispensary, 166, 167, 203, 206, 211-212
Department of Education, New York State, 122, 123, 124
Dickinson, Emily, 18
Dodge, Charles W., 67
Donovan, W. N., 37, 54
Dossenbach, Hermann, 184, 185
DuBois, W. E. B., 95
Dunbar, John, 83

Eastman, George, 57, 79, 82, 86, 110, 140, 156-177, 203, 213, 239, 241
Eastman House, 184, 242-244
Eastman Laboratory, 57, 69, 161-163, 177